BEAUTIFUL
WASTELAND

BEAUTIFUL WASTELAND

The Rise of Detroit as America's Postindustrial Frontier

Rebecca J. Kinney

UNIVERSITY OF MINNESOTA PRESS
MINNEAPOLIS • LONDON

Published by the University of Minnesota Press
111 Third Avenue South, Suite 290
Minneapolis, MN 55401-2520
http://www.upress.umn.edu

Printed in the United States of America on acid-free paper

22 21 20 19 18 17 16   10 9 8 7 6 5 4 3 2 1

Library of Congress Cataloging-in-Publication Data

Names: Kinney, Rebecca J.
Title: Beautiful wasteland : the rise of Detroit as America's postindustrial frontier / Rebecca J. Kinney.
Description: Minneapolis : University of Minnesota Press, 2016. | Includes bibliographical references and index.
Identifiers: LCCN 2016003047 | ISBN 978-0-8166-9756-4 (hc) | ISBN 978-0-8166-9757-1 (pb)
Subjects: LCSH: Detroit (Mich.)—Public opinion. | Public opinion—United States. | Popular culture—United States. | Frontier and pioneer life—United States. | Racism in popular culture—United States. | Detroit (Mich.)—Social conditions. | Detroit (Mich.)—Economic conditions. | Detroit (Mich.)—Race relations. | City and town life—Michigan—Detroit. | Urban renewal—Michigan—Detroit.
Classification: LCC F574.D44 K56 2016 | DDC 977.4/34—dc23
LC record available at http://lccn.loc.gov/2016003047

Contents

INTRODUCTION

Building a Beautiful Wasteland

> Detroit right now is a great American story. No city has had more influence on the country's economic and social evolution. Detroit was the birthplace of both the industrial age and the nation's middle class, and the city's rise and fall—and struggle to rise again—are a window into the challenges facing all of modern America. From urban planning to the crisis of manufacturing, from the lingering role of race and class in our society to the struggle for better health care and education, it's all happening at its most extreme in the Motor City.
>
> —John Huey, Time Inc. editor in chief, October 2009

In the summer of 2009, the editors of Time Inc. purchased a house in Detroit. John Huey, editor in chief, announced the purchase, as well as a yearlong series of articles called "Assignment Detroit," in an editorial letter to readers included in the print and online versions of *Time* magazine's October 5, 2009, "special issue" on Detroit. Huey frames the move as a chance to understand the city, telling readers, "As a story, Detroit has been misunderstood, underreported, stereotyped, avoided and exploited for decades."[1] Huey then explains that Time Inc., its editors and staff members, would become "stakeholders" in Detroit, with their plan over the next year to "flood the D-zone with journalists, photographers, videographers and bloggers" from its network of news outlets, including not just *Time* but *Fortune, CNN Money, Money,* and *Sports Illustrated.* The purchase of the home would enable journalists from across the news organization to live and report from Detroit in the home that they affectionately named the "D-Shack."

The nickname is revealing. Huey's letter describes a house with three stories, five bedrooms, and three and a half baths, in addition to both a basement and a yard; the accompanying photograph pictures a charming blue brick home with new windows, flower boxes, landscaped trees and bushes, and the hint of a backyard trellis. The house, in other words, is nowhere near a "shack." It seems to offer a pointed contrast with the ubiquitous images of Detroit's blighted and decaying homes. However, by naming the home a "shack" and emphasizing the fact that the purchase price of $99,000 was "about $80,000 above the average price of a house in the city limits," *Time* joined the long list of news outlets creating and fueling the narrative of Detroit as a devalued place, even as they tried to sell the story of Detroit on the upswing.[2] Semantics aside, however, during their year in Detroit, the company's journalists produced a lot of content, including "roughly 300 print or online stories, 48 video reports, and over 750 blog posts" across the print and online editions of Time Inc.'s brands.[3]

I begin here not merely to critique *Time*'s social experiment but because, in recent years, John Huey's impulse seems ubiquitous. He is just one of a seemingly endless line of people, not just journalists but bloggers and photographers, artists and tourists, big business and advertisers, drawn to the complex contradictions of Detroit—its storied past and beautiful buildings and its infamous decline and abandoned factories. Huey talks about the pride of Detroiters but does so beneath a shadow he presents of Detroit's broken present, telling readers: "Not all that long ago Detroit was one of the richest places in the country. . . . Today it struggles for its life." Huey pronounced that *Time* would report Detroit "differently," yet he offered an angle that has been used again and again: "We want Detroit to recover and find its way into the future." He announced that they would "bring a sense of surprise, discovery, enlightenment, horror, joy, inspiration and fun to the reality of Detroit." And then, just in case readers did not understand *Time*'s noble intentions, he added: "[The] reality is that Detroit, like all other cities, is human."[4] These pronouncements, however, smack of the same old stories that have been told about the city for years: the past as epic, the present as bleak, and Detroit as broken. Even as *Time* seeks to humanize Detroit, the irony of course is that over the years the media has been responsible for circulating and disseminating this notion of Detroit as dehumanized.

I grew up in Royal Oak, an inner-ring suburb that hugs Woodward Avenue, Detroit's main north–south thoroughfare.[5] Royal Oak is close enough to the city that a ten-minute car ride down Woodward could carry you the six miles to Detroit's northern boundary, or twenty minutes on the freeway could take you the seventeen miles to the Renaissance Center, which sits along Detroit's southern boundary, the Detroit River. To people familiar with southeastern Michigan, this geographic location identifies me as a metro Detroiter.[6] To everyone else, I am more simply a Detroiter. And whenever I tell people where I am from, they proceed to tell me what they know about the city: its spectacular decline, and that they learned about it from an online gallery of photos by *Time* or the *Huffington Post,* from a news story they read in the *New York Times* or *USA Today,* or a segment on the *Colbert Report.*[7] All this is to say that much of what is known about Detroit comes from stories that are read, or seen, or heard in passing. Such is the case for pretty much any aspect of life, of course. Stories are the way we make sense of the world. But when it comes to Detroit, the content of those stories, and the drama with which they are pronounced, takes on a particular significance. I have heard pronouncements of the city's impending death for as long as I can remember, predating the Internet and probably even my ability to read. Indeed, I first heard these stories coming from people like my grandparents, my mom, and others in my inner-ring suburb, who *were* Detroiters but who left the city proper in the 1950s and 1960s for the adjacent suburban periphery. The way they told it, downtown Detroit was a magnificent city back in the day—all glitz and glamour complete with Sunday best, including a hat and gloves for a trip to Hudson's department store. Then, when I moved from Michigan to California in the early 2000s, people were often surprised that first, I was a metro Detroiter—"There are Asians in Detroit?" is a question I get again and again—and second, that I had made it out alive: "You must be so happy to be out of that hellhole," one particularly memorable coworker exclaimed. However, after nearly a decade of this mix of pity and surprise and lament, the conversation began to change. Starting sometime in 2009 or so, friends, acquaintances, and strangers began to change their tune. "I hear amazing things are happening in Detroit." Or, "Detroit sounds like such a haven for artists and creative work, I want to go there someday." Yes, I was aware that the city was changing. But for me, the city has always been changing. It has always been both awful and wonderful, bleak and thriving. So the shift in the cultural conversation was particularly fascinating, and I needed to understand why people suddenly wanted to know about Detroit and celebrate the possibility of its resurgence. Though it seems like a cliché, this is where this book begins, with the seemingly banal small talk of everyday life. Even as I have heard the pronouncements of Detroit's dysfunction and doom for as long as I can remember, I am most interested in their wide reach and continued dissemination, and in the seductive appeal they still hold. And as a corollary to the tales of Detroit's death, I have been especially intrigued in the last half decade or so to also hear the stories of its rebirth. As the stories of my city seem to reach a fever pitch, my questions seem all the more resonant: Why Detroit? Why now? And, for that matter, what Detroit is everyone talking about exactly?

Running through all these stories is the undercurrent of neoliberalism. David Harvey defines neoliberalism as a political economic theory intended to lessen state intervention to allow the market to thrive, "by liberating individual entrepreneurial freedoms and skills within an institutional framework characterized by strong private property rights, free markets, and free trade."[8] Yet while one of the most important tenets of this philosophy is the idea that access to property, markets, and trade will be attained by those individuals best adapted for the marketplace, it is clear here that the continual embrace of this rhetoric of individual determinism and success that neoliberalism enables is deeply dependent on privileged access to capital. Indeed, I concur with Lisa Duggan and Jodi Melamed, who each argue that neoliberalism, although seen as a universalizing project, is one that further obscures the ways in which race, gender, and citizenship are implicated in the process of capitalism.[9] As will be shown throughout the book, the idea of Detroit as a postindustrial frontier is meant to be a racially neutral neoliberal project—a project that relies on a postracial outlook—yet it is steeped within the race-saturated rhetoric of the frontier. Ultimately, the racialization of place is not a symptom of capital but is produced by and in relationship to capital.

The writing of this book took place under the shadow of the country's worst economic depression in eight decades and an especially bleak time in Detroit's economic history. The federal bailout of two of Detroit's signature companies, General Motors and Chrysler, in 2008; the city's takeover by a state-appointed emergency financial manager in March 2013;

its July 2013 filing for Chapter 9 bankruptcy (the largest municipal bankruptcy filing in U.S. history); and its months-long slog through the challenges to its legality and plans of adjustment that culminated in approval of its plan of adjustment in December 2014, enabling Detroit to begin to restructure postbankruptcy—all of this served as the background to the chapters that follow. In less than a decade both the city's signature industry and the city itself have become a living symbol of financial crisis: Detroit is not only a broke city but a broken city. Yet even as these awful events unfolded, they also provided fertile ground for yet another narrative. Detroit has fallen so hard, and so far, that it can now become a "comeback city"; the poster city of economic crisis (and many other kinds of crisis) is now a space of possibility, or as I describe it—a *beautiful wasteland.*

Embracing the Frontier; or, How a Wasteland Can Be Beautiful

Detroit has been seen by some as a wasteland for at least the last forty years—but a wasteland of a particular kind, a postindustrial wasteland. Indeed, this familiar trope is one that the *Time* announcement leans on heavily. This Detroit is constructed via narratives of devastation wrought by deindustrialization, the departure of productive white businesses and people, and government corruption and incompetence. These all work in combination to render the city in literal and symbolic ruin, a place of "tragedy." Yet what I note in this book is the shift of the tenor of the depiction of Detroit. An example of this shift can be seen in the very cover for *Time*'s special issue announcing "Assignment Detroit." The cover (Figure 2) features the title of its lead story, "The Tragedy of Detroit," by Daniel Okrent. Notably, this very same title graced an earlier cover of the *New York Times Magazine* (Figure 1). Although the two magazine covers, published nineteen years apart, bear the exact same title, their visual and narrative compositions render two very different cities through two very different representations of "The Tragedy of Detroit."

New York Times Magazine's July 29, 1990, cover story, a feature by Ze'ev Chafets, was an excerpt from his book *Devil's Night: And Other True Tales of Detroit.* Published well before the current media fetishization of Detroit, the article was symptomatic of the common construction of

Figure 1. *New York Times Magazine* cover, July 29, 1990. Photograph by Christopher Morris.

Figure 2. *Time* magazine cover, October 5, 2009. Photograph by Yves Marchand and Romain Meffre.

Detroit as a place of ruin and depravity, a vision of the city crystalized in a local practice of widespread arson on the night before Halloween, referred to both temporally and in practice as "Devil's Night."[10] The cover image (Figure 1) centers on an African American boy, head turned away, looking back at what can only be described as ruins. The image evokes representations of the aftermath of 1960s urban rebellions.[11] With the stamp of the article's title, "The Tragedy of Detroit," in thick, bolded typeface, the closely cropped imagery of a destroyed home and an African American youth are framed as the central elements of the "tragedy." Tellingly, the viewer does not see the young man's face, even as his torso and head comprise about a third of the image. Instead, the proximity of the young man to the camera and the angle of the shot offers an outsized vision of a generic young black adolescent, looming large adjacent to the ruination. The proximity of typeface and young person in relationship to ruin draws a visual connection between the anonymous young black man—who is either perpetrator or victim, it is not clear which—and the destruction of Detroit. The composition of the burned-out home, in contrast to the young man and the typeface, is not shrouded in shadow but prominently lit from above at the center of the image, highlighting the tragedy at hand. The image leaves opportunity for interpretation, but the title's position places "The Tragedy of Detroit" quite literally on the young man's back. The anonymous young black man stands in as representative of the population of Detroit, which in the 1990 census was 76 percent African American.[12]

In *Time*'s 2009 "The Tragedy of Detroit" cover (Figure 2), the city's tragedy is clearly different, both in scale and in emphasis. There is no single blighted home, no looming black body. Instead, the twenty-first-century tragedy is one of large-scale deindustrialization, symbolized by a desolate industrial park. Rather than linking the tragedy of Detroit to a young black body, as in the forefront of the 1990 image, the only people in the 2009 image are two tiny figures, ghostly in their appearance and symbolically miniscule amid the hulking remains of the 3.5 million square foot Packard Automotive Plant. This cover suggests that the tragedy is wrought by large-scale factors—the scale of the buildings and the complex itself seem stand-ins for the even larger, all-encompassing twin threats of deindustrialization and globalization. The two figures are thus survivors in this landscape of postapocalyptic emptiness. The two figures are visible, despite the many elements of the cover, because of the cleared space in the center of the photograph, in contrast to the debris that clutters the side of the road. This cleared road serves as a literal path toward the horizon. The figures are on this path, walking into a future—blue skies and uncertainty but likely "better" than the debris of destruction they are leaving behind. The text also emphasizes this possibility of revival. The title of the cover story "The Tragedy of Detroit" is printed prominently in the center of the image in bold typeface that looms large over the entire image. The tagline of the article (How a great city fell—and how it can rise again) is printed in a smaller, thinner typeface and is placed below the title and above the two figures, directly linking the figures not to the fall but to the possibility for rise.

It is the tenor of difference between these two covers and their conceptions of what Detroit was, is, and has the potential to be again that this book takes up as its central point of interrogation. The visual sentiments of these two covers with the exact same title reveal a shifting narrative of the destruction of the city as a result of individual action in 1990 in contrast to global processes of labor and manufacturing in 2009. These two covers also reveal with startling clarity the shifting imagination of Detroit's decline and decay as directly linked to blackness in the 1990s and the possibility for Detroit to rise again in the late 2000s notably marked by an absence of association with the city's black population. I will explore throughout the book this shift in sentiment marked by the racially coded signification of the return of white people and the seeming disappearance of black people in the 2010s narrative of Detroit's comeback. This shift is gestured toward in what emerges in the twenty-first-century depiction of the city, what I conceptualize as the representation of Detroit as a *beautiful wasteland.* Rather than a city marred by grotesque remains and pathological residents, what emerges in the twenty-first-century depiction of Detroit is the city's perceived emptiness and the idea of Detroit's ruin as beautiful. As will be shown, the representation of Detroit's landscape is imagined anew, through narratives of its beauty, not as the "bombed-out shell" it once was but as a latent and underdeveloped frontier. Indeed, we are now coming full circle, returning once again to the possibility of Detroit's historic rise.

Rendering the city as beautiful, even while broke and broken, relies on the notion that Detroit is not actually without potential; beauty operates as a modifier to suggest a productive possibility for new investment and new investors. This beautiful wasteland can be seen most readily, for example, in the widespread dissemination and interest in the spate of photographs of Detroit architecture, especially the once-glorious, early and mid-twentieth-century structures now in various states of disrepair. The buildings are admired for their beauty and for their hint of both past grandeur and future potential: they are architectural "gems" with "good bones" but in need of careful and proper attention. In short, there is promise in its peril. It is through the simultaneous portrayals of Detroit as a beautiful wasteland, both desirable and desolate, that the narrative of ruin and rebirth stand not in opposition but as interdependent. Tellingly, the tension of productive possibility, of emptiness and beauty, is dependent on the settlement of contemporary Detroit by primarily white outsiders. It is through this narrative shift that the idea of Detroit not as a postindustrial wasteland but as a postindustrial frontier emerges.

However, before Detroit became a postindustrial frontier, it was first a frontier. Detroit has been a frontier for at least three hundred years. For most of its history that frontier has been geographical. Detroit in particular, and later Michigan more generally, was an important borderland for the French, British, and Americans in the eighteenth and nineteenth centuries.[13] Detroit long served as part of the French settlement in North America, until 1760, when it came under British rule during the French and Indian War. And although the Treaty of Paris ended the American Revolution and on paper ceded the Northwest Territory to American rule, the British occupation of Detroit did not end until the Americans took over Fort Detroit in 1796. After its admission as the twenty-sixth state in 1837, Michigan was cemented as the northwest frontier of the United States, the edge of the nation birthed by the American Revolution, and Detroit was a fort settlement along one of the most important waterways of this western boundary. The significance of this geographic role diminished as America spread westward, even as "the Detroit-Windsor gateway is the busiest commercial land border crossing in North America,"[14] with an estimated $500 million in trade crossing every day between Detroit and Windsor, Canada.[15] Although Detroit's geographic role as frontier diminished, Detroit's ideological role as frontier continued to grow. In the late 1800s and early 1900s, Detroit was a frontier of technology, industry, and innovation as headquarters for some of the nation's most prominent industries.[16] And a hundred years later, Detroit has emerged as the icon of the postindustrial frontier.

Twentieth-century Detroit stands in as a key example of the industrial heights and declines of U.S. manufacturing. The rise of the auto industry provides both an economic framework and a mythic narrative that facilitated the rise of the city as a whole. Industrialization served as a frontier of expansion historically in Detroit, fostering a critical mass of businesses, capital, workers, and materials that stimulated not only population but new industry and technology. Detroit's early population growth was due to a number of industries. The city served as the home to nationally recognized manufacturers of railroad cars, paint, pharmaceuticals, and stoves and kitchen ranges, among a host of other industries, long before it became the home of the automotive industry.[17] The eventual development of the auto industry itself owes to this diversity of manufacturing and industrialization. These successful industries facilitated a climate that generated the two most important elements of innovation: a critical mass of curious and creative people and the financial backing to support experimentation and new inventions. However, the richness of this period of automobile experimentation, growth, and competition is most frequently boiled down to the story of Henry Ford and the Model T. So while Henry Ford is the most famous of this cohort, the auto industry emerged through the successes and failures of Ford as well as numerous others who experimented with the "horseless carriage." These others mostly live in obscurity outside of historians of Detroit and the automotive industry.[18] Once the technology and production of the automobile became possible, the industry grew enormously as demand for the automobile increased. And as the automotive industry grew exponentially, so did the population of Detroit. In the first half of the twentieth century, Detroit's population grew enormously—for every person counted in the 1900 census, there were 6.5 more by 1950—from 258,704 people in 1900 to 1,849,568 in 1950.[19]

The story of Detroit's growth is the archetypal story of the nation's growth. Detroit's rise to national prominence in the early to mid-twentieth century is a marker of the modern industrial moment of Fordism, Taylorism, and the growth of capitalism. The 1910s and 1920s in Detroit were defined by the ramping up of its increasingly successful industries and the time of Ford Motor Company's widely touted, but difficult to achieve, promise of a five-dollar-a-day factory salary.[20] Foreign migration began to slow with the advent of World War I and was largely curtailed with the passage of the 1924 Immigration Act. The promise of jobs and opportunities made Detroit a destination for sojourners and families from states to the south and to the east, as well as from Mexico and Canada, both of which were exempt from the 1924 quotas. Jobs were abundant. If you wanted work, chances were you could find it. And if you were a white man, you had a very good chance of finding decently paying work.[21] Detroit's second big migration happened during World War II as more people came to Detroit to work in and power the factories that had transitioned from making cars to making war munitions. After the war ended, Detroit again had jobs aplenty as the automotive industry met pent-up consumer demand for new goods after the austerity of the Depression and war years. The result was that Detroit became, at least for some, the embodiment of a new version of the American Dream: if you worked hard you could own a house and a car.[22] This narration of rise of the city serves as the setup for a precipitous fall.

While the Detroit of the early and mid-twentieth century marked the rise of the United States as a global moral and economic force, the arsenal of democracy, and the American workers who powered that force, the Detroit of the late twentieth century served as the reminder of the United States' shift from a leader in production to a leader in consumption.[23] It is only in retrospect, not surprisingly, that the fall of Detroit seems so clear. In fact, the 1946 "Detroit Plan" hinged on slum clearance and redevelopment to accommodate continued population growth. However, the 1950s in Detroit, as in cities across the country, was a decade of change. During the Depression and war years new house construction had come to a near standstill. A building boom ensued to keep pace with the growing demand of the post–World War II baby boom. However, what Detroit city planners did not anticipate was the suburban location of much of this new housing and the sizeable population shift that would occur. People and companies began to migrate to the adjacent suburban periphery, preferring the vacant land and the newer structures rapidly being constructed outside the city proper. Detroit began its decline of population and reputation as early as the late 1950s, and it rapidly accelerated after the late 1960s.

The diminishing reputation of Detroit parallels the decrease in its white population and the increase in its black population. The damage, both physical and psychological, of the 1967 urban rebellion, the construction of the heavily fortressed Renaissance Center complex, the movement of Motown to Los Angeles, and the continual decrease in the domestic interest in American cars all served as cultural fodder for the narrative of decline. By the 1980s, Detroit was an easy punch line.

Detroit's implied narrative of rise and fall, as the city moved from a symbol of American greatness to a symbol of American urban crisis, is nowhere clearer than in the numerous nicknames and quips about the city in the 1980s: for example, "murder city," "most dangerous city in America," "Detroit: where the weak are killed and eaten." In the 1980s and 1990s, as Steve Macek argues, popular culture and news media were essential in establishing the cultural resonance of fear of postindustrial urban space. Social policy and media representations worked together to produce a "moral panic" about the U.S. city, resulting in a "culturally authoritative discourse on the urban crisis" that produced Detroit and other postindustrial cities as "landscapes of fear."[24] The crisis of Detroit was apparent in the nightly local news broadcasts I watched growing up and in the fear of the city in the suburban imagination by admonitions not to drive into Detroit alone, and when in the city to walk quickly from wherever we parked our car to our destination. I grew up with the shadow of Detroit in my backyard and in the stories of its epic heights and massive collapse as family history. Even as the story was told and broadcast across the globe, it too was the story being told at home, a tale of destruction, devastation, and death of this "once great" American city.

As a postindustrial city, Detroit is frequently conceptualized as a new American frontier, nearly empty and therefore an ideal space to fill with our continued national preoccupations about progress and mobility. At first glance, the western frontier might seem a world apart from Detroit today, but the link is stronger than we might think. The frontier, one of the most powerful and enduring American narratives, signifies both progress and possibility; it is a physical location, but just as important, it is a way of orienting ourselves toward the world, a means of looking forward both temporally and ideologically. It is a place to stake claims and (maybe) realize success, but perhaps more important, it is a place to locate dreams.

The narratives of progress that fueled and facilitated the settlement of the American West, and are now so entrenched in our culture, work here to reaffirm our attachment to stories of American exceptionalism, expansionism, and determinism. I will show in the chapters that follow how these deeply familiar stories of the frontier operate in the "renewal" of Detroit, iconic "Worst City in America." The concept of frontier operates in Detroit as a marker of anticipation of the city's ascent—a perpetual possibility just around the corner. This is seen in the hopeful descriptions of what will "save" this postindustrial city: revitalization, redevelopment, reuse, rebirth. In each case the underlying assumption is that space is being "underutilized" but that with the right new people, or new ideas, or new infusion of cash, the city can be returned to its former productivity. I link these concepts together through the notion of a postindustrial frontier. The compound phrase is meant to reference deindustrialized urban place as a space of newly imagined possibility.

I draw my conception of postindustrial frontier from Neil Smith's framework of the urban frontier. Smith frames the gentrification of New York City as what he calls a revanchist act—recovering and reclaiming the city, taking back the city from those who are deemed as ill-using it, namely the working class, the poor, and people of color—through the consolidation of public policy and private capital that privileges development.[25] For Smith the frontier is not only an ideological marker but also an economic marker of financial investment, rooted within the legacy of America's western frontier. His work argues that the new urban frontier, like the western frontier, is not actually advanced through "pioneers, homesteaders, and rugged individualists," despite our many myths to the contrary about intrepid men and stalwart women who brave the unknown; instead, advancement happens through the "actions of collective owners of capital."[26] As I will show, overcoming the American myths of individualism and recognizing the vast, though often unseen, actions of capital is a central backdrop to the work of this book. Of central concern is that development itself is never strictly an economic position; as much as the market is seen as a "neutral" location, in fact it is entangled with cultural narratives. Thus, I will return again and again to disparate aspects of culture, using the stories that are told and retold as a means to understand the structures of value—how place is deemed possible for death or rebirth, wasteland or frontier. And in Detroit, its story is inseparable from the story of racial formation in the United States. As I will explain, the frontier narrative blankets contemporary narratives of Detroit, seen in the continuing dichotomies of empty space / occupied space and productive/unproductive landscapes, which are, in turn, deeply steeped in racial conceptions of place.

George Lipsitz argues that "the lived experience of race has a spatial dimension, and the lived experience of space has a racial dimension."[27] Lipsitz places those lived experiences within material and cultural landscapes, arguing quite literally that "racism takes place" in the social fabric and spatial imaginary of everyday life.[28] More specifically, we can trace the way that racial formation operates through both public policy and popular culture.[29] Racialization is not the result of uneven development but in fact an organizing principle through which uneven development manifests. One of the main goals of the book is to show how the dominant story of Detroit's rise, though a story that hinges on privileged access to institutional benefits based on whiteness, is frequently told as a story not about race. However, the story of Detroit's decline, which is a continuation of the story of privileged racial access to suburbanization, for example, is frequently told as a story of the destruction wrought by black integration of the city. Another goal of the book is to show the ways in which our contemporary conversations about the past are key locations to analyze the continued investment in white privilege, despite proclamations that racism is over.

It is the cultural narratives surrounding both the story of rise, and perhaps even more important, the story of fall, that will be the central point of analysis. On the one hand, the narrative of Detroit's rise seems to be ideologically linked to generic American tropes of hard work and success: Detroit is celebrated, as will be shown, as a city of working-class immigrants and migrants, drawn to the city by the fire of determination and possibility. And on the other hand, the narrative of Detroit's decline seems entangled with notions of urban crisis and a culture of city corruption. The backdrop for both of these narratives—rise and fall—is the racialized narrative of movement and growth in U.S. history more generally. The mythology of America as a "nation of immigrants" creates a standard narrative that excludes the more complicated migrations of many due to transatlantic slavery, upheaval created by global structures of capitalism and warfare, not to mention those who did not migrate to America at all. In a similar fashion, cultural narratives that recirculate an origin myth of Detroit conceal a much more complex reality not only of the past but also of the present. By looking at one of the most racially polarized cities in the country, we will try and tease out the very complicated and messy relationship between racial formation and spatial formation in the United States.

The Stories We Tell

This book is not a historical accounting of the role racism has played in Detroit's economy or culture or daily life. Rather, here I will analyze the stories told about Detroit's past, present, and future in the contemporary moment. With each story told, there are other stories that are not told. With each memory that is retold, and reinforced, there are others that are forgotten. I do not attempt to fill absences in memories of the past. As a result, a crucial part of this investigation is the relationship between what is reinforced and what is ignored as Detroit is made "new" once again. At its core, my investigation centers on the ways in which the discourse about Detroit has shifted dramatically in the twenty-first century by looking at popular culture.[30] Yet I argue that this new discourse about twenty-first-century Detroit is, in fact, a redeployment of long-standing American narratives of hard work and determination as a race neutral project; it is indeed privileges of whiteness that enable it to be cast as racially neutral.

The book looks to a cross-section of cultural narratives to index what is not always visible in policy statistics, to explore what is often left out of the official archive, and to understand what the silences and fissures reveal not only about today but about the past and the future. It is tempting to view racial formation in the United States through a lens of historical and juridical "events." In the contemporary moment wherein the law is conceptualized as "colorblind," this structural-only approach is even more limiting. My students often question how and why racism still exists if we have laws and policies meant to address racism; certainly, we can all point to historical legislation that would suggest that racism is, indeed, over. And yet evidence of our daily lives belies the naïveté of such a suggestion. To me, this question is an important one that I address regularly not only in the classroom but also in everyday conversations with friends, family members, and acquaintances. If racism is legally over, how then does it persist? An answer can be found, I think, in cultural narratives, in the spaces in which we live our daily lives and in the tales that we hold dear. As Lisa Lowe demonstrates, "Although the law is perhaps the discourse that most literally governs citizenship, U.S. national culture—the collectively forged images, histories, and narratives that place, displace, and replace individuals in relation to the national polity—powerfully shapes who the citizenry is, where they dwell, what they remember, and what they forget."[31] Culture serves not only to help understand narratives of race but also to locate the discourses that undergird the production of racialized place. Helen Heran Jun suggests that "we can read culture not merely to identify ideological shortcomings but to understand that irrespective of intention and impulse, every text can be read for the inevitable contradictions it attempts to manage or reconcile."[32] Therefore the inherent contradictions in popular narratives are the key points of my analysis, as it is in these places and moments where the invisible is illuminated.

In each of the chapters that follow I look to particular cases of popular culture in order to analyze the persistence of racial formation in narrative tropes. Each of the chapters engages a story that is readily familiar in both content and form. I look to our everyday exchanges: an Internet discussion thread, photographs, a commercial, documentary films, and news media. Indeed, the power of each of these sites of analysis lies in the contradictions and complexity just beneath the surface of these seemingly straightforward slices of everyday life. Just like all the stories we tell, the sites of the book are all the more powerful because they are unique yet commonplace and representative of both the obstacles to and the possibilities of dreams.

The city of Detroit, which eventually grew to encompass 139 square miles of land and 1.8 million people, was a place where dreams were built. Even our biggest, most unifying one of all—the American Dream—was, we might say, "Made in Detroit." This can be seen in my own family. My maternal grandparents, neither of whom attended high school, both came to Detroit from the southern United States in order to seek work. In 1943, after several hard years due to the Depression and war, my maternal grandmother's family made the difficult decision to move north from Murray, Kentucky, where they had a small farm and a grocery store. My great-grandparents were unable to find work and returned to Kentucky after a few months, but my grandmother, at the age of sixteen, was allowed to stay in Detroit and work as a shampoo girl in a beauty shop run by her aunt. She went to beauty school, got a license, and worked in the shop until 1946, when she got a job on the line at the Chrysler Hamtramck plant. In 1947, when she met my grandfather on a blind date, she worked in a grueling job on the line where, because of her small size, she was assigned the job of jumping in and out of trunks installing wiring. My grandfather arrived in Detroit in search of employment in 1946 after serving aboard a Navy ship in the Pacific during World War II. Unlike my grandmother he did not have any extended family in the city. Although he grew up in Roanoke, Virginia, he, like a brother who headed north to Baltimore, sought work in the northern factories given the stagnant economy in their hometown. He soon found a job in the foundry at Ford Motor Company. My grandparents married in 1947. Due to the postwar housing crunch they lived first in a hotel apartment in downtown Detroit. Prior to the birth of my mom in 1949 they moved to a small house in Highland Park, the community that originally grew to house the thousands of workers that powered the 120-acre Ford Highland Park Plant during its operation from 1910 to 1928. Eventually, with access to steady jobs and the assistance of a VA-backed home loan, they were able to build a modest suburban duplex and moved to Royal Oak in 1960.

Yet even as my family's story is one shared by so many Detroiters, my personal story, growing up in metro Detroit in the 1980s and 1990s, as a Korean adoptee in a white family, makes the story of Detroit all the more complex. In a region bifurcated by a deeply divided history of race in starkly black-and-white terms, to grow up at a time and in a place where there were very few Asians and to be neither black nor white gave me a unique perspective. As early as I can remember I was aware of my difference, what I would later attribute to the fact that the community I grew up in was overwhelmingly white.[33] And when we would go to my mom's work in downtown Detroit I would also be aware of the difference between the city—its overwhelmingly black population, shuttered skyscrapers, and empty streets—and my community with its overwhelmingly white population, modest one-story homes and businesses, and busy sidewalks full of kids playing and people walking dogs. In both places, always acutely aware that I was neither white nor black, I wondered why two communities, just a short car ride away from one another, were so different in terms of people and the built environment. As I grew older I often asked this question not just of my family but in my high school history classes and in college ethnic studies and urban studies classes. I received many answers, most typically explained by "white flight" and "racism," elaborated upon through narratives of suburban development, the 1967 Detroit riot, and the declining auto industry. But none of these answers fully sufficed to explain the emotional schism so many former and current Detroiters expressed between the city of the past and the city of the present.

As a first-generation college student at the University of Michigan, I was all too aware of the even bigger schisms between Detroit and its suburban periphery, and between different races and classes in the United States more broadly. Then, as I worked in nonprofit organizations focused on community development first in Detroit and then San Francisco, I began to find many more answers—uneven access to education, housing, and transportation, development that displaces existing communities, and gaps in social services. Yet none of these fully sufficed by themselves; they did not account for the ongoing emotional power of narratives of place. This book then will take us through some of the most steadfast stories of Detroit, narratives of exodus, ruin, rebirth, possibility, and rise, as a way to analyze the enduring complexities of the stories we tell of America. In the chapters that follow I analyze the narratives of Detroit as parallel to the narratives of the national story of American postindustrial cities. Even as we cannot seem to reconcile what happened in the twentieth-century past beyond a story of rise, decline, and the possibility of rise again, the cyclical and transformative story of Detroit is one that is clung to as the possibility of the future. The unfolding of the book suggests that the story of twenty-first-century Detroit represents a continuing cycle of rise and fall, throughout its long and complex history and present.

I begin by looking backward to the stories told of Detroit's decline. Chapter 1, "It's Turned into a Race Thing: White Innocence and the Old Neighborhood," examines a most twenty-first-century location of public narrative—an Internet discussion board—in order to analyze the narrative of Detroit's nostalgic past. I am interested in the ways in which the past is frequently remembered as not about race, even as we have the benefit of decades of research that shows the relationship between race and place in America. An Internet thread on the website City-Data.com, "I found my old house in Detroit today," provides a place to analyze the narrative of exodus that is so much a part of the story of Detroit's mid-twentieth-century decline in order to reveal the significance of the past as a way to illuminate the continuing significance of race in the twenty-first century.

Although chapter 2, "Picturing Ruin and Possibility: The Rise of the Postindustrial Frontier," moves backward chronologically, to photographs of Detroit taken by Camilo José Vergara in the late 1980s and 1990s, I argue that these images were central to producing a narrative of ruin about the city of Detroit. In his Detroit images, and in his statements about the city, we see how structural racism and unequal access to the spoils of capitalism are written out of the narrative of postindustrial urban space, replaced with a simpler narrative of progress and decline. Vergara's images of the landscape in particular suggest that Detroit's ruin and potential for rise is a natural process, contributing to the common discourse that affirms the rise and fall and rise again of Detroit.

Chapter 3, "Fanning the Embers: Branding Detroit as a Phoenix Rising," provides the connective tissue between the storied past of Detroit as a location of workers and the narrative of rebirth of the twenty-first-century city. At its center is the mythic tale provided by the 2011 Chrysler "Born of Fire" commercial. The narrative tale of a rebirth of a city, and by extension the American auto industry, in the face of epic decline makes the story of Detroit the ultimate comeback tale—a phoenix rising from the ashes of destruction.

The conceit of the postindustrial frontier relies upon the continuation of a narrative of possibility in the face of hardship. While chapter 3 touches on this with the cinematic and narrative quality of a mini-movie, chapter 4, "Flickers of the American Dream: Filming Possibility in Decline," revisits this theme through the cinematic portrayal of Detroit and Detroiters in two documentary films from the early 2010s: *Deforce* (2010) and *Detropia* (2011). The premise of documentary film enables the narrative of possibility through the persistent belief of real Detroiters. Tellingly, even as the present is represented as a time of decline and difficulty, the persistence of the belief in a "better" future is the hopeful conclusion that filmmakers return to again and again.

And in chapter 5, "Feeding Detroit's Rise: Provisions for Urban Pioneers," I turn to the narrative of rise. The fascination with Detroit in the twenty-first century is due not to its ruin but to the evidence of Detroit as possible. This chapter looks specifically at the narrative of the rise of a "new Detroit." This rise is best seen in media portrayals of contemporary Detroit's "hungry" creative class, the billion-dollar investment of Dan Gilbert, and the media frenzy around the opening of a Whole Foods Market in Detroit and the company's use of that store as a national platform against "racism and elitism."

As will be shown throughout the book, the central tropes that *Time* highlights in the magazine's year of reporting serve as a good summary of the last half century of sentiment about Detroit, and about the nation more broadly. The stories of Detroit are interesting because as *Time* pinpoints, a story about Detroit is more than a story of the city—it is an "American story." Again and again, here and elsewhere, the city is depicted as a symbol of our stunning capacities to ascend, of the depths to which we can fall, and (just maybe) to the hope that we may rise again. This book then is my attempt to reconcile the many narratives of Detroit's rise, fall, and potential for rise again, not simply as individual memories or as the results of official policy but as widespread narrative tropes of American determinism and the racial logics that underwrite these stories. As the chapters will show, even as the visual, statistical, and historical evidence all point to the fact that in Detroit, the American Dream has long failed, it still serves as a location of speculative fascination, an ongoing love affair with the possibility of what could be, based on a rose-colored idea of what it used to be. In the book we will explore how and why, even in the face of the stark reality of poverty, blight, and failing schools and social services, the dream of Detroit is revived, again and again, with great earnestness. I focus on the narratives of exodus, ruin, rebirth, possibility, and rise that frame Detroit's story in order to provide insight into the unresolved place between the mythology of unfettered access to the American Dream and the uneven ways that reality plays out.

In June 2014 Karen Dybis, a local Detroit writer who blogged for *Time* during "Assignment Detroit," weighed in on the five-year anniversary of the purchase of the *Time* house. In the article, whose title says it all—"Five Years Ago, 'Time' Bought a House Here . . . and So Much Has Changed since Then"—Dybis pointedly asks where the magazine is now that the city is on an upswing. She argues that Detroit of 2014, with its new developments and investments, is more interesting now than it was in 2009. She also concedes that "maybe good news doesn't sell as well as bad news." Dybis's perspective of Detroit on the rise is not unique, as the stories of the book show. The positive changes that Dybis notes in her article are the backbone of narratives of Detroit's rise: the new businesses large and small now in Detroit, the sustained interest and increase of newcomers, and, most importantly, "there is a life, a vibrancy, a commitment to this revitalization."[34] What is of interest, though, are the ways in which even as so much has indeed changed, the stories told about the city are so much the same—that Detroit *now* is full of life and vibrant, which can only support a corollary that Detroit *then* (whether five or twenty-five years ago) was dead and listless. This book however, does not support these simple pronouncements of life and death, rise and fall (and rise again); rather, it asks: Why is Detroit such a compelling story? What is it that the narrative of Detroit, in its story of rise, fall, and potential for rise again, tells us about the seductive rendering of the promise of possibility in America? Dybis, in her five-year reflection, and Huey, in his editorial letter, hint at the answer: it is the city's evidence of a full range of human life and experience—its epic highs and devastating lows—that sets up Detroit as a perfect backdrop to continually reimagine the American frontier.

CHAPTER 1

It's Turned into a Race Thing

White Innocence and the Old Neighborhood

> All I tried to do was share a story about finding my house in Detroit, hoping other people would share their stories of finding former homes in Detroit, and all the fun they had living there and whatnot. As with all the Detroit threads, it's turned into a race thing.
>
> —Remisc

> The fantasies of the past, determined by the needs of the present, have a direct impact on the realities of the future.
>
> —Svetlana Boym, "Nostalgia and Its Discontents"

The website www.City-Data.com bills itself as an informational website that collects, analyzes, and integrates data directed at prospective home buyers from a variety of sources and encourages users to both research city demographic profiles and to submit their own questions and experiences on user forums. On March 18, 2010, a user named Remisc began a thread titled "I found my old house in Detroit today" on the Detroit-based forum.[1] Remisc details her experience looking for the old house she raised her kids in, and finds it absent save for the "teal foundation" and the "remains of the pillars of my front porch."[2] Just a few hours later, other users begin to chime in, discussing their own experiences looking for a home they had previously lived in and "finding" it in a much-altered physical state than they remember. The way that this thread unfolds represents a microcosm of the complex ways in which Detroit is remembered and recalled in the contemporary moment. For example, it is only when a couple of users offer an oppositional reading to the thread's sentimental view of a past that idealizes segregated Detroit as the city's glory days that Remisc and others suggest that the thread has turned into "a race thing."[3] While it might seem surprising to start a discussion on such an important topic as the process of racialization in contemporary representations of Detroit by exploring an Internet forum, in fact such a beginning is a perfect way to demonstrate the ho-hum and the hyperbolic, the divisions and the intersections, and most importantly, the ways in which the narrative of Detroit's present is dependent on the memories of Detroit's past.

In the "I found my old house in Detroit today" forum we see how institutional racism of the past—which enabled whites to accumulate property, among a host of other privileges—is narrated as "not about race," yet the decline of the city is narrated as "about race." This difference not only exposes the invisibility of institutionalized benefits attached to whiteness in the collective memory of former residents but also situates the narrative itself as a location of racial formation. Although the scholarly literature has well documented the relationship of property accumulation and whiteness in the United States and Detroit specifically,[4] the absence of acknowledgement of this history by most of these users demonstrates how that relationship, although backed up by irrefutable data, functions outside the standard story of home ownership in the United States. My intention is not simply to point out the ways in which the memories of individuals fail to match up with the historical record—something every one of us is guilty of, in one way or another. Indeed, the role of memory is not to mimic the historical record. Rather, I analyze the ways in which nostalgic memory is a lens through which racial innocence is created and maintained, both intentionally and unintentionally. As Svetlana Boym suggests, "Modern nostalgia is a mourning for the impossibility of mythical return, for the loss of an 'enchanted world' with clear borders and values."[5] Ultimately, this nostalgic longing is a way to see the continuing process of racialization in the United States.

The stories many of the users tell, and the way the most vocal forum members situate the idea of race as explicitly not about whiteness, must be considered within the large and unruly space of Internet forums, one of the many venues of popular culture that reflects, produces, and performs racialized narratives about the built environment. The Internet, and especially user forums, are profoundly public spaces of exchange, and thus locations that reveal what people are thinking about. And what we find, again and again, is a persistent view in which racism in particular is coded as a personal experience rather than part of a larger social system. I am by no means suggesting that a similar type of rhetoric does not occur in offline spaces, because in fact it does. I argue here that the City-Data.com Detroit forum, in other words, is a social system that replicates and creates a normative narrative of the invisibility of white privilege as it intersects with Detroit history. The online conversation runs alongside and in dialogue with the offline conversation; the location of the forum enables access to an ongoing conversation that is unmediated by notions of "political correctness."

City-Data.com is an informational website that collects, analyzes, and integrates data from a variety of sources and makes money from paid advertising on the site. The website, which hosts the forums, is primarily a resource for real estate–related information, a comprehensive database of everything from recent home sale prices, maps, and weather averages to demographic data about residents including race, income, and education, as well as overall community profile information about cost of living, crime data, and school rankings. The site is functional, above all else, and this interface serves as one of the ways it constructs itself as a place of data, concerned with nothing more than the seemingly neutral delivery of statistics about home buying, community composition, and neighborhood value. As websites become more slick and image-heavy, perpetually encouraging viewers to "like" and share content, the City-Data.com forums are intriguing: the design is barebones, the structure anonymous. The anonymity of the City-Data user profiles—which lack personalized avatars, and even basic profile information—speaks partially to the platform of the website but also to the users' relationship to the Web interface of the user forum, pictured in Figure 3.

Each user chooses their own profile name and this is how the user is represented in posts and threads. Things like location are customizable, and many of the posters to the Detroit forum have something vague like "Michigan," or "the Lakes," while others choose "Proud Detroit resident" or nothing at all. The ranking and join date reveal how long the user has been part of the forum, the number of individual posts they have contributed, and how those posts have been read. Finally, reputation is the times

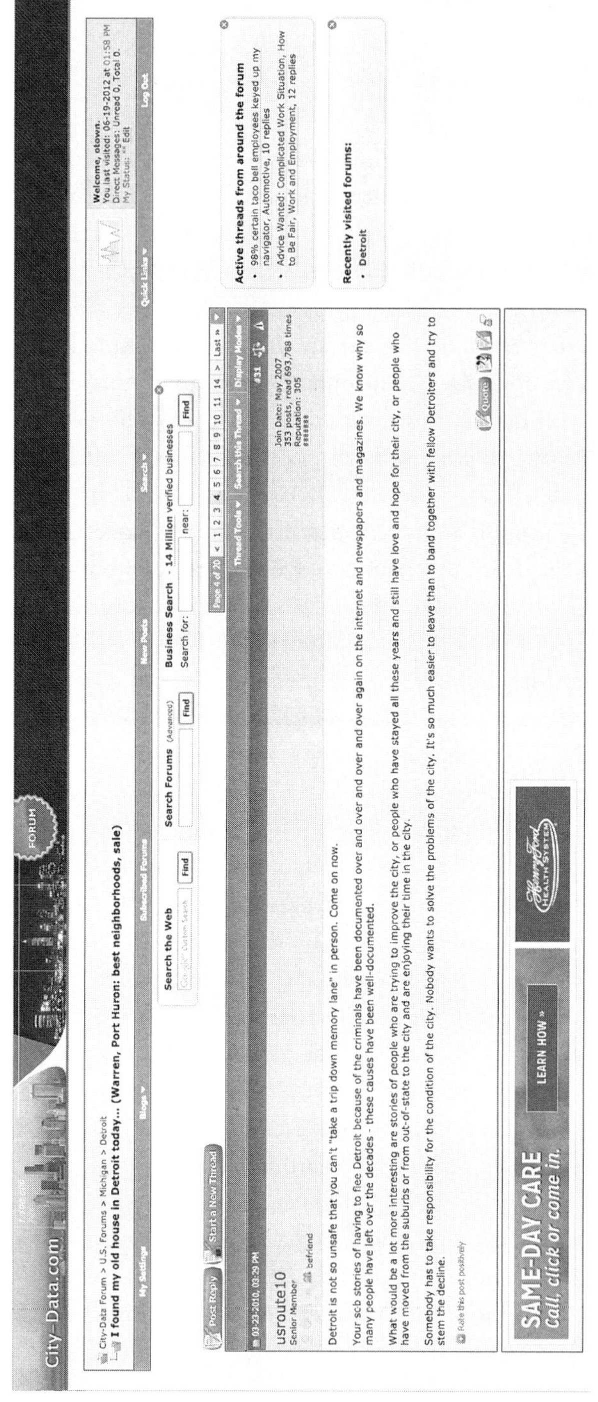

Figure 3. City-Data.com user forum interface. Photo by author, December 13, 2014.

that a user's posts have been rated positively cumulatively, not for individual postings. The basic structure has remained unchanged in the period from June 2010 when I joined the forum through my most recent visit in March 2016. Even more remarkable is the consistency of the interface despite the marked shift in user access to the Internet and networks more generally due to increased mobile connectivity and increasingly "smart" phones. By point of contrast, when the "I found my old house in Detroit today" forum began in March 2010, the widely popular photo-sharing and social networking service Instagram had not yet been developed.[6] However, even in 2010 the City-Data forum interface was considered antiquated, in marked contrast to sophisticated sites that ran complex applications including streaming video and images.[7] Therefore the form of City-Data most likely draws a user who is not necessarily interested in a sleek interface or the social networking component of many of today's more successful websites where users share at minimum a representative photo or image and quite often even more personal information when comments are directly connected to one's Facebook or Twitter profile.

In the period between March 18, 2010, and October 14, 2014, exactly 194 separate comments were posted to the "I found my old house in Detroit today" thread.[8] However, the bulk of the activity of the thread is comprised of the first 109 posts wherein a new post is written at least once per day from March 18 to April 1, 2010.[9] The analysis of this chapter is based on the initial activity of the Web thread, these first 109 posts. After this time there is a marked drop-off of frequency of activity with periods of weeks and months with no posts.[10] Overwhelmingly, given the title of the thread, "I found my old house in Detroit today," the majority of the posters self-identified as former Detroiters,[11] with a handful who did not identify, and a few who were from other nearby Rust Belt cities (Youngstown, Ohio, and Windsor, Ontario). It becomes clear through the discussion that the term *former Detroiter* is coded by the forum users as referring to someone who is white. The seven posters who contributed the majority of posts self-identified as five former residents, one current self-described black resident (usroute10), and one self-described white "trailer park" suburbanite who still spends a fair amount of time in the city.[12] Of the former Detroit residents, four self-identified as white (Remisc, SCBaker, MaryleeII, and scolls) and one self-identified as black (reconmark). Their self-identified racial background is important in how the other users conceptualize one another in relationship to themselves and as the discourse of "us" and "we" and "you," "they," and "them" emerges. Such assumptions are crucial in terms of how these users interact with one another and see each poster's stake in the narrative of Detroit. The most frequent posters share at least one memory, and often multiple memories, about a Detroit neighborhood, and what are invariably referred to as the halcyon days of Detroit. What is of note, however, are the ways in which the memories are coded as "appropriate" or "inappropriate" to post regarding "I found my old house."

What we find, in this presumably "anonymous" digital space, is a conversation in which everyday attitudes that are often hidden and filtered by political correctness are laid bare. The most vocal posters articulate a narrative of loss and destruction of homes as personal attacks by interlopers (who interfere both in real life as well as on the forum) against their homes and neighborhoods. Although initially the Internet was conceptualized as boundless, a space untethered from the restrictions of offline place, the discourses produced online are deeply linked to our existing social structures.[13] Even the early language describing the Internet, the "information superhighway," "cyberspace," or "electronic frontier," speaks and affirms a virtual space modeled after "real" place. The notion of "superhighway" in particular is an apt spatial signifier. In Detroit, the highway both enabled the growth of the suburbs and rationalized slum clearance projects, all in the name of urban renewal; thus the building of highways engineered a crucial shift in the city's population and its social and physical trajectory. In many ways, then, the configuration of the "information superhighway" serves to enable and rationalize projects that on the one hand seem not about social structure but on the other are already implicated in the social structure. In this chapter I show how a discussion in virtual space shapes the memory of actual place, and in turn this demonstrates the ways that the stories people tell about race and place perpetuate the process of racialization.

Longing for Home: The Nostalgic Pull of the "Old Neighborhood"

All of us are, at one time or another, pulled into reminiscing about a past time or place. The lament for the "old house," which both begins the City-Data thread and circulates through it, reconfirms the powerful pull of nostalgia for an imagined and idealized past. Indeed, Boym's discussion of the Greek roots of the word nostalgia—"*nostos* meaning 'return home' and *algia* 'longing'"[14]—clarifies the relationship on this thread between an individual's search for their old house and a much broader cultural longing for what once was, often conceived of as an idealized time and place of childhood. This particular discourse, the representation and longing for the past as a "better time," echoes Renato Rosaldo's conception of "imperialist nostalgia." He describes this concept as a paradox in which someone "deliberately alters a form of life, and then regrets that things have not remained as they were prior to the intervention. . . . In any of its versions, imperialist nostalgia uses a pose of 'innocent yearning' both to capture people's imaginations and to conceal its complicity with often brutal domination."[15] Indeed, here it will be clear how racial privilege is rewritten not just as an innocent time but in a way that frees users from culpability. As Rosaldo states, "The relatively benign character of most nostalgia facilitates imperialist nostalgia's capacity to transform the responsible colonial agent into an innocent bystander."[16] An overarching narrative of the thread is the account of segregated Detroit neighborhoods as innocent and carefree locations for the former Detroiters on the thread. Rosaldo's conception provides a lens to analyze the naturalization of white privilege in the memory of segregated spaces of childhood as idealized spaces of safety and prosperity.

The "I found my old house in Detroit today" thread begins on March 18, 2010, when a user named Remisc creates a new topic in the Detroit forum titled "I found my old house in Detroit today . . ." In this first post, Remisc shares,

> I found my old house in Detroit today . . .
>
> . . . and I was horrified. I found the street, but all I found at my former address was a teal foundation and the remains of the pillars of my front porch. I used to feel safe in my neighborhood, but I was scared just trying to find my own former home. I drove up and down the streets where I used to let my children play. They're now full of remains of burned down homes, caked with garbage, and infested with assorted stray animals. I moved out of Detroit 17 years ago, when the neighborhood was still pretty OK. I'm still in shock that all that could happen in under 20 years.[17]

This initial post sets the tone for what is to come—an emphasis on destruction and "horror" and "shock." Implicit here is the suggestion that the neighborhood itself has fallen victim to a disease—"burned down homes, caked with garbage, and infested with assorted stray animals"—in direct contrast to an imagined idyllic space where children used to play. The notion of past Detroit as different from present Detroit is clarified by the idea that when Remisc moved out of Detroit the neighborhood was "pretty OK." In this narration of what Remisc found, this user established not only a lament for what was but an inquiry into the destruction that led to the end of what was. And so a discussion ensues that contains memories of Detroit neighborhoods and their past, alongside narratives of the subsequent destruction of this past through a hazy lens of "imperialist nostalgia."

The posters who are most vocal about their old neighborhoods are self-aware of the seeming racial singularity of the neighborhoods, as either primarily black or primarily white. My analysis is most interested in the narrative of racial nostalgia that operates alongside the scholarship on institutional racism and housing in the United States. The discussion herein is not an attempt to suggest that users' memories are incorrect in the face of history; rather, the significance of their commentary lies in its role as a place to access the feelings and actions of everyday people who are not racist villains but in fact likely represent a fairly banal cross segment of the population. In this way the user comments illustrate a disconnect between the letter of the law and everyday social practice. For example, it has been illegal to discriminate based on race in public and private housing since the passage of Title VI of the Civil Rights Act of 1964 and the Fair Housing Act of 1968, respectively. Yet the Fair Housing Center of Metropolitan Detroit has repeatedly shown, through the fair housing testing it has carried out since 1977 and the more than four hundred subsequent housing discrimination lawsuits it has assisted in, that housing discrimination in metropolitan Detroit still occurs.[18] While the retelling of historical events often necessitates a definitive rendering of housing discrimination as illegal after the passage of the Fair Housing Act of 1968, a self-disclosed memory of the past can serve as a potent indicator of the disconnect between legislation and actual practice.

Many of the memories and narratives shared in the thread uphold a nostalgia for what was a segregated past. In Detroit, similar to cities throughout the north, the history of racial segregation begins in the early twentieth century as a formal social process but a not-yet-codified legal practice. As Detroit dramatically grew in population from 285,704 people in 1900 to 1,849,568 in 1950, the demand for housing far outpaced the available housing stock, especially in the decades of the Depression and World War II when construction came to a virtual standstill even as population growth continued.[19] Some studies suggest that because of the small size of the black population in Detroit before the large migration of African Americans during the interwar years, there was relatively little racial segregation as the size of the population allowed for small "clusters."[20] However, the historian David Allen Levine disputes this and indicates, "Detroit before 1915 was hardly an integrated community. Long before the onset of the Great Migration, most blacks were clustered in a clearly defined residential area on the city's near east side."[21] This pattern of residential housing segregation continued to grow, and increasingly mob violence and terror faced blacks who attempted to move outside the informal boundaries of segregated neighborhoods, most infamously marked by the 1925 case of Dr. Ossian Sweet.[22]

Detroit's local enactment of Depression-era New Deal legislation focused on housing Americans effectively codified the practice of segregation into city policy as carried out by the Detroit Housing Commission (DHC), established in 1933.[23] As part of its work, the DHC conducted the "Detroit Real Property Survey of 1938" to assess the housing stock and occupancy of the City of Detroit, providing evidence of a clear pattern of racial segregation in Detroit, as shown in Figure 4.

The importance of highlighting the existing pattern of racial segregation in Detroit is crucial, as the DHC began to make recommendations for where to build public housing in the city. With long waiting lists for Detroiters of all races, the DHC adhered to a policy of segregated occupancy. As each development was built, the decision whether it would house black or white residents was widely anticipated. The waffling of the DHC of designating the new Sojourner Truth housing project first for whites and then blacks led to a violent protest by white neighbors when African American families attempted to take occupancy on February 28, 1942, resulting in dozens of injuries and over two hundred arrests.[24] For many, the Sojourner Truth incident is seen as an early indicator of the racial vitriol that would become apparent in the 1943 race riot. In April 1943, in the wake of the Sojourner Truth Homes controversy and a few

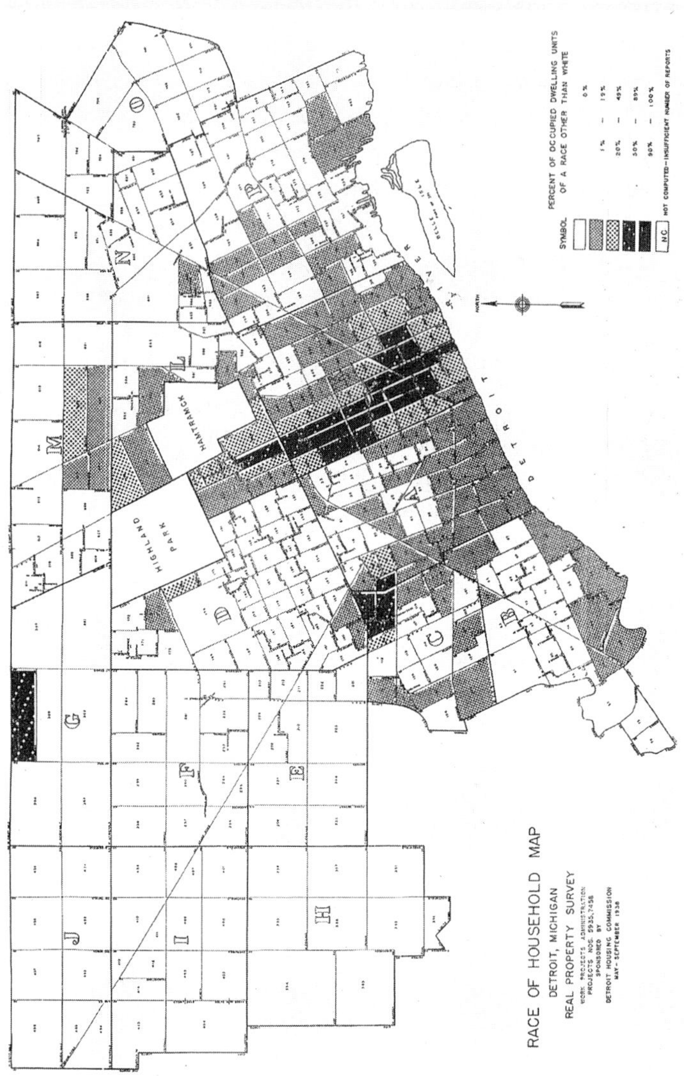

Figure 4. Race of household, Detroit Real Property Survey, 1938. City Plan Commission Papers, courtesy of Burton Historical Collection, Detroit Public Library.

months before the June 1943 riot, the Detroit Housing Commission adopted its first statement of record as to its policy of racial occupancy. This statement declared: "The Detroit Housing Commission will, in no way, change the racial characteristics of any neighborhood in Detroit through occupancy standards of housing projects under their jurisdiction. . . . [The DHC] reaffirms its policy of respecting neighborhood racial characteristics and will not sanction any deviations from this position that could lead to internal conflict during this war period."[25] In so doing the Detroit Housing Commission institutionalized racial segregation, relying on the already existing custom of racial segregation to rationalize the practice of segregated public housing. While not creating segregation, the formation and enactment of government policies based on the existing practice served to legally formalize segregation. Therefore, the DHC's position reflected the practice of the private market, which already operated according to the National Association of Real Estate Brokers, which formally adopted in 1924 an article in its "Code of Ethics" that formally forbade members "from introducing into a neighborhood members of any race or nationality whose presence will clearly be detrimental to property values."[26] The private market, long segregated through practice and preference of white homeowners, received formal support of segregation through the practice of redlining.[27] In this way the practice impacted entire neighborhoods, resulting in widespread disinvestment and decline in property values. Although this explicitly racial coding was removed from the Federal Housing Administration's *Underwriting Manual* by 1950, the practice was already firmly in place.[28]

Given the brief history of the practice of twentieth-century residential segregation outlined above, the City-Data thread plays an important role in explaining the transitions that emerged in a shifting racial landscape after African Americans began to integrate Detroit neighborhoods in the post–World War II years. The City-Data forum becomes a way to understand the memories of segregation and integration of Detroit as a lived rather than legislated experience. The most active participant on the thread is MaryleeII, and her posts are discussed throughout this chapter.[29] Through the course of the posts, MaryleeII self-identifies as a white former Detroiter of the baby boom generation who has not been back to Detroit in years. Throughout the duration of the thread, MaryleeII alternates between sharing memories of neighborhood institutions, places, and people and lamenting the loss of the neighborhood. A portion of MaryleeII's first post expresses both incredulity and camaraderie with Remisc's initial post:

> You actually went back and looked? I "visited" my former neighborhood by google map, I could barely recognize my old neighborhood, most of the houses are torn down and nothing but vacant fields. . . . I spent a lot of time just remembering the old neighborhood, the people who lived there, and spent the best years of their lives there. It was a solid, working-class neighborhood. My father, like many residents, found his way there after WWII, bought a home with his VA loan, got a job in the auto industry, and we all felt it would be that way forever. After all, we worked for the auto industry, we supplied the world with vehicles, and also the military. How could we fail and cease to be?[30]

At first, MaryleeII's memory of the old neighborhood and her family fits within the archetypal trope of universal citizenship, in which hard work and service to one's country makes possible the American Dream. In this model, which MaryleeII evokes, such "solid, working-class" values yield access to the middle class and to home ownership. This memory of the old neighborhood lives large for MaryleeII as she and another user, SCBaker, who grew up in the same general neighborhood in Detroit, share an exchange on the list of "do you remembers": "do you remember . . . that funky little hamburger place . . . the Cumminghams Drug right across from the Uptown, see a movie then go get a soda!"[31] In this trip down memory lane, SCBaker writes, "If I had only known what was to become of my beloved neighborhood, I would have taken tons of pictures when I had the opportunity. Unfortunately the images only remain in my memory."[32] MaryleeII agrees and writes, "We never thought to take pictures of the mundane, the everyday."[33] MaryleeII's version of history has been recounted by countless others, either members of the "Greatest Generation" or their offspring, for whom the post-Depression era brought not just victory in World War II but the economic victories of home ownership and a booming economy.

Yet MaryleeII's individual memory, like the common collective memory of access to home ownership in the United States, obscures the gulf between access to residential neighborhoods and home loans and mortgages for white and black Detroiters. The practice of mortgage lending based on neighborhood racial characteristics was widespread throughout the country: "Between 1940 and 1960 the rate of homeownership increased from 45.7 percent to 64.4 percent among whites but from 23.7 percent to 38.4 percent among blacks."[34] In the Detroit region, the numbers in the period directly following World War II are even more stark; of the 186,000 new homes constructed in metropolitan Detroit in the 1940s, only 1,500 were open to African Americans, and "as late as 1951, only 1.15 percent of new homes constructed in the metropolitan Detroit area were available to blacks."[35] What this means is that even as more Americans were becoming homeowners, African American homeowners were far outpaced by white homeowners. As Melvin Oliver and Thomas Shapiro have shown, the greatest transfer of wealth occurs in the passage of inherited property from one generation to the next, meaning that access to home ownership in America is directly linked to wealth accumulation.[36] Therefore, access to whiteness and the postwar housing boom ultimately enabled access to generational wealth accumulation.[37]

The above post by MaryleeII highlights the traditional version of American progress, emphasized via post–World War II policies that favored the housing subsidization of white veterans. Indeed, the federal government financed more than $120 billion worth of new housing between 1934 and 1962; over 98 percent of that housing was made available to white families, and less than 2 percent was available to nonwhite families.[38] And yet MaryleeII's comment mirrors the popular concept of these postwar efforts: that a loan or home mortgage, and ultimately the underwriting of racially exclusive development, was *not* a race-based government subsidy. As such, the dual takeaway central to this analysis is the way in which billions of dollars of government subsidy for whites is disappeared from the narrative of home ownership, both in this thread and in public discussion in general. However, when similar mortgages become available to nonwhites, they are characterized by some as government "giveaways."

This characterization is clearly expressed in a later post by MaryleeII ascribing home ownership of whites to fiscal responsibility and tenacity and homeownership by nonwhites as government handouts:

> My parents and grandparents actually paid for their homes. No government program, no special lets settle the score deals, just cash. They paid on their homes for 20 years. That meant paying every month, or you were evicted. No one cared about your sob story, pay or get out.
>
> We paid our homes free and clear, then were forced out due to the circumstances. No, we didn't create the circumstances, we were the victims. After a lifetime of hard work, we had nothing to show for it, nothing to sell, no equity, a total loss. Meanwhile, other "oppressed minorities" were literally given the homes we'd broken our backs to build and maintain. All sorts of HUD programs to shoehorn in the oppressed. Once they got there, if they got behind on their payments, no problem, just grant extensions.[39]

MaryleeII's statement exposes the underlying assumption that the VA loan she mentioned earlier is not a government program; instead, she characterizes her family's lifetime of "hard work" as what provided access to home ownership. And for "oppressed minorities" home ownership is due to government giveaways. Although it is not entirely clear which programs she might be referring to in regard to the giveaway of homes, her characterization of victimization of lack of equity after "a lifetime of hard work" here likely speaks to a below market return on a home sale when her white family moved out of an integrating neighborhood. This was not likely a result of actual neighborhood depreciation but more likely due to well-documented "blockbusting," a practice wherein real estate agents would initiate a sales panic by insinuating a sale or likely sale of a home in an all-white neighborhood to a black family, scaring white homeowners into selling homes at fire-sale rates in order for those agents to turn around and sell the property at widely inflated rates to black buyers.[40] Again, what is of interest here is not the historical recall of legislation, or unsavory practices by real estate agents, but the perception of a VA home loan as "paying for our home free and clear" and the characterization that nonwhite homeowners were receiving unfair benefits or privileges to access home ownership. In MaryleeII's posts she uses the terms *underprivileged* and *oppressed minorities* to signify blackness. Despite the rhetoric of home ownership as an aspiration for all Americans, there is a tenor of vitriol about the support of government-backed mortgages to enable nonwhite people to purchase homes.

In metropolitan Detroit, many of the new homes constructed in the post–World War II housing boom were built in the adjacent suburbs, far from the overwhelmingly old and dilapidated housing stock of the central city.[41] According to June Manning Thomas, "Builders constructed 178,000 new homes outside the city limits between 1950 and 1956," contributing to the suburban growth of metropolitan Detroit. Notably, less than 0.43 percent of these 178,000 new homes, "only about 750," were available to nonwhites.[42] In metropolitan Detroit, this trend continued well into the late 1960s: "In 1968, sixteen of the Detroit region's most affluent suburbs had no black homeowners, and most of the remaining communities had miniscule black populations."[43] Even as suburban growth became part of the American Dream, this dream was disproportionately reserved for white Americans. At the same time that black identity was cemented through prohibition of access to suburbanization, the identity of whiteness was expanding. David Freund's study of race and suburban development in metropolitan Detroit notes that "the people joining the 'white' exodus to suburban Detroit were a very heterogeneous lot, at least by pre–World War II standards."[44] In early twentieth-century Detroit, as in many other cities across the nation, nativism impacted housing for immigrants, most visibly evident in the ethnic residential enclaves of Jews, Poles, Hungarians, and Greeks that existed. However, suburbanization provided a key economic and geographic transition into American whiteness for European ethnics. As white privilege is obscured and stands in for the "typical" narrative of the GI Bill, mortgage, and access to work in the auto industry, these examples of racialized access are not seen as racially biased. This naturalization of privilege is a key factor of analysis in the City-Data thread, as it replays the experience of whites in Detroit as part of a common national narrative. This privilege is further naturalized in later posts that position racially equal access to home ownership as the extension of "handouts" or "privilege."

We Are Refugees: Remembering White Flight

Nowhere is the impulse to mourn the idealized time of the past more invoked than in the reoccurrence of the narrative that "we had to leave." The subtext of the forum is not simply about finding an old house; in order for such discovery to be possible, the individual had to at some point abandon that house. For example, MaryleeII explains in her second post to the thread, "What killed my neighborhood was the opening of the suburbs, they just had so much more house for the money. . . . When they built those nice, big homes in the suburbs people just . . . left our little homes to rot."[45] The decade after the end of World War II is a watershed moment in single-family homeownership in the United States. The pent-up demand for housing throughout the Depression and war years was finally able to be met as economic prosperity and the return of many workers from the war enabled a building boom unlike any other, evidenced by the sheer numbers of new construction. Becky Nicolaides and Andrew Wiese quantify this boom as follows: "Whereas only 142,000 housing units were built nation-wide in 1944, just two years later builders were hammering up over a million homes annually, 1.9 million by decade's end."[46] This pace continued, and Nicolaides and Wiese estimate that in the twenty years "between the end of World War II and 1965, the building industry constructed over 26 million nonfarm homes, most of them in the suburbs."[47] The ideal of the single-family suburban home is central to the dramatic twentieth-century population shift to the suburbs. In 1910 6.9 percent of the U.S. population lived in the suburbs; by 1940 that number had grown to 13.4 percent. In the post–World War II housing boom, by 1970 37.1 percent of the population lived in a suburban area and by 2000 fully 50.0 percent of the population lived in the suburbs.[48]

Being able to make a decision about where one lives is one of the invisible privileges of whiteness. The legacy of socially practiced and legalized segregation resulted in the maintenance of "white" neighborhoods by many under the discourse of "property values." Therefore, the City-Data forum is illuminating for the ways in which the economic argument for suburbanization that MaryleeII suggests above—"they [the suburbs] just had so much more house for the money"—is the first rationalization for white flight within the thread. Yet the everyday racism that underpins an economic argument is brought to light in the course of the forum. Typically the "newer home argument" takes precedence, but in the forum the idea that these "old houses" and neighborhoods were nice *until* integration happens supports then not an economic but a racial rationale for homes in the suburbs. As David Freund's work points out and my own experience growing up in an inner-ring Detroit suburb attests to, architecturally the oldest Detroit suburbs are "physically indistinguishable" from many working-class neighborhoods in Detroit defined by modest brick homes in the 1,200 square foot range.[49] When the homes in my inner-ring suburban neighborhood were built in the 1950s, they were most distinct from those in Detroit because of the racially exclusive access that was purchased with the new homes.

The thread is useful in illuminating an explicit preference for segregated neighborhoods not couched in the language of nicer or better homes. For example, SCBaker, a user who ultimately contributes twenty posts to the thread, states:

> I was born and raised in Detroit (East Side). I grew up during the late 40's, 50's and early 60's. Detroit was always segregated because most white people did not want a black family to move into their neighborhood. The white neighborhoods were quite successful in keeping blacks out but once in awhile a black family would manage to move in. Then the whole neighborhood would panic and begin selling their homes and fleeing to the suburbs. This phenomenon began happening in the 40's if not before. The 67 riots had nothing to do with white flight. The riots were not anywhere near the white neighborhoods. It began when the Detroit police raided a blind pig. There was an enormous amount of police brutality (ask any police officer from the 1st precinct back in those days) and I guess the raid was the "straw that broke the camels back."
>
> I graduated from Southeastern High School in 1961. When I enrolled there in 1958 there were 20% blacks, when I graduated there were 80% blacks.
>
> My parents sold their house and moved to East Detroit (Eastpointe)[50] in 1962. I went along kicking and screaming. I loved my neighborhood and didn't want to leave. I have fond memories growing up in Detroit and still love the City. I wish I could have lived there forever.[51]

In this first post by SCBaker, the work of memory lives large. The post reveals that SCBaker, like many of the other posters, is one of the "baby boom" generation, born in the 1940s and moved out of the city in 1962. However, he has clear perceptions of the movement of whites in the 1940s, hightailing it for the suburbs in the face of integration. In his own memory of high school, the shift of racial demographics of the student body further corroborates his experience of integration and white flight happening rapidly in his neighborhood in the late 1950s and early 1960s. Ultimately, he does not say why his own family moved to the suburbs but given the tone of the post suggests that his parents too may have been part of the neighborhood panic that ensued once their neighborhood was integrated. The idea that SCBaker went "kicking and screaming" suggests that his feelings about the neighborhood were different from his parents', that he did not want to go.

SCBaker's experience reveals the complexity of white attitudes toward integration, acknowledging institutional racism at work in both the brutality of the police as well as the segregation of Detroit neighborhoods. SCBaker's representation of "wanting to stay" in the face of integration suggests another perspective among whites, that not all fled and panicked, and perhaps he is suggesting that those who did were acting irrationally. SCBaker's personal experience reflects a dual narrative of white flight:[52] that there were both homes to be had in the suburbs and these suburban homes were not only available but served as a refuge from the panic of integration. Even as SCBaker did not want to go, he moved with his parents to Eastpointe and he eventually moved from Michigan in 1972.[53] SCBaker's experience chronologically falls squarely within the earlier part of the movement of suburbanization of white Detroiters. In fact, the decades-long out-migration of whites from Detroit, as discussed in the scholarly literature, is mirrored on the thread. Remember, the thread begins with Remisc's post, indicating a movement out from Detroit as an adult in 1993;[54] SCBaker moved from Detroit in his late teens in 1962. This means that the forum posters represent at minimum a spectrum of four distinct decades of exit from Detroit, which reflects the general population trends of the city and metropolitan area as a whole. For example, Joe T. Darden and Richard Thomas note that in 1960 the suburbs of Detroit were 96.2 percent white and 3.7 percent black, in contrast to the city of Detroit itself, which was 70.8 percent white and 28.9 percent black according to the census, revealing the disproportionately white population in the cities surrounding Detroit. This pattern continued throughout the end of the twentieth century: in 1970 Detroit city was 55.5 percent white and 43.7 percent black, and the suburbs of the city were 96.0 percent white and 3.6 percent black. In 1980 Detroit city was 34.4 percent white and 63.1 percent black, and the suburbs of the city were 94.1 percent white and 4.2 percent black. In 1990 Detroit city was 21.6 percent white and 75.7 percent black, and the suburbs of the city were 91.4 percent white and 5.0 percent black.[55] The population statistics bear out the increasing racial polarization not just between neighborhoods in the city proper but an increasingly segregated city and suburban periphery.

The historic population movement of whites from Detroit to the suburban periphery occurred alongside the passage of fair housing legislation. In fact, in the wake of the Supreme Court decision in *Shelley v. Kraemer* in 1948 and the passage of the Fair Housing Act in 1968, neighborhood patterns of racial segregation continued on a larger scale as the racial divide between the city and the suburbs became even more pronounced.[56] The majority of City-Data posters, like many who benefit from institutional racism, seem unaware of the factors that enabled their movement from Detroit. For example, SCBaker is well aware of the racially motivated shift in the out-migration of whites, including his family, from Detroit. Even as he does not explicitly reflect on the racially exclusionary housing practices in operation to maintain the whiteness of the suburbs, he tacitly conveys this reality in his description of whites choosing to leave for racially exclusionary suburban homes.

What results in the wake of fair housing legislation in Detroit then is the racial integration of the city of Detroit and the maintenance of racial segregation in the suburbs. The long-lasting impact of decades of segregation is nowhere clearer than in the 2010 population statistics of metropolitan Detroit: 2.9 percent of whites live in the city of Detroit and 97.1 percent of whites live in the suburbs, whereas 60.5 percent of blacks live in the city and 39.4 percent of blacks live in the suburbs, for an overall composition of the Detroit suburbs as 80.0 percent white and 12.2 percent black.[57] Meanwhile, the city of Detroit is 10.6 percent white and 82.7 percent black.[58] David Freund's work on national housing policy, and its particular application in post–World War II metropolitan Detroit, challenges the idea that suburbanization was simply the result of economic forces. The language of suburbanization, he reveals, undergoes a shift from the language of cultural preference to the language of the marketplace. Freund illuminates that white suburbanites were able to suggest that the rationale for racial exclusivity was linked to perceived threat to property values, insisting that "while they certainly did not want black neighbors, this did not make them racist."[59] As a result, the language of the marketplace enables suburbanization to be not about race but about economics. In particular, the recollection of "white flight" is one of the most complicated narratives expressed by users on the board. At its core a major theme that emerges from the debate is the recollection of black accessibility to home ownership as explicitly "about race" and white accessibility to home ownership as "not about race," exemplifying the ways in which whiteness is made invisible both in the legal facilitation of home ownership as well as in the memory of access to home ownership.

The debate about race and housing is an ongoing current throughout the thread, most clearly evidenced by the universalization of narratives of home ownership and access to home mortgages. However, one comment in particular sets into motion a conversation and debate about the remembrance of integration of neighborhoods and the racial rhetoric of white flight. MaryleeII responds to Remisc's tale of loss with a story of looking at a vacant lot in 2003 "where my house once stood." She continues, stating:

> Most of us have got on with our lives. We may have wonderful families, nice homes and a financially comfortable existence, but the destruction of our City and our first or childhood homes remain with us even if we have placed it far out of our minds. We still feel the loss, knowing we can never go back home.
>
> Thank you so much for starting this thread. I wish more people would find it and post their stories. Only those who have lived it can completely understand what we are feeling.
>
> Yes, many people had no choice but to leave. People have been killed, mugged, attacked or witnessed unspeakable horrors by trying to remain in their homes. Still, only to lose them to criminals and thugs in the end.
>
> I understand exactly. Its like we're refugees. I was chatting with a lady from Iran, everything she grew up with is gone, burned, destroyed. She can't go back if she wanted to. And she left due to dire circumstances, like we left Detroit.
>
> When you think about it, we are refugees. We didn't leave, we fled. We can't go back down memory lane, except via the Internet. Lately I've

> been reminiscing over old pictures, websites, etc, but there's no way I would ever go back there physically, simply because there isn't anything to go back to! My home, school, church, playgrounds, little businesses, are all gone. For those areas still remaining, well, its not worth the risk to take a trip down memory lane. I got out, stay out. . . .
>
> Hang in there, all my fellow refugees!"[60]

MaryleeII's post reveals the powerful tug of nostalgic memory that childhood homes represent; they are physical locations, but perhaps even more importantly, ideological places. Even though she states that the homes she and other posters arrived to are "financially comfortable" and that they have literally "got on" from the place of childhood, the emotional loss is palpable in this thread. This makes sense; the loss with which she begins this post many readers can likely identify with, recalling that when a childhood place of importance is developed or razed it changes the place of foundational memories into an unrecognizable location. For most, the ability to "go back" to a physical location and remember is a powerful source of nostalgia, and the inability to do so induces a feeling of loss.

What is of interest in the statement by MaryleeII is the perception that she and "many people" in Detroit "had no choice but to leave." The specter of crime and "unspeakable horrors" suggests that the movement from Detroit to the suburbs for MaryleeII was due to fear. In particular, it is the characterization of her experience and the experiences of her fellow white Detroiters as "refugees," akin to those of "a lady from Iran,"[61] that suggests an even more deeply harbored feeling of loss and persecution. The United Nations defines a refugee as a person, "owing to a well-founded fear of being persecuted for reasons of race, religion, nationality, membership of a particular social group of political opinion, [who] is outside the country of his nationality, and is unable to, or owing to such fear, is unwilling to avail himself of the protection of that country."[62] Even as most of us cannot quote the UN's precise definition of the term, the connotation of the term in the context of MaryleeII's post that white homeowners in Detroit were forced to leave due to fear, persecution, and destruction is palpable.

While the statement "Hang in there, all my fellow refugees!" may be read as hyperbole, the tone of "imperialist nostalgia"—and a lament that this person cannot go back because of a war-like destruction and persecution—presents a sentiment of blamelessness of departure of whites, situating the idea that they did not *choose* to leave but *had* to leave when Detroit became untenable. Part of the refrain of MaryleeII's posts that they *cannot* go back firmly reflects the belief that these former Detroiters were forced to flee, because of danger represented by their new neighbors, rather than representing that choice as a preference for the suburbs. In so doing MaryleeII recasts white homeowners as the victims of the housing system wherein a seemingly idyllic segregated neighborhood where she rode bikes and patronized the many businesses along the street was destroyed (physically, socially, economically, and ideologically) by integration.[63] The mourning of the individual childhood home and memory of the home serves symbolically as a lament of the loss of white privilege of racially exclusive neighborhoods. In their representations of the shift of Detroit, the forum users readily access the main popular narratives of Detroit's decline: white flight and black integration. Yet rather than separate narratives, the overlapping impacts of population movement by whites who *could* leave the city left behind an increasingly black city with a declining population and corporate and individual tax base—not the result of black home ownership but the result of white access to increasingly valuable suburban property.

"Back on Topic": Maintaining the Invisibility of Whiteness

On the "I found my old house in Detroit today" thread, the ongoing tension that frames the conversations is the sentiment that the Detroit of today, marked by destruction and decay, is markedly different from the Detroit of the past. Most of the users who post their memories of the city do so from locations outside the city. Although there is an underlying tension of the lament for the "old home" and the racialized undertones, the thread does not truly blow up until MaryleeII's comment situating herself and other former Detroiters as "refugees." In response to that posting and the ensuing debate, the pace of posting picks up as seventeen different users contribute seventy-six posts during the next week.[64] In the first two days alone, eleven different users contribute forty-four posts as the conversation grows increasingly heated.[65]

The first response to MaryleeII's post calling upon the other users to "Hang in there, all my fellow refugees" comes from usroute10. Rather than replicate the stories of crime and destruction, usroute10 asks MaryleeII and the other users who posted Google and Yahoo maps links of their old neighborhoods to visit the city in person, and see the city in a different light:

> Detroit is not so unsafe that you can't "take a trip down memory lane" in person. Come on now.
>
> Your sob stories of having to flee Detroit because of the criminals have been documented over and over and over and over again on the internet and newspapers and magazines. We know why so many people have left over the decades—these causes have been well-documented.
>
> What would be a lot more interesting are stories of people who are trying to improve the city, or people who have stayed all these years and still have love and hope for their city, or people who have moved from the suburbs or from out-of-state to the city and are enjoying their time in the city.
>
> Somebody has to take responsibility for the condition of the city. Nobody wants to solve the problems of the city. It's so much easier to leave than to band together with fellow Detroiters and try to stem the decline.[66]

Instead of contributing to the production of "panic" of the death and depravity of Detroit, usroute10 attempts to insert another narrative and disrupt the repetition of urban crisis. Usroute10 asks the forum users to think of those who have stayed or even moved into the city to express their continuing investment in Detroit and the possibility for another narrative—far less publicized—of Detroit on the rise. The narrative connects the pride of longtime Detroiters to boosterism about the city's rise, which is discussed further in chapter 5. Usroute10 fully acknowledges that the city has problems and instead asks the forum users to take into account the role that shrinking population, in which they and their families played a role, had on hastening a declining tax base in Detroit.

While members of the thread seem receptive to hearing positive stories, they push back usroute10's suggestion of focusing on stories of improvement. For example, while westender would "appreciate hearing current stories of improvement and positive directions," he also believes "that it is important to hear 'sob stories' and other historical anecdotes so that we don't repeat the bad outcomes of history."[67] Whereas the stories of improvement are interesting or appreciated, it is the "sob stories" that are deemed "important" as historical information. The idea then is that the thread in its formation is constructed to uphold a narrative of a destroyed city. On the heels of westender's response to usroute10 is an even more direct call from SCBaker to focus on the original topic of the thread:

> Why are you on this thread? Did you find your old house today? If so please tell us your story about its condition and provide pictures if they are available. If you have no old house to find then post your remarks on the appropriate thread.[68]

And there, in plainly typed language, is the clear statement that usroute10's call for stories of improvement or staying in Detroit are out of the purview of the thread. Rather, SCBaker is telling usroute10 that the thread is about a specific lament of an "old" house, not about new development, not about current residents, but a very clear call to provide, through story and image, proof of an old house. It is the idea of the "old house" that this hinges on, because as usroute10 wants to encourage discussions about still-occupied houses in Detroit, this particular thread is about finding an "old house," the memory of former homes rather than currently occupied dwellings. This distinction is a way in which the thread users articulate a possessive narrative of Detroit and imperialist nostalgia. The only stories that are deemed "appropriate" according to the most vocal forum users are those that can corroborate and mourn the narrative of homes and childhood places in states of ruin or decay. These users attempt to make a personal narrative into a collective memory of loss and destruction through the partitioning of what is an appropriate versus inappropriate topic of conversation.

It is, however, MaryleeII who fires back at usroute10's critique of her "sob story" with the following response:

> Three generations of the [*sic*] my family had nothing left but "sob stories" to tell. Someone has to take responsibility for the condition of the city?[69]

> Who built it and raised it to one of the industrial giants of all time? And who came in on their government sponsored "the white man did you wrong" programs? Oh, yes, I'll probably get banned from this board for this, but let it be said—Detroit, including my old neighborhood, was a fine place to live until certain "people" came in, sobbing all the way that they were "done wrong," social injustice, racial inequality, well, look what they did to it. Three generations of my family lived in the "old neighborhood" it took less than 5–7 years for those downtroden [*sic*] to destoy [*sic*] it beyond salvation. So its my fault because I left? Why did I leave it if was so wonderful? Who built it? And Who destroyed it? Blame the victim! Why—because you can't very well blame yourself![70]

The intensity of her thinking is palpable in her willingness to override her intellectual understanding of what she *should* say within the framework of politically correct discourse as evidenced by her comment "I'll probably get banned from this board," as she decides to state her opinion anyway. This post, which reflects a shift in tone as the grammar, syntax, and language becomes clipped, hurried, and full of typos, also provides an unveiled look at what MaryleeII actually feels beyond the screen of political correct discourse. Additionally, the use of rhetorical questions and exclamations at the end offers cues that she is very much on the defensive, responding with a repeated personal standpoint as "a victim" who previously had to flee and now is being revictimized as a result of a perceived attack that she is to blame for the decay of Detroit. While circular in logic, the point here is to show that this discussion is not necessarily about logic or facts but about the deeply personal memory of what former Detroiters believed happened to them and to Detroit.

This post provides insight into the division between what are multiple and competing reasons for white flight. While earlier MaryleeII expressed that many people left Detroit for the suburbs for newer, better houses for less money—a market-based argument—in this post three days later she presents a very different reason for leaving. The differing and multiple rationales she offers for leaving illustrate that reasons, as well as memories, are multilayered and, just like MaryleeII's recollections, messy. The writing then, both in content and form, suggests a larger struggle of competing memories—not that her previously expressed memories are untrue but that the perspective and recall of memories are not neatly packaged and may conflict with each other. Here she says that the neighborhood (and presumably its homes) "was a fine place to live." Indeed, this post clearly presents an idea that Detroit was built by families like MaryleeII's, raising it "to one of the industrial giants of all time." The houses did not immediately become less desirable from a market perspective, according to MaryleeII, until the shift in neighborhood residents from white to black. Beyond the work this post does in lifting the gauzy memory of white flight as a primarily economic argument is that it positions white homeowners as the victims of integration.

It is MaryleeII's memory of the destruction of Detroit represented in this heated response that enables access to a perspective that is often hidden in polite conversation. The idea of "who came in" to the neighborhood is clarified in the recall of those who accessed the old neighborhood through "government sponsored 'the white man did you wrong' programs." In this direct contrast between MaryleeII's perception of government programs available to her family and to black families, she situates a division in perception between access for whites and blacks in home ownership. Perhaps most indicative of underlying feelings of racial animus in the post is the use of scare quotes around the idea of "people" when she writes that her neighborhood "was a fine place to live until certain 'people' came in." Whether it is a slip of the keyboard or a typographical error, the idea here that in reference to nonwhite people there is a disdainful grammatical marking of whether or not certain people are indeed people is a possible interpretation of this use of punctuation.

Usroute10 challenges MaryleeII's circuitous language and urges her to articulate the racial narrative and claim it outright, stating, "MaryleeII, we (negroes) haven't destroyed those neighborhoods yet! By the way, why don't you say 'black people' in your above post. Those are the people to whom you are referring."[71] Furthermore, usroute10's invocation of the antiquated term *negroes* situates MaryleeII's "we" and "you" as part of its own antiquated racial discourse. The idea that MaryleeII's attitude is best captured by the use of *negro,* a term that diminished in popular use during the 1960s, alongside the rise of first *black* and then *African American* as parts of larger movements for equality, situates her narrative as a continuation of a time when widespread publicly and legally sanctioned racism was ubiquitous.[72] In addition, it simultaneously serves to link the continuing practice of interpersonal and institutional racism to the past through a momentary lifting of the well-veiled contemporary cloak of politically correct language.

Ultimately, in this remembrance of exodus the authority of memory emerges as the key debate of the thread. In the same post from usroute10 wherein he urges MaryleeII to say "black people," he begins by first responding to SCBaker's question asking if he found his "old house." Usroute10 states, "I live in the city. I am a homeowner. I see the slow decline of the neighborhood."[73] He goes on to share that the neighborhood to his north "is looking really run down—unkept houses, vacant housing stripped of aluminum siding"—and that the nearby elementary school will close and the nearby middle school closed a couple years ago.[74] Before he adds his reply to MaryleeII, usroute10 writes: "But I haven't been jaded yet enough to bail out on the city just yet. My house has been broken into, but I still stay. I just don't want to quit like everybody else did. The city is doomed if everybody leaves."[75] Usroute10 simultaneously acknowledges the decline and slow slipping away of his neighborhood and of the city. Yet in his characterization of refusal to abandon the city, he simultaneously situates himself as someone who could "bail out" but persistently stays. Additionally, the subtext of usroute10's rationale for staying indicts those who left as quitters and lays blame upon this group for the city's doom. He closes the section to SCBaker by including some websites and links to show "cool" information on what is currently going on in some neighborhoods.

In response to this, SCBaker writes a post that alternately acknowledges and thanks usroute10 for the weblinks and simultaneously suggests that usroute10 cannot know what the other posters like MaryleeII and himself feel:

> Just as I thought. You have not experienced the complete devastation of your neighborhood yet. It is just beginning for you and I understand your frustration. It appears you love your neighborhood and are saddened by what is going on around you. Some of us experienced the same feelings some 45 years ago and to finally lose in the end. . . .
>
> I know you think if everyone had stayed they could have prevent[ed] the decay. Possibly, but many tried to stay and paid with their lives and

> peace of mind. There was no one to help them protect their homes. The police simply [threw] up their hands. No one was safe in those neighborhoods. The hoodlums and criminals did not discriminate, everyone was a potential victim. . . .
>
> I do hope you and your neighbors can save and improve your neighborhood. It would be a wonderful ending. . . .
>
> Finally, I do not think it is proper to criticize others if you have not walke[d] in their shoes. I only hope that you are not forced to flee your home someday like so many others before you.[76]

SCBaker presents the idea that usroute10 cannot know and understand what the other users are feeling because the neighborhood has not been completely devastated, "yet." However, the idea is clear that, just as MaryleeII suggested previously, the destruction is imminent because of the "hoodlums and criminals." Again, the idea that the neighborhoods in which the posters grew up in and had to flee became increasingly unsafe is repeated here, but in contrast to MaryleeII's suggestion of "certain people," SCBaker pointedly notes that "everyone" was a potential victim. SCBaker's memory here of crime and destruction contrasts with his prior post that indicates he went "kicking and screaming" to the suburbs. Herein is where memory becomes tricky—the feeling of not wanting to go is also complexly intermingled with this recollection of fear and violence. In the end these both operate as the collectivization of the personal memory, and the writing of the post suggests that the purpose of this particular thread is to corroborate and present Detroit as either destroyed or in the process of destruction.

In the two days after usroute10 makes his post urging MaryleeII to "just say black people," users contribute forty-four more posts. Of these are fourteen separate posts between the original poster Remisc and another user, scolls, that focus primarily around sharing current and historical images and information about researching tax and property records.[77] Rather than an exchange of memories, this exchange is notable for its practical suggestion of how to research property records to learn who may have owned the home in the interim and breaking down some of the potential sources for research. However, alongside and interspersed in the exchange between Remisc and scolls is an alternate conversation between reconmark, SCBaker, MaryleeII, usroute10, ilovemycomputer90, RememberMee, meemy, omckenzie710, and malamute that is not about research or even memories for the most part, but rather is about race.[78] The tenor of the conversation can be summarized as primarily usroute10 and reconmark playing defense to comments made by SCBaker, MaryleeII, and ilovemycomputer90. For example, in response to MaryleeII's description of the violence and neighborhood decline her mother experienced,[79] usroute10 writes:

> Blacks folks came up north for better economic opportunity, to get jobs in the auto factories. I don't understand why too many of us have descended into crime, drugs, broken families, and low achievement, but we didn't come up north to rob and kill people. I really do feel bad for what your mother went through.[80]

As he has done previously, usroute10 illustrates that there are in fact problems in Detroit. Usroute10 and reconmark seem most interested in illuminating the racialized power structure that emerged between white and black Detroiters. At one point reconmark, in response to MaryleeII, writes: "Do you see where your ignorance lies, to you, it's all about what the blacks did!!"[81] Reconmark in this same post mentions two homes that he lived in in the past, acknowledging, "Yes both of these homes are gone now." Very clearly even as usroute10 and reconmark are mired in a back-and-forth war of words with MaryleeII, SCBaker, and the others, neither contrarian is suggesting that Detroit is not in decline, or that Detroit's present situation is less than ideal. However, they are both interested in illuminating a perspective of the city's decay beyond the personal narration of African American depravity as the cause of Detroit's decline. Yet it is an uphill battle as ilovemycomputer90 chimes in to state:

> Of course it would be stupid to blame ALL of Detroit's problems on blacks. But the fact is that Detroit's population is over 80% African American. It also happens to be one of the most dangerous cities in the U.S. Coincidence? I think not.
>
> My views on the situation has nothing to do with prejudice or racial sentiment. I'm simply looking at the facts.[82]

At the same time the user realizes that Detroit's problems are complex and are likely a result of multiple factors, ilovemycomputer90 ultimately falls back onto the idea that racial demography is proof enough of criminality and danger perpetrated by African American residents.

After two days and over forty back-and-forth posts, Yac, a City-Data forum senior moderator, steps in and posts the following, "Everybody please calm down. Agree to disagree, ignore each other—I don't care. Just don't turn an interesting and controversial (as it seems) topic into a flame war."[83] The controversy that the moderator attempts to quell is no less than the complex struggle between narratives of Detroit's past as it impacts the present. The call by Yac to "calm down" and "ignore each other" is unheeded in the next four posts. Reconmark posts directly after Yac and does not acknowledge the moderator intervention. Instead, reconmark posts a response to ilovemycomputer90 about the racial makeup of Detroit as evidence of the relationship between race and decline:

> When you cite the racial make up of the city you are simply citing the end result of all the racial, market, commercial, and socio-economic inputs that contributed to the city being 80% black.
>
> Those that are stuck behind include not only those who do not want to work but those tradesmen and skilled workers that no longer have a market for their skills.
>
> The largest exodus of opportunities for the majority of working blacks occurred when the automakers left the cities and blacks were refused loans to purchase properties in the suburbs.
>
> Now there are those who would put their thumbs in their ears in an attempt to deny this fact, but it only takes a second to verify this on your own.
>
> When you skim off the upper and most of the middle class employment opportunities Detroit is what you have left.
>
> When a cycle of segregation, racial animosity from both sides, a lack of personal drive, a sense of helplessness, and few chances at a coveted auto plant job are the norm, this is what we are left with.[84]

This response underscores an earlier comment that reconmark made indicating that he has "lived AND studied this situation [Detroit's decline] for many years."[85] Relying on both the historical and scholarly accounting of Detroit's history to frame his perspective of the city, reconmark is not seeking to suggest that Detroit is *not* in decline but that it is more than a majority black population that serves as evidence and proof of decline. What emerged thus far on the thread is the refusal by usroute10 and reconmark to acquiesce to the much-vaunted narrative of Detroit's past as an idealized time that was destroyed by shifting demographics. Users such as usroute10 and reconmark go out of their way to situate Detroit's history within a reality of institutional racism in home ownership, jobs, and education.

While this post from reconmark is met with partial agreement by ilovemycomputer90 and SCBaker,[86] MaryleeII puts forth another post that acknowledges that her neighborhood was victimized by violent crime after "the 'great equality' movement began."[87] Although she acknowledges that her neighborhood "had crime long before the first 'colored' person ever came, that's so true,"[88] she suggests that the nature of the crimes changed:

> Within a few years [after the "great equality" movement] you were afraid to go out in broad daylight. . . . A few petty burglaries is one thing, but rapes, muggings, arson, and murder were almost an everyday occurrence. . . .
>
> One group came and destroyed another's home, then shakes their head in wonder, why did they leave? Now look at the garbage hole I'm stuck with? Well, it wasn't that way when they came in.[89]

MaryleeII's redeployment of violence and crime as a very personal memory and experience is one that emerges again and again in her posts. While she offers memories of burglaries faced by her mother and a fire that resulted in the burning of a home in the neighborhood—both of which are by no means considered lightly here, and are in fact strongly negative experiences—it is her correlation between these acts of violence and crime and the integration of the neighborhood that is the central sentiment. While crime existed in the neighborhood before integration, it is the perception of the violence of the crime and the criminal actors that is of interest. I am not suggesting that MaryleeII's memories and experiences are not deeply felt and impactful; in fact, it is just the opposite. Yet her experience validates the idea that burglaries and fires are seen as violent only *after* integration. For example, in that same post she talks about burglaries in her neighborhood before integration when the theft of her father's car radio occurred not once but three times: "He finally rigged up an alarm, it went off and scared away whoever, no problem after that." In this instance, burglary is seen not as a symptom of the decline of neighborhood or violence; rather, it was "a stable neighborhood."[90] It is evident that MaryleeII believes that violence and ultimately the decline of Detroit is the fault of the racial integration of previously segregated neighborhoods.

After this post, Remisc states simply, "Yikes. This thread is getting out of hand."[91] And in many ways the parallels of white–black vitriol that emerged in the battle over Detroit's actual integration are replicated on the thread itself in the discussion of memories and experiences of that time period. The parallel unfolding of the memory of the time and the time itself offers an indication that the stakes of these memories, as much as they are about the past, are also about how we imagine the present and the future. This comment by Remisc ushers in a period of silence throughout the remainder of that afternoon and evening. The next morning, MaryleeII breaks the silence with a call to the board that begins, "Can we get back to the OT [original topic] and continue to post pictures & stories of old homes in Detroit?"[92] and concludes by asking fellow users if they have pictures of or remember particular businesses in her old neighborhood. Less than forty minutes later, reconmark chimes in with the following post:

> Yes, let's get back [to] the original topic, which was NOT black people ruined it all, don't work and had everything handed to them on a silver platter!!
>
> Anyone live around the Dexter and Boston area in the last 40 years!!
>
> It's hard to imagine that when I lived there we had bakeries, cleaners, a car dealership, and nightclubs.
>
> I learned to swim at the YMCA on Dexter and Grand River, there was also a city swimming pool next to my elementary school (Keidan Elementary) during the summer when it was hottest we would climb the fence and swim after closing hours.[93]

Reconmark's post begins with the pointed critique that black people did not ruin Detroit and speaks to the ways in which so many of the prior posts about users' memories of their "old house" end up assigning blame about the current state of that home, and drawing a link, whether explicit or implicit, between the ruined neighborhood and black integration. Reconmark asserts that this was not the original topic, either, and goes on to share memories about his old neighborhood, a place with a full spectrum of commercial and leisure activities. He recalls long, hot summer days that have nothing to do with violence but rather the joys of childhood. In this way, the balance of this post evokes the early posts on the thread of MaryleeII, SCBaker, and others when they shared remembrances of places and small businesses that formed the fabric of their childhoods, reconfirming the nostalgia that imbues all users' memories of the past.

A few hours later, SCBaker jumps back into the thread and, as all the users seem to want, attempts to have the last word on the topic of race. Rather than responding to MaryleeII or reconmark's contribution to the original topic, SCBaker replies directly to reconmark:

> Just had to get in one last dig, did you? Remisc began this thread to tell her story. Immediately she was criticized by usroute10. It was all her fault and others like her for the demise of Detroit. Marylee11 told her story and was attacked for her story as well. By the way, her first post did not include any defensive comments, she simply described her lovely neighborhood before its demise. She should have never been put in a situation of having to defend herself. First usroute10 and then you had to chime in and keep the racial strife conversation going. The two of you turned this thread into an ugly attack session.
>
> In reading your posts, I get the feeling that you felt gangs of "blacks" were justified marching into peaceful neighborhoods inflicting unspeakable destruction and horror against the innocent residents. While agreed, the black residents did suffer from unfair racial prejudices, violence was not the way to solve the problems. Violence, or the fear of it brought a once great dynamic City to its knees. Dr. Martin Luther King knew that violence was not the way. Too bad not enough people listened to him.

> There are so many stories to be heard and I hope more people will find this thread and post their stories without fear of being attacked.
>
> The moderators will close this thread if we don't cool it.[94]

SCBaker situates reconmark's post as an "attack" on MaryleeII and Remisc and jumps in to protect them, in the process replicating in the forum thread the idea of the white posters as under attack by "inappropriate" (black) posters. It is revealing that SCBaker reads dissonant voices in the thread that highlight the investment in whiteness as an attack. His version of attack is supported in the ways that memories of "lovely neighborhoods" that were all white are read as "simply described" and that "demise" after integration is not about race. His recounting asserts that particular memories of Detroit, much like Detroit history as frequently told, is removed from the understanding that race did play a part in access to home ownership. SCBaker and MaryleeII position themselves as the victims of "attack" within the thread itself that parallels the "attack" that they felt they were under in their neighborhoods, which "forced them to flee." Indeed, in SCBaker's characterization of "gangs of 'blacks' . . . marching into peaceful neighborhoods," it is unclear whether the reference here is to a particular event or a general characterization of the process of integration. Either way, the depiction of an all-out attack on "innocent residents" either as an act of war or a mandate for equality situates these memories of former white residents as the victims of integration and accuses usroute10 and reconmark of replicating an attack of these users' stories about the attack of their old neighborhoods.

As the conversation grows increasingly animated, the narrative that is being described about the transition of the physical places of Detroit is replayed in the forum's posts. Reconmark asks SCBaker for clarification—"who exactly were these gangs of 'Blacks' who committed these unspeakable acts??"[95]—and plays defense to continuing comments from a handful of users that suggest the decline of Detroit is placed squarely on the back of black residents and politicians. In a final exchange between MaryleeII and reconmark, MaryleeII writes: "Oh, geez! Can we get back to the OT—people finding their former homes in Detroit, and their memories? Let's make all this 'race talk' another thread."[96] To this, in his final post to the thread, reconmark writes: "Why do you keep asking to get back to the ot, and then making snide remarks??? Let's get back to the ot and leave the childish remarks behind!!!"[97] As this back and forth has escalated to this exchange, once again Yac, the moderator, returns to the thread, stating, "Back on topic folks. And no, it's not about race or your personal dislikes about other members. Thank you."[98] The City-Data moderator is able to post with authority of enforcement that the topic is "not about race" and urge posters to return to the "OT" of the thread. The forum attempts to maintain a perspective of fair and neutral community yet at the same time relies on individual users to monitor and set the precedence as to what is "appropriate" for discussion. What is of note here is not only Yac's directive to get "back on topic" but the secondary comment in which Yac defines the topic itself. In the comment, "and no, it's not about race," Yac in effect shuts down the conversation to dissenters who were critiquing the invisibility of white privilege. In so doing the dominant discourse about the invisibility of white privilege within the city of Detroit historically is redeployed through the work of memory and the maintenance of the "fantasies of the past."

The maintenance of white privilege as invisible is best illustrated with Remisc's reply to Yac's instruction to get "back on topic," which is the epigraph that opens this chapter: "All I tried to do was share a story about finding my house in Detroit, hoping other people would share their stories of finding former homes in Detroit, and all the fun they had living there and whatnot. As with all the Detroit threads, it's turned into a race thing."[99] The idea of white privilege as invisible and not about race in the end is the final word on the topic as reconmark and usroute10 do not add any additional comments on the thread. After this post from Remisc, the thread continues on, slowing down in pace yet still active as eighty-eight new posts are made in an ensuing four-and-a-half-year period from March 31, 2010, to October 14, 2014.[100] The subsequent posts trickle in slowly, with periods of weeks and months in between posts. The conversation never returns to the pace discussed in this chapter and never turns back toward this type of dialogue about the decline of the city. Instead, the subsequent posters primarily contribute as Remisc had intended when beginning the thread; they offer stories of neighborhoods and memories of the past against the backdrop of the decay of the present.

Fantasies of the Past Laying the Groundwork for the Future

It is not at all surprising and in fact it is fitting that here, on a website centered on the economics of housing, memories of economic prosperity and decline are recalled via the shift from segregation to integration. In many ways then the "culture of fear," which both created and replicated narratives of declining neighborhoods and property values because of integration, shows up online. The hostility that erupts within the thread in many ways is a replication of the long-standing black–white divide in metro Detroit that is marked most physically by the geographic segregation between city and suburbs. At the most basic level, this thread is about the memories of white flight from the city to the suburbs by former white residents. The majority of users here share personal recollections of what their neighborhoods were like before and after integration and draw a conclusion that after they left, Detroit collapsed. Rather than relying on a scholarly or historical framework of the declining tax base and population, the major shifts in Detroit's infrastructure at the level of homes and neighborhoods is rendered as a result of an increasingly black population.

This conversation therefore serves as a powerful replication of the process of making whiteness invisible—the continual emphasis that "race" only matters when it concerns people of color. As I have explained, any comment that seeks to disrupt the invisibility of white privilege is accosted as turning the conversation into a "race thing," despite the fact that history and other users show that access to housing in Detroit was indeed a "race thing." If other users want to talk about how neighborhoods are still thriving, about childhood memories that don't fall inside this narrative, and defend the coded (and not so coded) racial attacks being thrown around, then their responses are considered outside the original topic, as a critique of white privilege is seen as making the conversation "about race." The enforcement of users and moderators to propel a conversation that is seemingly "race neutral" disavows the institutional investment that whiteness is granted in terms of the subsidization of private home ownership. This "neutrality" is reinforced both in the nostalgia and in the policing of comments on the board itself. However, while some users share their nostalgic memories for the past, saying that the thread is not about race, they rely on an entirely race-based logic of black criminality and depravity to explain the "demise of Detroit." At its core, the calling into question of white privilege is a "race thing," but living within a cloak of invisibility of white privilege is race neutral.

As the subsidization of home ownership and suburbanization of whites is rendered as "not about race" both historically and in the memory of the past, the invisibility of white privilege continues to flourish, both at a material and (importantly here) an ideological level. This unfiltered (though not unmediated) forum provided a location to analyze how collective memory around race, segregation, and white flight is reproduced, providing access to discourse that is increasingly closeted off-line. The importance of the forum thread is in its ability to show the continuing legacies of the memories of the past in representing the present. Throughout the book I will continue to illuminate the fantasies of Detroit's past greatness *and* destruction as central to the story of Detroit's present and future.

CHAPTER 2

Picturing Ruin and Possibility

The Rise of the Postindustrial Frontier

> My photographs, exhibitions, and articles on downtown Detroit helped begin a national dialogue on the future of urban ruins. Without pretending that structures in the process of being discarded can retain their former economic and social importance, I continue to argue that their power as symbols remains strong. They are an essential part of understanding America.
>
> —Camilo José Vergara, *American Ruins*

> It is true, of course, that *all* forms of representation call forth questions of responsibility and perhaps of descriptive accuracy, but those evoked by photographic representation are unique. The apparent truth value of photography and film has made them powerfully effective vehicles for reportage and commentary. Of all photographic practices, social documentary—the self-professed truth-teller, implicated in modernity and part of its "life world"—is the one in which the underlying issues of social power are accessible to contestation.
>
> —Martha Rosler, "Post-Documentary, Post-Photography"

During the 1990s areas of postindustrial cities conceptualized as "urban ghettos" served as spatial locations to focus scholarly study of "the underclass." The consolidation by both federal and state governments of neoliberal policies, prioritizing privatization and ideologies of personal responsibility, resulted in a scaffolding of the logic of "the market" onto and into government policies.[1] Most famous among these were summations that wide-scale poverty, crime, and joblessness in America's urban cores were the result of either structural failure or the redeployment of the "culture of poverty."[2] This ideology reemerged in scholarly and journalistic accounts, frequently framed as the "culture wars." While causes and solutions were hotly debated, what was typically agreed upon was that postindustrial cities were locations where the "truly disadvantaged" lived and that those who lived in these places were overwhelmingly black.[3] The debates often focused on race as either the outcome of spatial segregation, resulting in an "American Apartheid," or an outcome of location—that those in postindustrial cities were poor because "work disappeared."[4] Either way, the voices from all angles, both in the scholarly conversation as well as in the everyday narrative described in chapter 1, seemed to verify that central cities were disproportionately poor and disproportionately black. And as the conversation raged onward, representations in the 1990s of the U.S. city as a location of crime, arson, and decay created what Steve Macek calls a "landscape of fear" that extended to both the city itself and its inhabitants. Detroit and its majority black population were often equated as prime examples of this landscape of fear in both local and national news media, as seen, for example, in Figure 1 discussed in the introduction.[5] More broadly, the period marked the third consecutive decade of disinvestment in U.S. cities, resulting in a decreased tax base, declining government services, and a large-scale disregard of infrastructure. The U.S. city of the 1990s, as Jason Hackworth argues, was left ready and primed for growth and investment that produced ever-increasing uneven development and social polarization.[6]

In this chapter I analyze the ways in which the narrative of Detroit as a landscape of fear shifts to a landscape of possibility through photographs of the city in states of emptiness and ruin. While this type of imagery runs rampant in the 2010s, the shift I locate here emerges in the 1990s. This offers a sharp contrast from the more typical representations of that time period as a landscape of fear teeming with danger to a city in near emptiness full of possibility in its ruin. The photographs and narrative statements of Camilo José Vergara are central to the shifting representation of Detroit from a landscape of fear to frontier. As I will show, Vergara's photography offers a new way of looking at the postindustrial city that emerged in the 1990s.

My focus on Vergara's work, then, is important as the first nationally prominent imagery to offer postindustrial Detroit as a space of beauty and lays the groundwork for the spate of imagery that reached a fever pitch in the last decade. Indeed, in 1995 Vergara argued that Detroit was envisioned by others as a "throwaway city," yet he intended to show the potential in ruin.[7] Significantly, Camilo José Vergara's visual presentation of a derelict built landscape in ruin as an object of beauty predates the contemporary interest in ruin photography by nearly two decades. In his images, Detroit is not full of danger but evocative in its near emptiness. Vergara's images serve as a precursor to the photography genre that emerged in the late 2000s and early 2010s, colloquially referred to as "ruin photography" and sometimes "ruin porn."[8] Although Vergara continues to photograph Detroit, his more recent images of the city have been eclipsed by the visually arresting and more widely distributed work of photographers like Yves Marchand and Romain Meffre and Andrew Moore.[9]

Vergara's work ushered in a particular way of looking at the postindustrial city, walking the line between artistic imagery of urban landscapes and documentary-style photojournalism of urban life. Vergara's images and narratives operate within the already established role of documentary photography in providing access to and information about those considered a part of, yet apart from, American life.[10] His images, and the narrative he assembles around them, consciously recall the works of late nineteenth- and early twentieth-century American photographers, such as Jacob Riis and Edward S. Curtis, in which photography operates as a medium of "truth," as a mode to bring American "others" into the consciousness of mainstream America. Some have gone so far as to describe Vergara as "the Jacob Riis of our time."[11] As Alan Trachtenberg argues, however, the photograph itself is significant not only for what it shows but for what it says about the historical and cultural context in which it is made.[12] In this chapter I study the role of Vergara's work in shifting constructions of Detroit as empty of "productive" capital and people yet full of possibility in ruin. I argue that this shift is connected to long-established racial logics that underwrite ideas of places of promise and places of fear in the American landscape.[13] The ideology of the majority black city of Detroit as empty, abandoned, and in ruin, which gains traction during this time, was and continues to be deeply implicated in conceptions of racialized space. By examining some of the earliest visual narratives of the postindustrial city as empty, I show the context for the spate of narratives currently in production about Detroit's potential as a frontier.

The "New American Ghetto Archive"

Camilo José Vergara is well known as both a social documentarian and an artist. In 2002 he was selected as a MacArthur Fellow and received the prestigious, no-strings-attached "genius" grant, and in July 2013 he became the first photographer to receive a National Humanities Medal. According to the National Endowment for the Humanities, which awards the medal, Vergara was chosen "for his stark visual representation of American cities. By capturing images of urban settings over time, his sequences reflect the vibrant culture of our changing communities and document the enduring spirit that shines through decay."[14] The acclaim from the National Endowment for the Humanities is in regard to the content as well as the form of his images. This distinction is important, as the documentary image-making is a key piece of achievement. Vergara has gone on record stating that he is not an activist, nor is he interested in making change in the neighborhoods he records. According to an article about the announcement of the award, "He thinks of himself as a 'snooper' whose job is to simply record what he sees."[15] Yet his framing and subjectivity can and should be considered as a stylized reflection of a moment—particularly framed, captured, and filtered by the camera, his gaze, and artistic choices.

The New American Ghetto (1995) and *American Ruins* (1999), which form the focus of analysis in this chapter, helped to build his reputation as the country continued to locate postindustrial cities as the center of urban crisis.[16] Vergara explains that *The New American Ghetto* "grew out of the 'The New American Ghetto Archive,' my collection of over nine thousand color slides that I began taking in 1977 for the purpose of documenting the nation's major ghettos," an archive that features, in addition to Detroit, Los Angeles, New York, Newark, Chicago, Gary, and Camden.[17] Although the "New American Ghetto Archive" formally begins in 1977, Vergara did not officially photograph Detroit until 1991. At the time *The New American Ghetto* was published he counted 260 slides of Detroit.[18] He explained that he had only been to Detroit a handful of times, stating: "Four years ago I decided to add Detroit to the collection. Instead of doing a systematic documentation of the entire city—impossible, my being able to spend only five days a year photographing there—I chose to concentrate on the city's downtown and some of the wide commercial thoroughfares, areas most affected by the process of disinvestment."[19] The language in which he writes about adding Detroit to the collection gives the impression that it and the other cities he photographs are like artworks to be collected and owned. The statement reveals that although Detroit is part of the collection, he was not as familiar with the city as others that he had lived in or visited consistently since the 1970s.[20] *American Ruins* is a continuation of the same project and presents additional images from the growing collection of the "New American Ghetto Archive," showcasing both older and more recent images spanning from 1977 to 1998. It is the Detroit-specific narrative compiled in these two books that I focus on in this chapter. Of the fifty-one images of Detroit in *The New American Ghetto,* four images are dated 1987, suggesting that although Vergara *visited* Detroit in 1987, he did not intend to methodically capture the city until 1991. The other forty-seven images included in *The New American Ghetto* are dated between 1991 and 1995. In *American Ruins* there are eighty-two images of Detroit. Of these, seventy-eight were taken between 1991 and 1998. Of the remaining four images, three were captured in 1987 and one is dated 1985.

Given the geographic diversity of the "New American Ghetto Archive" as a whole, the organizing principle of the archive for Vergara is that all of these locations represent "the poorest and most segregated urban communities in the country. . . . My choice of locations coincides with areas called 'hyperghettos'—places where at least 40 percent of the population lives below the poverty level."[21] For Vergara, then, poverty and segregation are the two most definable characteristics of a ghetto. In the mission to provide documentation of the ghetto, through sheer volume of images produced Vergara creates and manifests the ghetto as a location most starkly defined by poverty and blackness. Therefore, the publication of the archive not only reproduces; the archive itself also produces a relationship between spatial location, poverty, and blackness.

The compilation of the archive is an attempt to record the life cycle of what Vergara terms *the American ghetto.* He states, "The visual and written record that I have begun enables us to mentally reconstruct neighborhoods that are disappearing and to better understand the lives of the inhabitants of shattered communities."[22] He consciously follows in the footsteps of the "social reformers of the late nineteenth century [who] expressed a belief in the power of urban environments to shape lives."[23] And much like earlier reformers, the perspective is intent on shedding light and fomenting change through the production of urban environments as locations of difference. He writes:

> Ghettos, as intrinsic to the identity of the United States as New England villages, vast national parks, and leafy suburbs, nevertheless remain unique in their social and physical isolation from the nation's mainstream. Discarded and dangerous places, they are rarely visited by outsiders, becoming familiar to the larger population only through television and movies. Ghettos are pervaded by abandonment and ruin; they openly display crude defenses and abound in institutions and facilities that are rejected by "normal" neighborhoods.[24]

At the same time that Vergara situates the ghetto as central to the identity of the United States and the other places he names, he suggests that ghettos are exceptional for their "social and physical isolation." Although Vergara explains that the ghetto is "rarely visited by outsiders," he himself acknowledges that American ghettos have a long history of being explored by social reformers, moral reformers, academics, and adventure seekers since at least the late 1800s. Vergara thus follows in a long line of what Chad Heap calls "urban slummers" who left behind the banalities of their middle-class reality to look, partake, moralize, and slum in immigrant, racially segregated, or "vice" neighborhoods.[25] In the late nineteenth and early twentieth century, social documentarians worked to produce images and narratives—muckraking and informative—to provide information to those outside these places.

The Chilean-born Vergara began photographing Rust Belt cities while completing his bachelor's degree in sociology at the University of Notre Dame in South Bend, Indiana, in the 1970s. He continued his record of American urban life after moving to New York City to pursue a doctorate in sociology at Columbia University, which resulted in the completion of his master's degree in 1977.[26] Given this background, his images and essays lay at the intersections of photojournalism and academe. Of the eight books he published from 1989 to 2013, three were published by university presses.[27] Indeed, his first book shares a coauthor credit with the venerable urban historian Kenneth T. Jackson. Rutgers University Press published Vergara's first single-authored book, *The New American Ghetto.* Its marketing and praise categorized it as a cross-over scholarly and popular urban studies and photography book. Yet it in many ways escapes classification in either genre, absent both the scholarly context and conventions of academe and the large, full-page images of a popular photography book; in fact, there is only one full-page-sized photograph in its 235 pages.

Vergara's representation of Detroit as sparsely occupied and nearly empty contrasts with more common depictions of the "urban ghetto" as overcrowded, representing a significant ideological shift. Vergara's images therefore operate as initial "proof" of narratives of Detroit as ruined and empty. This shift from representing Detroit as a site of urban nightmare to a nearly empty city reconverting to pastoral landscape lays the visual foundation of Detroit as fertile ground, a concept that will be embraced full scale in the narratives of redevelopment that emerge in the 2000s, discussed in depth in chapter 5. Important here is the way in which the Detroit of the 1990s was *not* empty, despite Vergara's visual representation. The 1990 census officially counted over one million people, making Detroit the seventh most populous city in the United States at the time Vergara's first Detroit photographs were published.[28] In the face of clear numerical heft, the representation of Detroit as empty, symbolic of a postindustrial wasteland, is deeply linked to the racial tropes of place and renders a majority black population that was previously seen as hypervisible, now seen as invisible, nearly disappeared. While "white flight" was long considered an adequate explanation for the absence of white Detroiters, Vergara's depiction of the overwhelming emptiness of the city of black as well as white Detroiters was new. This ideological shift in depiction is essential to the work of reimagining the city as possible for development in the contemporary moment.

Vergara's earliest published Detroit images date to the mid-1980s. Figure 5 is among these early images and is central to what I delineate as the visual shift in representations of Detroit to a place of emptiness. At first glance Figure 5 evokes a rural vernacular with blooming wildflowers that fill the image from foreground to horizon in the distance complete with a wood-sided house on the left side of the image. The presence of a paved rather than dirt or gravel road running directly in front of the house and its parallel concrete sidewalk disrupts the pastoral rendering of the scene. And it is the caption—"In a once crowded area west of Rosa Parks Boulevard (formerly Twelfth Street) the 1967 Detroit Riot began. This neighborhood in a 1987 photograph resembles the Midwestern prairie"[29]—that draws a contrast between image and history of the place. The most often circulated images of the 1967 riot featured city streets filled with crowds of primarily black people looting, looking on, running in all directions alongside the tanks and faces of primarily white national guardsmen brandishing rifles with the imagery of burning and burnt-out buildings in the background. In contrast, Vergara represents the epicenter as an evocation of "the Midwestern prairie."[30] The stop sign prominently featured in the foreground then, more than artifact, finds an intentional placement here to literally mark the STOP of a growing and populated urban environment.

Figure 5. Vergara's representation of Detroit as Midwestern prairie. Camilo José Vergara, *untitled*, 1987. Reproduced with permission from Camilo José Vergara.

The juxtaposition is startling not only as it disrupts the idea of what "Detroit" looks like but also as it shifts the idea of what a center of "urban riot" looks like twenty years later. Rather than a neighborhood of businesses, buildings, and people, the area looks nearly deserted. Important then is the message of disappearance in the wake of the unrest. Rather than a visual archive of a prior social landscape of the burnt-out remains of the riots akin to the type of image depicted in Figure 1 in the introduction, Vergara's *untitled* ("Midwestern prairie") renders that past as completely disappeared. This contrast is all the more notable given that Figure 5 was taken in 1987, just as linkages of images of blackness, crime, and poverty were taking hold against the backdrop of neighborhoods that two decades prior were locations of urban unrest during the "long hot summers" of the late 1960s.[31] While images of Detroit as urban prairie abound in the late 2000s and 2010s, Vergara here is nearly two decades ahead of the curve. Vergara's representation of open landscape and the prairie leans heavily on the American fascination with the openness and possibility of the frontier and represents the earliest iteration of the postindustrial city as a literal American frontier. The promise of the postindustrial city is therefore in the disappearance of the black population that two decades prior had rebelled against ongoing racism. Although the actual population demographics of 1980s Detroit do not bear out this narrative, as per the 1980 census, Detroit was the sixth most populous city in the United States.[32] Figure 5 stands in as one of the earliest images that introduces the possibility of Detroit as a regenerative frontier.

Vergara has created a body of work that reconceives the city through the contrast of the natural and the constructed; the notion of the built environment of "the city" is unsettled through its juxtaposition with the natural environment. In 1999 Vergara explained that his aim as a photographer was to record "the evolution of the built environment in the country's largest and most devastated ghettos."[33] His language of "evolution" speaks to recording changes over time, which is one of the hallmarks of his work.[34] I also interpret the language of evolution as a way to suggest that the process of ghettoization to frontier is somehow a natural progression. Much of the work of ruin imagery operates to represent the reemergence of nature taking over once-grand buildings. This suggestion of reclamation by nature reaffirms the narrative cycle of development wherein man exerts control over nature (and those who are naturalized as part of the landscape) in the conquest of place and develops and cultivates land—and if that development is not maintained nature will reassert its force. At work in Vergara's Detroit portfolio is the idea that the "evolution" of the built environment is actually one of de-evolution to frontier.

Detroit Ruin as Archive of the Rise and Fall of Capitalism

The aesthetic quality of Vergara's images is not the central focus herein. Indeed, there is a marked difference between Vergara's style of photojournalism and the art photography of Marchand and Meffre and Moore. Rather, my engagement with his work suggests that his images of "the ruins of Detroit" are essential to crafting a visual narrative of possible other uses. The photographic representation of the city in ruin finds historical antecedents in the history of painting. As Nick Yablon states, "Since at least the seventeenth century, ruins—both real and imagined—have elicited pleasure as much as gloom."[35] Thus, today's ruin photography enters an already established visual and ideological realm. The cultural geographers Caitlin DeSilvey and Tim Edensor offer a caution that the "persistent tendency to privilege visual concerns . . . making the ruin illustrate particular aesthetic or philosophical constructs . . . neglect[s] the ruin's non-representational power to activate memory and sensation and downplay the significance of the lived presence of ruined spaces and places."[36] Yet it is precisely the power of visual representation in building narrative that makes ruin photography such a powerful genre. Indeed, the ruin takes hold as a representation for what it is not. For example, images of a ruined building not only show ruin but also represent a narrative about a historical time predicated on an idea that there was once a fully functioning, non-ruin building. The power of the representation of ruin is that the building is now important in its nonfunction as a ruin. DeSilvey and Edensor argue that the overemphasis on the visuality of ruin does not attend to the "relational, material, spectral and (non-)representational qualities of space and experience."[37] Therefore, they suggest that the continuing emphasis on the visuality of ruin to stand in for complex and regionally specific processes collapses larger social processes. While in the chapter I work to uncover the specific narrative collapse that is taking place in picturing ruin and social processes, I am most concerned with illuminating that which gets collapsed—namely the ease with which places where the poor and especially poor people of color live are narratively produced as ghettos and ruins.

Camilo Vergara's images do the symbolic work that collapses a complex past and present along standard narrative lines of Detroit's industrial heights and precipitous decline. In the representation of ruin there is always the evocation of non-ruin, the suggestion of achievement. As I quote in the epigraph that begins this chapter, he writes, "My photographs, exhibitions, and articles on downtown Detroit helped begin a national dialogue on the future of urban ruins. Without pretending that structures in the process of being discarded can retain their former economic and social importance, I continue to argue that their power as symbols remains strong. They are an essential part of understanding America."[38] As such, the importance in capturing ruin for Vergara exists because it is physical evidence of the *downfall* of economic and social importance. The work of ruin photography can stand in as the visual narrative of the idea of the rise and fall of capitalism.

Vergara's Detroit images primarily capture the places and locations that grew as a result of twentieth-century population growth—homes, businesses, storefronts, and places of worship. In this he is able to evoke a robust populace of the past through images of deteriorating or vacant structures. *Brush Park along John R. Street, Detroit, 1998* (Figure 6) originally appeared in *American Ruins* as the opening image in a section titled "The Disinherited Mansions of Brush Park." Vergara's caption for this image reads, "Brush Park along John R. Street, Detroit, 1998. The city skyline contrasts with the cluster of ruined Victorian houses."[39] *Brush Park along John R. Street* offers an overview of the neighborhood from a higher vantage point, looking down both at the "disinherited mansions" as well as at Detroit's downtown in the distance. Yet the neglect that he suggests in the caption is not immediately visible in the photo. We have to look closely to see boarded-up windows; only one roof is clearly damaged. However, the most visible part of the photo, filling the lower two-thirds of the image, is the lush greenness of clusters of trees and recently shorn green lawns in full summer splendor. The trees, at two and three stories in height, are more prominent than the mansions themselves and have begun to encroach on their entryways and exteriors. In the top third of the image the viewer's eyes are drawn to the distant skyscrapers of downtown. We clearly see the juxtaposition of a visual narrative of reclamation of nature and the close proximity of the downtown central business district.

Brush Park was developed in the 1870s as a neighborhood for wealthy Detroiters intentionally more than a mile away from downtown on the Brush family's farmland. The family paid careful attention to the parceling of their land from farm to housing, "imposing restrictions on the type of housing that could be built and insisting on what were then large lot widths of fifty feet,"[40] thereby ensuring its status as an enclave for the wealthy, away from the noise, chaos, and overcrowding of downtown. However, as the city grew to the north, west, and east, Brush Park quickly filled in and its wealthy residents sought even more desirable locations. Vergara writes, "Moving is a time-honored way to improve one's condition in the United States. People migrate to suburban space for more space and greenery and to feel that they have greater control over their environments."[41] Vergara's sentiment here could be applied to Brush Park; many prominent families who lived in the stately mansions of Brush Park did

Figure 6. Vergara's representation of Victorian houses in ruin. Camilo José Vergara, *Brush Park along John R. Street, Detroit, 1998*. Reproduced with permission from Camilo José Vergara.

not leave or abandon their Detroit residences because of economic collapse but left precisely due to the increasing economic opportunity that Detroit's growth provided, as they sought newer and larger residences in more fashionable neighborhoods in Detroit or further out in the suburbs. Although representing a different time period than that discussed in chapter 1, this movement to a more fashionable or better neighborhood can also be motivated by class- and race-based anxieties. Yet it is precisely the photographic record of decline and decay of Detroit's once-magnificent homes that serves as the visual shorthand to support the trope of Detroit's magnificent rise and spectacular fall. However, that story is overly simplified. The reality is that many of these homes turned over, became subdivided into apartments, and fell into neglect as occupancy neared 100 percent of available housing stock during the peak of Detroit's concentration of wealth and population in the first half of the twentieth century, not in the period of deindustrialization. The original occupants of the Brush Park mansions moved elsewhere not because of economic collapse; rather, economic growth enabled movement to other neighborhoods.

However, this visual imagery is more powerful and accessible as the story of decline of capitalism. Like so many visual representations of ruin that DeSilvey and Edensor discuss, ruin stands in for the failure of capitalism in the postindustrial city. The visual signification of the decline of industry is provocatively represented through the still-standing factories, buildings, and homes that are in various states of blight and decay. Therefore the visual image of ruin reinforces the presumption that shifts in capital yield a large-scale abandonment of the city, thereby intimating the structural argument that the poverty and decline of the city is largely a result of the disappearance of work. Vergara corroborates the story of his images with the remembrance that he "happened to come to the United States during a period when people and capital were abandoning the cities, at [a] time when the economy was relocating to the suburban periphery and domestic industries were expanding to locations all over the world."[42] Especially for the case of Detroit and the automobile industry, Vergara's statement speaks to the idea that the U.S. city is in decline not because of the failure of capital but because of the expansion of capital. Therefore, what he marks in the images and the statement is in fact evidence that capitalism is working in the way it is meant to work—by generating profit for shareholders and investors. What Vergara records then is not the failure of industry but what might be interpreted as capitalism working to its fullest potential, with 1990s Detroit as a large-scale example of disaccumulation, a part of the cycle of surplus and crisis. The geographer Ruth Wilson Gilmore draws the links between surplus and crisis as follows:

> In political economy, surplus and crisis derive from a single, extremely complicated, relationship. The purpose of capitalist business activity is to make a profit, and profitability is dependent on both keeping wages as low as possible, while selling all goods produced. In fancy terms, this means that implicit in capital's imperative to accumulate is an equal necessity to disaccumulate. Systemic failure to disaccumulate constitutes crisis.[43]

Therefore, Vergara's representation of 1990s Detroit's buildings and landscapes stands in as both witness and evidence of the shift in capital, an index of accumulation and disaccumulation. The images are evidence therefore not that capitalism has failed—quite the opposite. Rather, the images show the uneven impacts of capitalism's success, wherein poor black Detroiters are rendered a surplus. In effect this record of crisis of disaccumulation in 1990s Detroit sets up the current cycle of accumulation in the 2010s as discussed in chapter 5.

The stark portrayal of Detroit in the 1990s reveals the long-lasting divisions between race, class, and spatial location. Although Detroit proper was envisioned as abandoned by industry and white flight, the American auto industry was (and is still) headquartered in Detroit and metropolitan Detroit. Census data from 1990 reveals that Detroit and its metropolitan area was "more residentially segregated than any other U.S. metropolis."[44] Centrally important to the well-documented spatial segregation of the region is also the segregation of wealth. As Farley, Danziger, and Holzer show, even as the city of Detroit "ranked first in terms of poverty," the metropolitan region, which includes the suburban ring, was "among the nation's most prosperous."[45] Therefore, the representation of the primarily black city as crumbling and in ruin omits the racialized prosperity of metropolitan Detroit at large. At the time Vergara was photographing Detroit in the 1990s, metropolitan Detroit as a whole was one of the most prosperous in the country, while also one of most racially and economically segregated regions in the country.[46] The symbolic narrative represented by *Brush Park along John. R Street* (Figure 6) and *Row Houses on Alfred Street, 1998* (Figure 7) and their depictions of once-opulent homes in decay is that industrialization, and particularly the rise and fall of the U.S. automobile industry, resulted first in the large-scale accumulation of wealth and then, when the industry fell, the abandonment of the city. Therefore, the visual presentation of Detroit in ruin makes invisible the wealth and population that thrived in the metropolitan region as a whole, what Andrew Highsmith calls "metropolitan capitalism," that caused the metropolitan area, rather than the city itself, to grow.[47] And as I showed in chapter 1, this invisible growth of the metropolitan area was racially exclusionary. This narrative of abandonment constructs the city as empty and serves to obscure the ongoing presence of Detroit's majority black population.

The representation of the poverty of 1990s Detroit is all the more startling through the juxtaposition of the evidence of the extravagant wealth of the past. In *American Ruins,* one of the two-page spreads of "The Disinherited Mansions of Brush Park" features four images of the "Row Houses on Alfred Street,"[48] one of which is reproduced here (Figure 7).

Vergara characterizes these row houses, like the other once-opulent residences of Brush Park, as "gems of devastation."[49] In so doing he continues a narrative of abandonment of Brush Park, situating the neighborhood as a cast-off, yet beautiful, artifact of the past. *Row Houses on Alfred Street, 1998* features three people gathered in front of the house. Two people are sitting on a fallen tree trunk that has provided a perfect front-row seat to the houses, their backs to the camera. These two are passing something between them. The third person stands facing the camera, back to the houses, but gazes off to their right in the direction of the corner market that is not visible in this image but appears in the other images, as they include the street that runs perpendicular to Alfred Street. The three people seem to be relaxed, immersed in their socializing. It is their casualness, the ordinariness of their gathering, that suggests they are unmoved by the decline all around them, in contrast to the presumed viewer who consumes the image with both fascination and surprise that the hulking ruin in the background is considered so banal by the subjects in the

Figure 7. Vergara's representation of the "disinherited mansions of Brush Park." Camilo José Vergara, *Row Houses on Alfred Street, 1998*. Reproduced with permission from Camilo José Vergara.

foreground. The image works to place the people in the image even further away from the consumer of the image. The inclusion of seemingly indifferent people gathering in the shadow of ruin serves as a device to highlight the difference not only between the places where the presumed viewer lives and the landscape that Vergara portrays but also between the viewer and the people who live alongside these "gems of devastation." For the viewer, the devastation is raw and provocative, and by portraying what looks like the indifference of local denizens, Vergara emphasizes Detroit's landscape as a location of difference and a sparsely populated population unmoved by what Vergara presents as widespread devastation. The depiction of near-emptiness and the seeming nonchalance of those who remain suggests the possibility of new use through what Neil Smith calls a willful revanchism, or taking back of the American city.[50]

Vergara's 1980s and 1990s imagery is key in facilitating a narrative shift of the city as nearly empty in its depiction of ruin and abandonment. The new American ghetto as Vergara captures it is represented as a vestige of capitalism vis-à-vis old buildings left as relics of a past time. Rather than a "culture of poverty," he presents Detroit as a largely empty and abandoned landscape, an important motif in the genre of ruin photography. Vergara's work emphasizes and creates a narrative that the opulent buildings are the sole remnants of the wealth of this once-powerful city. His is not the nightmarish gaze of a "landscape of fear" but rather a panoramic look at the city as a space of possibility for reclamation. We see, again and again, the longevity and fortitude of buildings, which survive in spite of the national media's death knell for Detroit and its postindustrial counterparts.

From Ruined Possibilities to the Possibilities of Ruin

Camilo José Vergara's work in the 1990s was central to the creation of a genre of postindustrial ruin photography. Detroit's location as an epicenter for ruin gazing and image making was cemented in the 2010 publication of the two most defining books of this contemporary vision of Detroit as ruin: Yves Marchand and Romain Meffre's coffee table book *The Ruins of Detroit* and Andrew Moore's *Detroit Disassembled.* Both were released as catalogs that accompanied major art exhibitions, showcasing Detroit's decline as an object of art and beauty. Images from both collections were featured prominently in online news sites and are widely available in online image catalogs. This visual "fetishization" of Detroit happened in full force in the years after 2008, not coincidentally as the nation fell deeper into recession.[51] As industries have declined and unemployment increased nationally, Detroit's operation as an icon of the nation has been thrust further into the spotlight. Vergara's images of Detroit in ruin laid the groundwork for these later photographers, much as earlier images of urban tenements and the American West laid the groundwork for Vergara's images.

Vergara conceded the unpopularity of his proposal to preserve Detroit in ruin when he reflected, "From homeless person to professor, there is unanimity among Detroiters that skyscrapers have no future as ruins. My proposal of keeping twelve square blocks south and west of Grand Circus Park as an American Acropolis—that is, to allow the present skyscraper graveyard to become a park of ripe ruins—is seen by most as at best misguided and at worst a cruel joke."[52] Yet this outlandish proposal may in fact be one of the reasons that his work generated so much of its early buzz. His specific naming of Detroit and other postindustrial cities as "urban ruins" announced a new envisioning of these places. Much as the ruins of the Acropolis evoke a particular relationship to the past, Vergara's proposal sought to highlight the value in what he terms *ruin.* That Vergara situates downtown Detroit as a "skyscraper graveyard" underscores the notion that Detroit is in effect a dead city. Yet Vergara's images themselves tell a story not of death per se but of still-existing life. Ultimately, his portrayal of the landscape shows Detroit as possible *because* of the depth of its ruin, which lays the groundwork for a full-scale narrative of possibility.

The Work of Giants Moulders Away/Detroit Skyline (Figure 8) is notable for its inclusion in both books, captioned in *The New American Ghetto* as "The work of giants moulders away" and in *American Ruins* as "Detroit skyline."[53] It captures Detroit's rich architectural heritage of beaux-arts, art deco, and modern buildings, foregrounded by a landscape of emptiness and ruin. *The Work of Giants Moulders Away/Detroit Skyline* captures a portion of the city from a vantage point that evokes Michel de Certeau's "totalizing eye" from above, transforming the experience of everyday life

Figure 8. Vergara's representation of the Detroit skyline. Camilo José Vergara, *The Work of Giants Moulders Away/Detroit Skyline,* 1991. Reproduced with permission from Camilo José Vergara.

as voyeur. Rather than reproducing the city as a pedestrian at the ground level, which would capture what de Certeau situates as the "true systems whose existence actually makes the city," this particular view is from several stories above ground level, most likely taken from the roof of the Park Avenue Hotel.[54] Although Vergara states that the reason for moving from street level was due to safety, he appreciates the perspective it provides, explaining, "I began systematically to shoot from high viewpoints. They offer many angles from which to photograph the urban scenes below, views of what lies behind walls and windows and on the tops of buildings. This new perspective, from above, helped me in my goal of achieving more complete and clearer documentation."[55] Vergara's representation of "seeing from above" illuminates James Scott's concept of "seeing like a state." Scott argues that the modern state organized its territory to "get a handle on its subjects and their environment" and ultimately "when allied with state power, would enable much of the reality depicted to be remade."[56] Scott suggests that the "formal scheme" of state organization "always ignores essential features of any real, functioning social order."[57] Yet it is Vergara's emphasis on this "view from above" that simultaneously disallows individual inhabitants to be seen and enables the evidence of human use in an otherwise empty landscape. For example, in looking at the dirt lots depicted in the lower right-hand corner and the middle-left section of *The Work of Giants Moulders Away/Detroit Skyline,* two dirt paths—small enough to be made by pedestrians or bicycles—bisect the clearly plotted squares of land. Upon closer inspection the lots that at first glance seem to be "empty" all bear visible traces of pathways created and utilized outside the formal structure of the paved streets. And at closer examination still at least one of the specks dotting the foreground seems to be a human form. The optics then that disallow visualization of individual people enable a narrative of presence of people, even in their visible absence. This absent presence depicted in Vergara's 1991 image of Detroit anticipates the common "post-apocalyptic" imagery of Detroit by nearly two decades. As Detroit in the 2010s "vanished" in the census and on the big screen,[58] Vergara's images of the vanished city emerged two decades earlier.

In this image Vergara's camera captures a view looking southward toward the skyscrapers of downtown at the top of the image. The tallest towers in the distance have almost been cropped out of view. Yet Vergara's photograph also offers a perspective downward, capturing in the foreground nearly vacant lots that are dotted with cars, trash, rocks, squat buildings, and near-empty streets. It is this scene that occupies over half the frame—begging the question of the role of skyscrapers in the background and in both of the titles, given that the focus of the frame is a downward look at the lots and one- and two-story buildings in the foreground. The focus of the image suggests that rather than in ruin, Detroit's downtown is densely populated with buildings tightly packed into the background, and in many ways the lots in the foreground look very much like speculative land—that is, getting ready for new buildings, which could be suggested by a title like "Detroit skyline," indicating the flatness of a foreground that anticipates new buildings. Although the intimation that the "work of giants moulders" positions the skyscrapers in the background as undergoing a slow decay, it still does not offer context for the focus in the foreground. The office buildings and skyscrapers serve as both a visual and an ideological frame of the picture of Detroit that Vergara enforces—that of an empty space.

The Work of Giants Moulders Away/Detroit Skyline first appears in the concluding pages of *The New American Ghetto,* as part of Vergara's discussion of Detroit in ruin, which serves as a conclusion to the book as a whole. The arc of the book thus offers a clear link, a narrative progression, from Detroit as "American ghetto" to Detroit as "American ruin." For *The New American Ghetto,* Vergara features the image as a way of symbolizing the slow disintegration of the city—the "work of giants" is crumbling before our eyes, captured on film by his camera. This final section of the book is provocatively titled "American Acropolis or Vacant Land? The Future of Detroit's Pre-Depression Skyscrapers." In *American Ruins* the image is included in a two-page, four-image spread titled "An Alternate View of the Detroit Skyline." It is the placement and Vergara's cataloging of images that provides a discursive frame for a reader to understand the image. Yet his representation of ruin is evocative in its suggestion of the possibilities that can emerge from ruin.

A reading of *The Work of Giants Moulders Away/Detroit Skyline* from bottom to top or top to bottom provides a space for different interpretations. A reading from bottom to top suggests a forward motion from underdeveloped land to the skyscrapers of downtown. A reading from top to bottom suggests a sliding forward, a slow erosion of the city. Either way, the angle from the foreground to the background of the image is so steeply graded as to simultaneously suggest an arduous pathway forward and a slippery slope backward. A reading from foreground to background emphasizes the natural evolution of the empty landscape, which seems to be slowly consuming the skyscrapers, those icons of past greatness, as suggested by the close crop of the horizon. The horizon line, then, rather than shaped by the openness of big sky and endless possibility, is defined by the buildings. The skyscrapers stand in as economic potential and wasted economic opportunity—simultaneously both and neither.

The Incomplete Archive

Camilo Vergara situates the "New American Ghetto Archive" as an "uninterrupted dialogue with poor communities, their residents, and the scholars who study them."[59] Yet rather than a conversation with poor communities, he states that his "photographs are intended to offer a visual journey through cityscapes and interiors, accompanied by a narrative spun largely from my direct observation, accounts given by ghetto residents themselves, and historical records."[60] In this respect the books appear to be intended not as a conversation *with* the communities depicted on the pages but as a way to engage and inform those outside these communities. In this way, Vergara's representation of Detroit as an empty city in ruin, regardless of the opinion of people who live and work in the city, is interwoven throughout his depictions. Although Vergara writes of the importance of talking to and recording the perspectives of residents, he often utilizes those perspectives as evidence of a local myopia. For example, Vergara states in *American Ruins:*

> Few people admit that the buildings in which they live or work are actually ruins. A former headstone showroom in Detroit has its wraparound windows sealed and painted white, and its front yard is overgrown, giving the impression that it has been mothballed. Above its entrance, against black marble, is a fading gold star. Yet someone in the building answered the phone and responded to my questions by saying: "I work on cars. I'm very busy right now." Left to decide whether or not the building was a

ruin, I took another look at the faded gold star against the black polished stone and decided that it was.[61]

Although Vergara is aware of the relationship residents have with a place and includes these interactions and their voices in the text, he seems to think that they are denying an obvious reality. Even though someone uses this building as their work place, even though the response to his intrusive questioning is "I'm very busy right now," Vergara still makes the decision to call this and other buildings "ruins." If the people who live or work in the buildings that Vergara deems "ruins" refuse to call the building a ruin, then one could conclude that the building is in fact in use and therefore not a ruin. Yet it is Vergara's contention that the people being probed are simply in denial, characterized by the idea that "few people admit that the buildings in which they live or work are actually ruins." He does not consider the opposite perspective: that as an outsider, he has a very different vision of usable space.[62] In this example, even as the person who answered the phone told Vergara, "I work on cars," indicating a clear use as well as pace of work in "I'm very busy," Vergara still decided that ultimately to his eye, the building is a ruin. This ultimately raises the larger questions that emerge throughout *Beautiful Wasteland:* Who decides what is ruin and what is non-ruin? And what are the motivations and impacts of these assertions?

While Vergara includes the words of the occupant of the building, he does not hear the words. So while the people who occupy the places that Vergara has labeled "ghetto" and "ruin" are clearly speaking, Vergara is not listening. And herein lies the contradiction of Vergara's images and their articulation of emptiness and ruin. He engages the people who live in the neighborhoods and the places he photographs; yet he refuses to hear. Not only does he not listen, he continues to project an image of emptiness and abandonment when those who live and work in the places he photographs are clearly stating that Detroit is not empty, not abandoned, and life, commerce, and living are still happening—despite popular perceptions of ruin and abandonment. Rather, Vergara projects his interpretation of the locations he photographs as abandoned ruins and ghettos.

Vergara's representation of the people and places he photographs as out of sync with the worldview he is producing in his written and visual texts appears clearly in his discussion of Detroit's David Broderick Tower in *American Ruins.* An image of this building, *The Top of the David Broderick Tower, Detroit, 1998,* is featured as part of a four-page spread under the name "Four Vacant Skyscrapers."[63] One of the inset images also includes a photograph of the Broderick Tower's caretaker in the defunct penthouse bar of the building. The image is captioned, "Jessie Willie Sr., the building's eighty-one-year-old caretaker, in the bar of what was the penthouse apartment in the David Broderick Tower, 1995."[64] In the accompanying text, Vergara writes:

> For thirty years Jessie Willie Sr. has been the David Broderick Tower's caretaker and my guide to the building. When he started he had a staff of nine. Now he is alone. . . . Recently the present owner invited nearly a hundred people to watch fireworks from the roof, and they left behind many empty bottles and cans. In his early eighties, Jessie can hardly walk. His back hurts, and he has trouble getting up the stairs to the roof. Picking up these bottles is, for him, an impossible task, so he just looks at them and gets angry at the people who dumped them.
>
> Jessie is probably the last person to identify with this proud tower. He must feel left behind. "There is nothing wrong with this building," he told me, and to prove it, he turned on lights and opened windows and closets. On the way down, when I expressed mild concern that we might get stuck in the elevator, he made it run fast, proudly explaining that it could go even faster. Yet I feel that Jessie has given up trying to convince people of the building's soundness. I imagine him carrying on a sort of ritual dialogue with the building: "What's wrong? Why don't they like us anymore?"[65]

In this recollection, Vergara's narrative clearly seeks to equate Jessie Willie Sr. to the David Broderick Tower—linking man to building, arguing that the man's physical state represents the infirmity of the building itself. He makes the connection that Jessie "can hardly walk" and that the elevator barely works. While Vergara represents Jessie Willie Sr.'s words, he couches them between his own subjectivity. Vergara's recollection of the moment constructs Jessie Willie Sr. as simultaneously childishly petulant, defiant, and a proud symbol of the past. Jessie Willie Sr., Vergara's local escort, is telling him clearly and specifically that "there is nothing wrong with this building," which seems to be backed up by the fact that the building's owner invited "nearly a hundred people" to the building's roof. Yet Vergara's text seems to suggest that in the moment he humors Willie Sr., he uses the recall of this exchange to provide readers with an example of how out of touch and defunct Detroit and Detroiters are. Vergara includes Jessie Willie Sr.'s perspective as a way to underscore the alternate reality of Detroit and concludes the short essay not with Willie Sr.'s perspective but with a Chicago historian's perspective of Jessie Willie Sr.'s "plight."[66] This then becomes a double displacement of Jessie Willie Sr.'s perspective as expert, first by Vergara and then by an outside academic expert. It becomes clear that while Vergara is asking questions, he is not listening to the answers he receives and instead prefers to create an image of both building and man as "left behind." In so doing he forwards a perception that the people and buildings that continue to stand in Detroit remain as outmoded and out-of-touch relics.

When Vergara published and exhibited his photographs, constructing Detroit as "empty" and proposing those twelve square blocks of downtown as a monument to ruin, he cast aside the million people who were living in the city of Detroit, relegating them to little more than a surplus of twentieth-century industrialization. Yet the places he showcases, in their non-emptiness, despite his narrative of emptiness, produce an uneasiness, a ghostly representation of place and people. That uneasiness parallels the uneasy way in which America's racial divide, so much a part of our past and still so potent in our present, cannot be easily resolved despite endless attempts. The people who haunt these images, passing through the frame or standing just outside it, are visual evidence that we have not yet reconciled with the realities of our past. I see these figures as icons of nonconsensus, evidence to counter the standard narrative of Detroit as abandoned and empty. Vergara's work clearly establishes the city as not empty, but in his images and narratives he represents those who are left behind as out of sync as evidenced by his cavalier representation of their words and opinions.

In particular Vergara's fascination with the symbol of the city in ruin is clear when he proposes to preserve Detroit's downtown core as "a grand national historic park of play and wonder, an urban Monument Valley."[67]

In the setup to this proposal he hits on the still common sentiment that Detroit's ruin is beautiful, stating:

> Detroit's downtown moves me like no other place. There, for the first time in history, large numbers of skyscrapers that were planned to last for centuries are becoming derelict; a cluster of semi-abandoned structures rises like a vertical no-man's-land behind empty lots. Supposedly immutable structures of reinforced concrete are falling into decay. . . . I propose that as a tonic for our imaginations, as a call for renewal, as a place within our national memory, a dozen city blocks of pre-Depression skyscrapers should be left standing as ruins: an American Acropolis.[68]

This proposal to preserve Detroit's downtown as a memorial to the past—a "ruin park"—was met with anger and annoyance from everyday Detroiters, the city's government, and economic backers.[69] However, Vergara's proposal to close and preserve the downtown core was essential to crafting a narrative wherein the postindustrial landscape is understood as empty yet valuable for its symbolic structures of an industrial past and its possibility of regeneration in its future, which will come full circle in chapter 5. Vergara metaphorically links the postindustrial landscape to the "natural" landscape of the West, announcing "the end of the city" nearly one hundred years after Frederick Jackson Turner announced "the end of the frontier" in his seminal 1893 essay, "The Significance of the Frontier in American History." By relying on imagery of Detroit as both an Acropolis and a Monument Valley, Vergara situates the postindustrial city as simultaneously a city in ruin and the natural landscape of the frontier. Monument Valley—situated on Navajo tribal land near the Four Corners region and a natural environment of towering sandstone buttes rising over the windswept plains—has long stood in for visual imagery of the American West, significantly as a backdrop for many of the images famously compiled by the American photographer Edward S. Curtis in his effort to photograph a "vanishing race." Curtis created a forty-thousand-image archive of what he called "The North American Indian." This archival project consumed his life's work.[70] In many ways, then, Vergara's suggestion of Detroit as Monument Valley—as towering structures dotting a windswept landscape of emptiness—is a powerful allusion to the photographic history of picturing America, and an attempt to situate his own project within that legacy. In both cases the landscape is clearly not empty, but the value to outsiders is presented through the vanishing population of the past.

By way of postscript to the stories above I offer two accounts from the vantage point that twenty years provides.

On July 20, 2014, the eighty-fifth birthday of Mike Ilitch—a Detroit native, founder of the Little Caesar's Pizza chain, and owner of the major league sport teams the Detroit Tigers and Detroit Red Wings—Olympia Development of Michigan, a company owned by the Ilitch family, announced a $650 million plan to develop a forty-five-block area into an "entertainment district."[71] Anchored by a new stadium for the Detroit Red Wings, the district will serve as a connection between Midtown and downtown Detroit. In an announcement that ground breaking would begin on September 25, 2014, Chris Ilitch, CEO of Ilitch Holdings, explained, "The 45-block entertainment district stitches together surrounding assets into charming, walkable, livable neighborhoods" and has been "fifteen years in the making."[72] And central to the location, the roughly six-block area that is planned as the footprint for the Ilitch-owned Detroit Red Wings arena actually consists of the lots pictured in Vergara's photograph *The Work of Giants Moulders Away/Detroit Skyline.* Up through the mid-2010s the lots in the image served as pictorial examples of "abandonment" even as up until late 2014 they were heavily utilized as surface parking lots for patrons attending events at the Fox Theater and on Tigers and Lions game days.[73] Park Avenue Hotel, the location from which Vergara took this photograph, was imploded on July 11, 2015, to make way for the new development; as of March 2016 the construction of the Detroit Red Wings arena is well underway, slated to "be finished by the start of the 2017 NHL season" and "be named in about two months."[74]

It is also now crystal clear that Jessie Willie Sr. was right when he said that "there is nothing wrong with this building." In December 2010 *DBusiness* announced that the David Broderick Tower had completed its more than $50 million proposal for the renovation of the historic building and would begin work immediately.[75] The plan was for luxury housing on floors 5 through 34 and restaurants and office space on the lower floors. The exterior of the building would be cleaned and restored with a complete renovation of the interior of the building. The newly renovated Broderick Tower opened for occupancy in November 2012, and five days after opening all 124 apartments, ranging in price and size from $650 for a 650 square foot studio to $5,100 for a three-floor penthouse, were fully leased.[76] An inquiry in July 2013 revealed only two openings for September 2013, one for October 2013, and a wait list for fourteen other units with unspecified move-in dates. The range on these seventeen available units was from $950 for a 508 square foot studio to $3,985 for a 1,920 square foot three-bedroom penthouse.[77] Jessie Willie Sr. was right in 1995; it only took a twenty-first-century development boom to create a market for high-rise luxury apartment living in downtown Detroit. Had Vergara listened and heard Jessie Willie Sr., he may have predicted downtown Detroit's future not as an "American Acropolis" but a heavily gentrifying market—both capitalizing on the beauty of the building itself and the reconversion of Detroit, which I return to at length in chapter 5.

CHAPTER 3

Fanning the Embers

Branding Detroit as a Phoenix Rising

> "Born of Fire" debuted at the 2011 Super Bowl. . . . The two-minute commercial, which was also a Super Bowl first, ignited a spark throughout the United States, as many felt a connection to the attitude and work ethic portrayed in the scenes and narration. The spot reflects where the brand is headed and pays tribute to its industrial roots. While the commercial focused on Detroit, in many ways, it encapsulated the spirit of the country and the comeback of the Chrysler brand.
>
> —Chrysler Corporation

> It is impossible to look at modern advertising without realising that the material object being sold is never enough: this indeed is the crucial cultural quality of its modern forms. If we were sensibly materialist, in that part of our living in which we use things, we should find most advertising to be of an insane irrelevance. . . . It is clear that we have a cultural pattern in which the objects are not enough but must be validated, if only in fantasy, by association with social and personal meanings.
>
> —Raymond Williams, "Advertising the Magic System"

One of the biggest stories to emerge from Super Bowl XLV, played on February 6, 2011, had nothing to do with the teams on the field. It was a Chrysler commercial. At the time of its release it was the longest and most expensive ad in history, with an estimated production budget of $9 million and taking up two full minutes of airtime; the commercial was so grand it had a title as ambitious as the project itself: "Born of Fire."[1] The commercial was well received by audiences and media alike. Tim Nudd, senior editor of *Adweek,* not only considered it to be one of the best ads of the Super Bowl, but one of the ten best of the year.[2] Nudd places it on his top-ten list, calling it "the year's toughest, proudest, most defiant advertisement" and explaining, "It offered a gritty defense of a city, an industry, and a way of life, single-handedly bringing some of the old swagger back to Detroit and attacking those who would doubt the city's heritage and conviction—or its ability to produce a worldclass luxury vehicle."[3] Nudd was not alone in his praise and it won the preeminent advertising-industry award, the Grand Effie, for selling "the product, the category, and the city,"[4] as well as an Emmy Award for "Outstanding Commercial." Super Bowl XLV was watched by 111 million people, which at the time made it the "most viewed telecast in U.S. broadcast history," theoretically providing enough justification for the recently bailed-out company to spend an estimated $12 million on airtime alone.[5] But perhaps even more remarkable is that, in the first month after its debut, the advertisement had over nine million views on YouTube alone.[6] The popularity of the commercial seems obvious: the combination of beautifully mundane images, combined with a narrative of hard work and determination, all propelled by the pulsing backbeat of Eminem's award-winning song "Lose Yourself."[7] But the real meaning and, I believe, the real reason for the commercial's popularity was in its underlying message. While ostensibly the point of the commercial was to create buzz and sell the Chrysler 200, a midmarket sedan with luxury car aspirations,[8] the star of the commercial was not the automobile or Eminem but the city of Detroit. Detroit was, and is still for many, the ultimate symbol of both the nation's industrial heights and its postindustrial collapse.

In so many ways then the commercial calls on "Detroit" to stand in as a symbol for so many things, good and bad, local and national. It begins with images that reinforce a typical vision of the city: gray factories billowing smoke and crumbling building façades, shot in muted tones against a gray skyline on a cloudy winter day. The barren trees captured at the edges of frames underscore the idea of a frozen and depressed landscape. As the pace of the commercial picks up, the images begin to stabilize and the narrator begins to unveil this story. In the next two minutes we are led through a city in motion, a city that is not set in a Hollywood-esque gaze of soft light and languid panoramas but captured in cool light and seen through fast-moving and jerky editing splices. The unsteady work of the camera, the quick cutting from scene to scene, and the narrator work together to simultaneously destabilize and throw off balance what we may know about Detroit and readies us for a new story about Detroit. The narrator in his opening dialogue acknowledges head on that Detroit is "a town that's been to hell and back" and challenges those watching to see the city differently, to understand that this unnamed hell is not the only story about Detroit. For the first seventy seconds the ad is filmed almost entirely in a first-person point of view. The stately buildings of downtown and public art—the steel fist that is the *Monument to Joe Louis,* Diego Rivera's *Detroit Industry* fresco, and *The Spirit of Detroit* statue—appear onscreen as the narrator discusses "our" story. As the viewer takes in a neighborhood of modern middle-class homes (in direct contrast to the imagery of abandoned and blighted Detroit homes described in chapter 2), the narrator states, "That's who we are. That's our story. Now it's probably not the one you've been reading in the papers," a dig at all the "parachute journalists" who swoop in, photograph, and report on the city's demise.[9] Rather, this narrator shows a neighborhood, lawns and homes blanketed in snow, and a high school football team in matching blue sweatpants, hoodies, and gloves, running head-on into the blowing snow. We see Detroiters at work, readily identifiable by occupation in the clothing they wear: a greeter outside a building in an opulent uniform nodding in recognition as the camera passes by, a police man waving people through traffic, and a professional man glancing over as he crosses the street. We are not the unseen audience gazing upon them; we are in fact part of what Jane Jacobs might call the "sidewalk ballet" as the camera works as a proxy, these three men nodding in direct recognition of us.[10] In so doing the commercial operates within an existing perception of Detroit, and by extension the nation, as the viewers have been folded into the action of the ad, as the underdog—as the determined and hard-working individual in spite of the narrative being written. At about seventy seconds into the commercial the point of view shifts from first person to a five-second bird's-eye shot of the front of the car gliding beneath—the movement suggested by the changing reflection in the vehicle's shiny exterior. This shift in perspective serves as a bridge to shift from the gray daytime light to nightfall and a movement from narrated voice over to the crescendo of the song that was in the background now filling the commercial.

The penultimate action of the ad reveals that we have not been driving the car around the city; rather, the car is driven by none other than Detroit's native son Eminem. In the final scene the viewer watches as Eminem enters the near-empty Fox Theater and takes the stage to say: *"This is the Motor City. And this is what we do."* The Chrysler ad thus reframes a narrative of globalization through an emphasis on the comeback of Detroit as an underdog, ultimately suggesting that Detroit, and the United States more generally, will prevail. Notably, however, the (implicitly) white man will prevail not as a worker but as a member of the professional class, the ideal consumer of the Chrysler 200. Chrysler's ad consciously visualizes a new way to imagine Detroit and, by extension, the nation's future. Yet it explicitly relies on the storied past of the American automotive industry and its working-class origins. Even as the advertisement is driving the audience into the promise of a new future, it does so by looking through the rearview mirror, at a point behind, the same fantasies of the past discussed in chapter 1: a rosier time when jobs were plentiful and working men could earn a good living.

Born of Fire

Given its name, "Born of Fire," the motif of fire reoccurs in the ad to underscore an elemental productive power. Yet fire itself is absent from the commercial—instead it appears in the narration and is visually suggested through the appearance of smoke in numerous places throughout the commercial. Smoke is the aftereffect of fire, suggesting that the commercial's intent is to show the result of productive power, a deeply entrenched force that burns despite hardship. The use of fire as a symbol of both destructive and productive force is telling, since it is relevant not only to industrial manufacturing but to Detroit's history. In June 1805 a fire burned almost the entire French settlement at Fort Detroit to the ground and sparked the penning of the city's motto, *Speramus meliora; resurget cineribus,* which translates to "We Hope for Better Things; It Shall Rise from the Ashes." The fire, while destroying the settlement, situated the mythical rise of the phoenix—a creature that according to Greek myth died and was reborn from its own ashes—securely within Detroit's history. The trope of fire burned brightly again a century and a half later, as the Detroit rebellion and hundreds of fires burned over the course of five days in July 1967. The Detroit Rebellion, its many images of a major metropolis on fire and the aftermath of burned homes and gutted businesses, was seared into the national consciousness. The "fire" of the rebellion is narratively situated as the definitive pivot of Detroit's decline and popularly considered the catalytic moment of the mass exodus of whites from Detroit's urban core. Even for those not familiar with Detroit's history, fire operates as an element of change and mutation, the transformative element not only for industry but for humanity. Chrysler's "Born of Fire" commercial redeploys a vision of Detroit's fiery past, through the suggestive idea that it is "a town that has been to hell," in order to play against the half-century-long narrative of Detroit's destruction and replace it with a recycled and updated story of phoenix-like rise.

The years following the 2008 auto-industry bailout are often heralded as the beginning of Detroit's renewed rise, and the phoenix-like myth of the automobile industry as "back" circulates and gains traction through cultural tales like the Chrysler commercial. The narrator of the commercial, Michigan resident Kevin Yon, with his grizzled and raspy voice, begins by challenging the viewer: "I got a question for you. What does this city know about luxury? What does a town that has been to hell and back know about the finer things in life?" The commercial references this most ingrained narrative of Detroit, a collective understanding of decline that the millions of people watching presumably have about what Detroit has been through, literally and figuratively. Just as Detroit's fall stands in for the larger decline of both U.S. industry and the U.S. postindustrial city in the last half of the twentieth century, in the second decade of the twenty-first century Detroit's rise stands in for a larger narrative of possibility. Stories about the city's potential for rebirth are emerging everywhere, from *Food & Wine* magazine, which I discuss further in chapter 5, to President Obama's 2012 State of the Union Address, in which he told the nation, "We bet on American workers. We bet on American ingenuity. And tonight, the American auto industry is back. What's happening in Detroit can happen in other industries."

The "Born of Fire" commercial was the flashy kickoff of Chrysler's larger ad campaign, titled "Imported from Detroit." This was the first national campaign in recent memory focused on branding a product through reliance on the brand of Detroit. The narrative embraced by the commercial, alongside President Obama's double down on the American auto industry a year later, and the rise of Detroit's "cool" factor are all examples of the idea that Detroit has made a comeback. Rather than a symbol of economic destruction, Chrysler positions the city as a prime example of "making it" despite all the odds; this is especially remarkable considering its release in 2011, while Detroit and the country at large were still in the throes of national economic recession. Although Chrysler was the first company to base a national campaign on Detroit, numerous others have since followed. A notable example is Bedrock Corporations, the Texas-based parent company of luxury goods and watchmaker Shinola Detroit, which chose to locate Shinola in Detroit because of the resonance of the brand of the city.[11] Shinola's creative director, Daniel Caudill, commented in a 2013 interview in *Forbes,* "We wanted people to respond to the integrity of the brand. 'Made in America' is a little generic, it's overused."[12] But "Detroit," as the company plays up in its personal story, evokes the storied past of the industrial worker in a once-great American city, and insists that Detroit, and American manufacturing, is not just a part of history but part of the future.[13] For the founder, "Made in Detroit" evokes a rich industrial past and history, much more compelling and specific than Made in America, a bold move made first by the "Born of Fire" commercial.

"Born of Fire" emphasizes not merely a "Made in the USA" campaign, a common industry response to competition from foreign automakers, but the idea of Detroit specifically as a place that is both of the nation and also somehow outside of it. The tagline of the commercial, and the larger campaign that it kicks off, is "Imported from Detroit." The idea here is that Detroit, once the center of the global auto industry, and often written off as dead, is a place where cars (and dreams) can be reborn. This place is gritty and determined; it has faced the worst kind of adversity, and now it is back. The commercial relies on, and perpetuates, a recycled cultural rhetoric of the power of the individual in the face of difficulty, selling the commodity as evidence of individual success based on hard work and determination. The phoenix myth of rising from the ashes relies on the idea of both past greatness and past destruction; this historical apex and nadir are what frame a renewed chronicle of ascent. Detroit's past greatness is nearly always evoked through tales of industrial dominance and the notion that there was a job for every worker who wanted to work.

When the commercial was released in February 2011 much of the nation was still reeling from the impact of recession, and 2011 would prove to be a year when "the 99 percent" staged public protests over the wealth and income gap in the United States as the Occupy Wall Street movement took shape in the later half of the year. Detroit proved to be a particularly resonant symbol in this time of economic struggle. Rather than rely solely on a celebrity endorsement (as so many other car ads do) to upsell the Chrysler 200 as the embodiment of glamour, or feature the car driving along a picturesque coastline, the commercial upended genre conventions and relied on the most infamously and ingloriously fallen city in the United States to serve as a backdrop for the vehicle. Detroit is utilized as a brand, one that works through the narrative of rise *and* decline. Indeed, Detroit is possible precisely because its epic rise and decline makes it the ultimate comeback story.

The Hell of Globalization: An Appeal to Middle-Class Nationalism

Filming began on January 4, 2011, and wrapped four days later, less than one month before the commercial's Super Bowl premiere.[14] During these four days in January, a cold winter landscape complete with blowing snow and gray skies served as the backdrop to images of factories billowing smoke and façades of partially demolished buildings before transitioning to iconic images of Detroit's monuments and downtown. This commercial begins in gray scale, shot as if with a handheld camera, shakily recording a frigid and seemingly motionless landscape. For the first six seconds of the ad, we hear nothing save for the deep bass vibration of an industrial-sounding, faintly metallic echo. The sounds and visual imagery are muted, frozen, and unidentifiable fragments, the visual and sonic palettes mutually reinforcing each other.[15] The jerky camerawork and the faint yet unidentifiable sound serve to immediately destabilize the viewers as we are thrown into an undecipherable landscape. The images in these first few seconds—a freeway underpass, barren tree branches alongside a blurry freeway sign, smoke billowing from the metal chimneys of factories—serve as nondescript visual markers of an industrial location that could be anywhere. However, as the camera steadies on a freeway sign that reads "Detroit I-75 North," the camera pulls back once again and shows other vehicles on this freeway all heading toward the city in the distance. These other vehicles combined with the billows of smoke in the previous shots offer a faint sense of life and gesture toward a narrative that goes beyond a dormant landscape. The imagery of smoke against the cold, frozen terrain serves as the commercial's symbolic hook, which is seen again and again as a framing device and suggests that despite the years of hardship, the city still has the deep burning fire to produce.

The voice of the narrator begins about five seconds in, laying over a long, cavernous echoing sound, and the camera begins to become more stable, still depicting the city as if through a car window. The voice begins a split second before a freeway sign tells us that we are, literally, on the road to Detroit. The narration is delivered slowly and with a raspy, gritty voice. Throughout the commercial the narrator maintains an unhurried tempo, as if his words are half of a conversation he's having with us. His monologue begins with questions: "I got a question for you. What does this city know about luxury? What does a town that's been to hell and back know about the finer things in life?" The leisurely unfolding narrative weaves together Chrysler's two-minute mini-movie. As he continues, the narrator provides context for the shifting images on screen: viewers realize that these images are visual evidence of the "hell" the narrator evokes; as the ad goes on, it becomes clear that these images are evidence of Detroit's knowledge of "the finer things." From a population peak in the 1950s of 1.85 million to the 2011 census estimate of 706,585, the literal shrinkage of the population is frequently cited as symptomatic of the "hell" wrought on the city, a demise most often linked to the U.S. automobile industry's declining dominance of the domestic market.[16] In other words, this hell is created by globalization. The establishment of this "hell" is essential for the operation of the phoenix myth, as the rise from the ashes relies on a prior moment of destruction—a symbolic (or literal) burning to the ground.

The commercial suggests that the driving force that propels this potential for rise is Detroit's character as unbreakable and resilient—both adamantly American and unapologetically tougher than other U.S. cities. The narrator firmly declares, "Now we're from America," and then continues, "but this isn't New York City. Or the Windy City. Or Sin City. And we're certainly no one's Emerald City." In so doing there is a suggestion of a steely determination in Detroit's makeup, something particularly "American" in a maverick sort of way. The narrative at work in the commercial, and the entire "Imported from Detroit" branding campaign of which this commercial kicks off, locates Detroit as both a part of and apart from the nation. The commercial simultaneously functions as one-part economic nationalism (Buy American!) and one-part badass comeback of the underdog (Buy Detroit because we're still here, even after you've written us off). The narrative that a prominent member of a global industry, a Fortune 100 company, is an underdog is laughable, but given Chrysler's history of government bailout and alignment with the city itself it somehow works—the commercial positions the storied American automotive industry as beaten down yet ready for a comeback, just like the city it evokes.[17]

The advertising agency behind the commercial, multi-award-winner Wieden+Kennedy, is the powerhouse that has in its portfolio the last three decades of iconic Nike campaigns ("Just Do It," "Bo Knows," and the "Livestrong" yellow wristband) among other award-winning advertisements. The genius of its "Born of Fire" ad is the way in which it shifts, in a span of two minutes, Chrysler's corporate narrative from a punch line into an anthem of American can-do, will-do spirit. Chrysler, long considered the weakest of Detroit's "Big Three" automakers—Ford, General Motors, and Chrysler—was twice pulled back from the brink of collapse, first by a government-backed loan guarantee in 1979 and more recently in the 2008 auto bailout.[18] But here it transforms that losing reputation into a rallying cry for the nation. This masculine feel-good story is also a clever attempt to position the domestic auto industry as on the brink of resurgence. Not only is the commercial a self-conscious ploy to brand the city and its signature industry, but the use of the motif of individual success through hard work is also likely an attempt to deflect lingering anger at the automobile industry in general. The U.S. auto industry faced stinging criticism as myopic and out of touch in the face of the 2008–9 government bailouts.[19] The development of "Born of Fire" is attuned to the genre-specific function that "advertising was developed to sell goods, in a particular kind of economy."[20] The emotional staging of Detroit's determination and grit in the face of deep-seated economic decline plays into the zeitgeist of early 2011. Aaron Allen, Wieden+Kennedy's creative director for the Chrysler brand, said of the commercial, "This is the Rocky story, but it's real."[21] And like the famous training montage of the eponymous boxer training in *Rocky*, "Born of Fire" relies on a powerful and pulsing anthem to underscore the journey, beginning in gritty neighborhoods and ending by ultimately ascending atop the platform of a cultural institution, the stage of Detroit's Fox Theater.

One of the most compelling parts of the commercial is its setup of the adversary. Rather than an internal opponent or even a domestic rival (Ford or General Motors), the ad campaign—right from its "Imported from Detroit" title—stakes its opponent as the foreign auto industry through the idea that Detroit cars are competitive with their imported counterparts. And even more readily, it calls upon Detroit as an "underdog" in the global automobile industry. This notion has long relied on the assumption that American industry is under "attack," whether by cheap labor or cheap goods, from somewhere in Asia—first Japan in the 1970s and today from China. The commercial relies on an already established cultural rhetoric that minimizes the actual link between U.S. industrial decline and the United States' political and economic commitment to neoliberalism, which privileges the free market and produces an increasingly privatized public sector with an increasing emphasis on market gains. The auto industry, like any sector, has periods of growth and retraction. The period of growth for this industry in particular seemed to only increase; from 1946 to 1979 total domestic production of cars increased from five to thirteen million vehicles.[22] It truly seemed as if the dominance of the U.S. automotive industry would continue forever. However, as Germany and Japan both began to export cars to the United States and their smaller models became increasingly attractive in a period of skyrocketing gasoline prices due to a global oil crisis, the market share of the Big Three began to decline from its all-time high of 95 percent of the U.S. market in 1955.[23] In the case of Honda, for example, sales of its subcompacts in the United States increased from 20,000 vehicles in 1972 to 222,000 vehicles in 1977.[24] Correspondingly, just as U.S. market share decreased so did employment in the U.S. automotive industry; between 1978 and 1981 automobile employment fell from 760,000 to 490,000.[25] The myriad of reasons for the loss of jobs ran the gamut then, as now, from decentralization and automation to higher costs for wages and benefits in the United States compared with lower wages abroad and shifting customer preferences. However, it is easiest to name the biggest threat to American corporations and workers as the "import" rather than the multiple and complex interconnected factors.[26]

In the decades of deindustrialization in the wake of the decentralization of the automobile industry, the notion that "American jobs" are being lost to workers abroad is felt in various ways across the country, but perhaps nowhere as acutely as in Detroit. This is partly, as is shown in chapter 4, because Detroit as the birthplace of the United Automobile Workers (UAW) was long considered a bastion of working-class jobs, a place where a high school education and a job on the line could provide access to a middle-class life. As the U.S. automobile market faced increasing competition from imported cars, anti-Asian, "yellow peril" rhetoric grew in the Detroit region, due to the perception that Japanese imports were the primary reasons that autoworkers were losing jobs. Perhaps the most infamous manifestation was the beating death of Chinese American Vincent Chin. On the night of June 19, 1982, Chin was at a strip club when an altercation broke out between Chin and two laid-off autoworkers, Ronald Ebens and Michael Nitz. During the altercation one of the assailants yelled, "It's because of motherfuckers like you that we're out of work," mistakenly assuming that Chin was Japanese. Ebens and Nitz pursued Chin around the city and beat him nearly to death with a baseball bat in a McDonald's parking lot. He remained in a coma for four days before dying on June 23, 1982. The initial sentence of the perpetrators—a $3,000 fine and probation—caused outrage and rallied pan-Asian activism both in Detroit and nationwide.[27] Ultimately, with pressure from activists, the federal government investigated and charged Ebens and Nitz with a violation of Chin's civil rights. After a guilty verdict, an appeal by the defense for a retrial followed, and eventually a jury overturned all previous charges. The two men never served a day in jail for the murder of Vincent Chin.[28]

Metropolitan Detroit in particular, as home to the corporate headquarters of the Big Three, has long championed a company town ethic to "Buy American," not simply as a nationalistic impulse but from an economic perspective of creating and maintaining jobs. However, the "import" is an easy target that absolves and shifts responsibility for job loss and market-share from corporations and government policies like NAFTA to a vague "foreign" threat, readily symbolized by imported vehicles. The irony, however, of the "Born of Fire" commercial, and the rhetoric of the automobile industry more generally, is that no one is "stealing" "American" jobs—they in fact are not disappearing but have strategically been moved and reconstituted by the companies themselves.

The Chrysler commercial seems to hint that the woes of the American workforce can be resolved by a shift from workers/producers to managers/consumers. "Born of Fire" foregrounds a tale of modernist progression from physical labor on the line to less physical and more intellectual professional and managerial labor. While the commercial begins with visual images of the "guts" of production—multiple shots of the mechanical outsides of factories, smokestacks, and old brick façades—it soon shifts to public artworks and aesthetically pleasing examples of Detroit's architecturally rich beaux-arts, modern, and art deco landscape. The use of montage—detail shots juxtaposed with lateral tracking shots—offers a literal suggestion of movement from industrial production to, as the narrator suggests, the "finer things in life." While the first part of the commercial works to briefly circulate an account of the industrial background of the city, the bulk of the commercial works to establish not the opulence that might be called to mind when invoking "finer things" but solidly middle-class luxuries—a nice home, professional clothing, a nice watch, and, obviously, a midmarket sedan with luxury aspirations. The movement suggested by the car signals the passage of historical time and space,[29] the motion signifying a narrative of progress, and the transition in visual imagery implies a shift from production to consumption.

The montage of shifting landscape in the commercial works to facilitate an understanding of a "different" Detroit, embracing its reputation as a place of crisis and foregrounding those trials as evidence of its success. As the imagery transitions from staccato shots of "typical" Detroit—as a weathered industrial and manufacturing center—to smoother camerawork and longer shots of signs of typical middle-class commodities of "success," longer and fluid images of the car itself begin to appear. At this visual and narrative transition in the ad, the voice-over underscores the changeover in the commercial as the narrator tells the audience, "That's who we are. That's our story. Now it's probably not the one you've been reading in the papers. The one being written by folks who have never even been here, and don't know what we're capable of." The images and the filmic techniques underscore the transition from a gritty, choppy, depressed landscape to longer and slower depictions of persistence and vibrancy, interspersed with images of the vehicle itself. The commercial's shift in cinematography and story mirrors a shift in the function of the automobile as a manufactured good produced by working-class labor to a commodity consumed by middle- and upper-class professionals.

This shift from worker to consumer underscores a separation of "unskilled" and "skilled" work through the idea that "skilled" labor is intellectual and "unskilled" is physical. The conception of working-class work and the working-class worker in the commercial is utilized as a motif rather than a reality. In the ad it is in fact middle-class labor that is actually materialized through the embodiment of the consumer of the car rather than the maker of the car. The intended consumer of the car is not a worker on the line but a manager or professional, as the people represented in the commercial are not the workers who would physically *build* this car but the people who would *buy* the car. The underlying message of the ad campaign is that the need to "import" a car from Asia or Europe is no longer necessary as luxury vehicles can be "Imported from Detroit." The commercial propels the idea that importing from Detroit is a way to actualize a phoenix-like middle-class rise from the ashes of the competition of globalization. The commercial suggests that the "hell" of the past (globalization) can be overcome by economic nationalism through the rise of middle-class America.

Smoke and Mirrors: The Erasure of Work and Workers

As the commercial opens, the image of a freeway sign indicating "Detroit-North" evokes the historical narration of the northern industrial city as a destination for generations of black and white southern migrants who moved north in search of work and whose descendants still populate Detroit and its metropolitan region. Detroit's position as the historical center of U.S. auto production ushered in a working-class American Dream for those who worked on the line as introduced by former Detroiters in chapter 1 and further discussed in chapter 4. The industry, and by extension the city itself, became synonymous with the working-class man who, through hard work on the line, could lift himself into the middle class and achieve those pinnacles of the deeply gendered and heteronormative American Dream—home ownership and a better life for his family. Indeed, the commercial's narrator links "hard work and conviction" to "the know-how that runs generations deep in every last one of us. That's who we are. That's our story." The narrator positions Detroiters, and by extension the automobile industry, as linked to a hard-scrapping work ethic that is passed from generation to generation. The ad frames automobile manufacture as an artisan craft, taught by a father to a son, rather than the mass-produced, highly decentralized, globalized process that it actually is, underscoring the nostalgic haze through which the commercial operates. The trope of generational know-how is potent, capitalizing on something that we all want to believe: that the hard work of one generation pays off and advances economic prosperity for the next generation. It reifies a notion that each generation should have, and is entitled to, a better economic and financial situation than the generation before. This idea is seen in the commercial's suggestion that Detroiters have evolved from producers to consumers, paralleling the transition of the American Dream generationally from physical to intellectual labor. The commercial epitomizes the job on the line as a means for achieving the American Dream, and the purchase of the vehicle as an actualization of the dream itself. Nostalgia for this past—like most nostalgia for the old days, as shown throughout the book—is remembered with fond affection and an uncritical recollection of a glorified vision of an abundance of easily accessible jobs and a collective amnesia over the reality of life on the line. Needless to say, the reality was and is far more complicated.[30]

Indeed, life on the factory floor was frequently brutal for all workers, its contours shaped by long hours, work speed-ups, and inadequate safety standards. However, in spite of these difficult and dangerous work conditions, which were by no means unique to the auto industry but common to work in general, tens of thousands of families undoubtedly made a living working in Detroit. But this particular fantasy of Detroit remained just that—a fantasy—for many recent immigrants, people of color, and black women in particular.[31] The uneven access to jobs for African Americans, not only in the automotive industry but in all classes of jobs throughout Detroit, was documented by Forrester B. Washington, executive secretary of Detroit's nascent branch of the National Urban League. Washington's 1920 report, *The Negro in Detroit: A Survey of Conditions of a Negro Group in a Northern Industrial Center during the War Prosperity Period,* is revealing for both the racial segregation of jobs but also common spaces such as lunchrooms and bathrooms.[32] Even more notable in the report is the brief discussion of the sexual violence—physical and verbal—faced by black women workers from supervisors and customers at the work place. Additionally, the report documents the repeated preference for lighter-skinned black women workers in hiring.[33] The differential hiring practices of white men and black men and the types of intersectional racial and gender-specific harassment that black women faced were not unique to Detroit. However, "Born of Fire" reimagines the past as a time of hard work and possibility for personal success, regardless of actual access to jobs.

While on the one hand the ad seeks to create a context of work and nostalgia for the worker, the absence of actual workers in the commercial parallels the ways in which workers are called to stand in for an idea of historically imagined work, as an absent referent, but not as actual representative subjects.[34] When workers are evoked, they are represented as static, dormant, and firmly located in the past. The commercial engineers the absent referent of workers through its use of close-ups of Diego Rivera's *Detroit Industry* (1932–33) frescoes and as a suggested presence in the structures and the structural remains of work—the façade of brick buildings and industrial plants billowing smoke. The camerawork, choice of imagery, and quick-cut editing disguise the fact that actual automobile production and automobile workers are entirely absent. Although Chrysler positions the collective "we" as producers of automobiles, no actual auto workers or automobile production appear in the commercial. In fact, the only representation of automobile production is when the camera focuses on a close-up of one of the most famous panels on the North Wall of Diego Rivera's *Detroit Industry* mural. The camera begins by zeroing in on an extremely close shot of two workers, one a black man bent over a metal bar, arm muscles taut as he pushes, and his ambiguously raced coworker's straining forearm muscles pulling the same unseen heavy load. This detail shot is followed by another close-up of two men, both "white" in 2011 parlance—one with blue eyes trained steadily on unseen work and the other with his back toward the viewers revealing a head full of red hair, eyes also trained on the work before him. The camera then pulls back and slowly pans along a broader view of the detail sections of the mural, clearly showing a multiracial workforce working in concert along the line. Even here the idea of racial integration on the line, while a big theme in the mural, was much less a reality. The three seconds devoted to the mural, and its emphasis in the commercial, occurs alongside the absence of actual work or workers; as such the reality of work is rendered as an artistic representation of a nostalgic ideal.

The use of this specific artwork to sell an automobile is especially ironic. The mural was commissioned in 1931, during the height of the Great Depression, by the Arts Commission of the Detroit Institute of Arts as a gift to Detroit. The mural was funded by Edsel Ford, son of Henry Ford and at that time both president of Ford Motor Company and board president of the Arts Commission. Although it might seem baffling that the president and heir of one of the most prominent industrial companies in the world should support the commission of Diego Rivera, who had "an international reputation . . . not only [as] the outstanding artist of Mexico, the most accomplished muralist of his day, but also as the best-known 'political,' specifically Communist, artist in the world."[35] Edsel and Eleanor Ford were lifelong patrons of the arts and champions of Rivera's work. The respect seems mutual as Rivera incorporated a kindly rendered image of Edsel into the South Wall fresco. It was at the behest of William Valentiner, director of the Detroit Institute of Arts, that Rivera was commissioned to carry out a fresco project that would represent "something of the history of Detroit, or some motif suggesting the development of industry in this town."[36] Rivera was initially contracted to paint only two walls of the Garden Court of the museum, but after his research and initial sketching, he requested and was granted permission to paint all four walls of the indoor courtyard. The now-named Rivera Court houses the twenty-seven-panel fresco mural, which measures almost 450 square yards.[37] Each wall touches on a different theme and each individual panel contributes to a symbolic motif of the interconnectedness of raw materials, humanity, technology, and labor. Rivera spent nearly a month of his three months of research at the Ford River Rouge complex studying, sketching, and observing automobile production in preparation for the project, spending other time at a Chrysler plant, Parke-Davis Chemical, Michigan Alkali, Edison, and various other factories, which is evident in the wide swath of technology and industry represented across the panels.[38]

While automobile assembly is the backdrop for the two largest and most prominent panels, there is only one representation of a completed car in the entire work. It is hard to find as it measures only about four inches in length within a panel that is approximately seventy-five feet long and seventeen feet high.[39] Its miniscule size in proportion to the panel and mural as a whole makes clear that the finished product, the automobile, is not the centerpiece of *Detroit Industry.* As art historian David Craven comments, "[Rivera's] subject in the murals would be nothing less than 'the human *spirit* that is embodied in the machine.'"[40] In so doing, Rivera highlighted the worker, and not the end commodity, as the main feature of Detroit industry. Both Rivera and the commercial downplay the car itself, but the Chrysler ad spotlights the consumptive symbolism of the automobile, erasing the workers, while Rivera spotlights the laboring symbolism of the automobile, placing the commodity as only possible because of the labor of the workers.

The section of the mural that "Born of Fire" features is part of the main North Wall panel that shows the production of the engine and the transmission. This detail shot of the mural shows a multiracial labor force straining as they deburr an engine block and transfer the engine blocks off the line for final assembly.[41] The North and South Walls of the fresco cycle, and the detail that the commercial highlights in particular, showcase the physicality and labor of the historic automobile production processes. In this way the mural, as well as the idea that the commercial seeks to evoke, is visceral—loud, hot, heavy—a departure from the technological and robotic process of manufacturing today.[42] The same ideas that Chrysler is seeking to stimulate are the ones that formed an initial critique of the mural at its unveiling: that the hot, dirty insides of the factory should not be showcased on the walls of a brand new major metropolitan museum.[43] Yet eighty years later, it is in fact precisely the artistic rendering of the "insides" of the factory that the commercial works to evoke. The choice to most directly link physical labor and automobile production to an artistic representation, not to a contemporary photograph or video portrayal of workers on the line, or even a historic photographic or filmic representation, places work and workers in the realm of the imagined past. This directorial choice underscores physical labor as something firmly situated in the past, and the fictional rendering of that labor via the representation in the mural speaks to the ways in which labor is idealized, both in 1933 and again in 2011. The use of the mural serves as an important context for the commercial; as the camera pans the mural, the line of voice-over that narrates Rivera's artwork reaffirms the images, telling viewers, "It's the hottest fires that make the hardest steel. Add hard work and conviction." This literally sets the stage that fire, the elemental power that induces the alchemy of raw material to commodity, is only possible with the intervention of humans. The choice to represent the ideas of "hard work and conviction" through an artistic rendering of a historicized manufacturing process underscores the nostalgic evocation of work and workers rather than its reality that the Detroit workforce has shrunken as many jobs on the line have been replaced by machines and have shifted from Detroit to other areas of the United States and decentralized parts suppliers all over the world.

Indeed, Rivera was tasked by the Arts Commission to create, as Linda Bank Downs writes, "symbolic or allegorical images . . . for the Detroit murals, not the stark reality of factory interiors."[44] Even at the time of the mural's creation, the images of workers were used not to symbolically represent actual workers but as the *idea* of workers in an imagined multiracial workforce that was highly productive and robust. In reality, the factory that Rivera would have observed would have been at much less capacity in terms of workers as production had been scaled back due to increasing competition and decreasing demand during the Great Depression.[45] Steve Babson in *Working Detroit* explains that in March 1929 the Ford Motor Company employed 128,000 people and by August 1931 employment was down to 37,000; labor historians estimate that 46 percent of the entire Michigan labor force was unemployed by 1933.[46] This imaginary workforce, deployed during the mural's initial construction during the Great Depression, is ironically appropriate for the 2011 commercial, as it was in both instances used for the same purpose: to evoke an idealized workforce.

In the Driver's Seat: Off the Line and behind the Wheel

As discussed previously, the commercial's point of view immediately aligns the gaze of the audience as the gaze of the subject of the commercial: the viewers are literally in the driver's seat when the commercial begins. Once we exit the freeway and are driving around the city roads, we begin to see the car in the edges of the frame—a side mirror, a rearview mirror—interspersed in the views of the city, and it becomes apparent that rather than in the driver's seat we are in fact a passenger in this car being driven around Detroit. Very tightly filmed shots of the exterior are interspersed—the grille of the car, the Chrysler logo, the steering wheel and in-dash navigation system, tires, and trunk—slowly unveiling a piece of the car, one detail at a time. This montage works to build anticipation of the closing scenes of the commercial when viewers finally see the car in full. These detail shots parallel the disembodied unveiling of the person driving the Chrysler 200. The driver is also revealed slowly: first a blurry profile cruising by in the car, the detail of a hand with a luxury watch casually positioned upon the steering wheel, the hint of eyes reflected in a rearview mirror. The revelation of the driver parallels the revelation of the car—the detail shots simultaneously creating mystery and anticipation in the slow uncovering of the car and driver. The driver is finally revealed, after multiple disembodied glimpses, to be Eminem, famous hip-hop artist and native son of Detroit.

The ultimate choice of Eminem to be the symbolic white man who drives the viewer around Detroit gestures toward the tropes of bootstraps, hard work, and determination at any cost.[47] Eminem's two lines of dialogue, "This is the Motor City. And this is what we do," link him to Detroit, as a representative native son, and link his actions to what the city "does." One of the most commercially successful hip-hop artists of all time, Eminem has also raised controversy for his lyrical perpetration of misogyny and homophobia. Additionally, some have suggested that rather than his whiteness as an obstacle to overcome, Eminem's ascent has paralleled past examples of white performers mimicking black cultural performers and rising to fame because of their white performance of black cultural forms.[48] As his fame grew, one of the primary ways that Eminem articulated his "authenticity" was by linking himself to what Loren Kajikawa calls "inner-city black subjectivity."[49] By linking himself to the postindustrial landscape of Detroit, he casts himself as a credible voice of hip-hop through his spatial location in the depopulated and crime-ridden urban core.[50] The ways in which *8 Mile,* a fictional yet loosely biographical film, paralleled his own rise to success led many critics to herald the film (and by extension Eminem's life) as a populist narrative of success against all the odds, a filmic portrayal of the American bootstrap tale.[51] Despite the actual demographics of Detroit—whose population was more than 80 percent black in 2010[52]—it is the successful, white rapper who will drive the city's rise from the ashes.

"Born of Fire" uses as its anthem a musical riff of the backbeat to Eminem's easily recognized song "Lose Yourself."[53] The Grammy- and Academy Award–winning song was the first track released from the soundtrack to *8 Mile.* Although the lyrics from the song do not appear in the commercial, the song's repetitive backbeat and sonic crescendo are laid down under the narrator's voice. The song at first seems to be a chronicle of the character arc of Jimmy "B-Rabbit" Smith, the protagonist and Eminem's character in the film. However, the lyrics consciously play with the double persona of Eminem on and off screen, stating, "and there's no movie, there's no Mekhi Phifer, this is my life."[54] Therefore, "Lose Yourself" may be read as both part of the film and also part of Eminem's larger personal narrative. In the film the song is utilized as a rousing call to action for the underdog. *Rolling Stone* magazine considers it one of the "50 greatest hip-hop songs of all time" and summarizes its placement on the list: "Eminem's biggest-ever hit plays like Rocky condensed into a five-minute song."[55] The hook of the song is set to a pulsing, urging drum rhythm that is enriched with simple repeating guitar and piano riffs:

> You better lose yourself in the music, the moment
> You own it, you better never let it go
> You only get one shot, do not miss your chance to blow
> This opportunity comes once in a lifetime yo. (repeat)[56]

In the commercial, the song's musical accompaniment is lighter, the pulsing backbeat set on an electric guitar punctuated with pronounced piano chords. In the original the increasing tempo and urgency of Eminem's lyrical delivery urges a sonic crescendo, and in the commercial a choral swell that begins almost imperceptibly reaches a full crescendo just in advance of the narrative climax—creating a tension in the commercial's story as we eagerly anticipate the conclusion to this two-minute mini-movie.

The commercial relies on our lyrical knowledge of "Lose Yourself" and of Eminem—both as a person and as B-Rabbit, the fictional character in *8 Mile*—as a scrappy fighter able to overcome his impoverished circumstances and make good on the "one shot" at the "once in a lifetime" opportunity. Though there is no direct allusion to it, I believe that the commercial even capitalizes on Eminem's perceived difficulty finding acceptance in the black hip-hop world, which forms one of the main obstacles for his alter ego in *8 Mile.* In the commercial Eminem becomes a stand-in for the embattled white worker who faces competition from unseen people of color around the globe. In the broader national context of vitriol over the bank bailouts and the auto bailouts, and in growing anger targeted at corporate elites, Eminem functions not only as a Detroit-raised megastar but, importantly, as a star that embodies working-class credibility. He is not a "trust fund baby," and although he is clearly part of the 1 percent, the idea that he "worked for it," as circulated by his public persona, symbolizes an egalitarian approach to success—his humble beginnings and persistence in pursuit of his career positions him within the narrative of the hard-working self-made American man. And in so doing, the affirmation of the bootstrap myth is complete; Eminem is compelling because according to the myth of egalitarian access it was not being a white man that enabled his success. Indeed, his race in *8 Mile* is perceived as an industry barrier he had to overcome. Therefore, rather than white masculinity as a factor that enabled access to success, it was his own individual determination. As he drives through Detroit, with his expensive watch in full view and in complete command of the city, he is a vision of hard work paid off.

The commercial's final scene begins with Eminem's arrival at the historic Fox Theater, where he parks the Chrysler 200 beneath a marquee that reads: "Keep Detroit Beautiful." The bright red of the car's taillights and the lights of the theater marquee shine brightly against the darkness of night, a marked distinction from the cool gray tones of the first eighty seconds of the commercial. This is the visual accompaniment to the sound of a choral swell against the backbeat of "Lose Yourself." The audience follows Eminem as he exits the car and enters the empty theater, where an African American choir is performing a choral melody onstage and the viewers understand that the vocal accompaniment heard earlier foreshadowed this scene. Twenty men and women are dressed in contrasting red and black choral robes on a stage flanked by rich red curtains, and wisps of smoke float above their heads. This transition to a rich and warm color palette suggests that we have been driving to the heart of the fire all along. Eminem walks through the theater and climbs atop the stage. He turns to face us directly and the shot cuts very close: Eminem is framed from the chest up, almost imperceptibly filmed from a lower angle so that he is slightly above eye level. We are just barely looking up at him. In the background, at the exact moment Eminem turns to face the camera directly, the choir members—in almost military precision—lower their hands and clasp them in front of their waists, bow their heads, and stop singing. They become a silent backdrop, heads bowed and eyes averted, as Eminem addresses us directly. He looks straight into the camera and delivers his two lines of dialogue: *"This is the Motor City."* He pauses slightly, and raises his hand to point a finger at the camera: *"And this is what we do."* His pointed finger serves to punctuate the dialogue and offer a directive. After he finishes, the camera lingers for a second as he walks out of the frame, exiting stage left. Then the scene cuts to the car idling in front of the theater, and the audience watches as the vehicle glides toward the camera into the night, down an empty, rain-sparkled street. As the car begins to fill the frame the shot closes in and text glides over the passenger door, which reads: "THE CHRYSLER 200 HAS ARRIVED." The car and text seamlessly fade to a black screen, and then "Imported From Detroit" appears, a single word at a time, each word gliding across the screen as smoothly as the car that has just faded to black and punctuated by a light tinkling on the high registers of a piano, a sonic reminder of both "Lose Yourself" and the "finer things in life."

Eminem's "performance" makes the viewers wonder: Who is this "we" that he is evoking? And what is it that this "we" does? As is clear, the audience is meant to identify with the subject of the commercial. Kevin Yon, the commercial's narrator, mentioned in an interview that Eminem's dialogue—*"This is the Motor City. And this is what we do"*—was his favorite part of the commercial, and that he gave over one hundred different readings of this line during the recording of his voice-over.[57] Ultimately it was decided that Eminem would deliver the line, underscoring the idea that what we do is linked to the rise of *individual* success based on hard work and determination, perpetuating the great American myth of meritocracy. The "we" then is set up not only in juxtaposition of the "they" of foreign auto industry competition but could also be analyzed in terms of the "we" of Detroit. As discussed throughout the book, this "we" is complex both in terms of the historical memory of Detroit's past and the plans for the development of Detroit's future. If the viewers read the Fox Theater, the location of the commercial's final scene, as a symbol of the city itself—in its individual history of rise, decline, and rebirth in the late 1980s—Chrysler's use of the location for the final scene is evocative: the empty seats are parallel to the idea of the emptiness of Detroit's landscape. However, the theater is not entirely empty; there is an African American choir performing onstage. As Eminem takes the stage his actions are uncontested by the choir—they do not make direct eye contact with him or with the camera. Only Eminem looks directly into the camera and addresses the viewing audience. These occupants of the Fox Theater are easily silenced, it seems, willing to acquiesce to the declarations of the white man who strides onstage; these robed men and women become an unsettling parable for who the "we" of the commercial is. The subliminal "we" of the commercial is crystalized in this final scene when the choir assembled onstage bows their heads as Eminem takes center stage. Is he speaking on behalf of the choir—are they part of the "we"? Or is the choir a "they" that will be overtaken? The majority of the people seen in the commercial and again on stage are black—which makes sense in Detroit's majority black population. However, the other people in the commercial serve primarily as background characters while it is the actions and gaze of Eminem, the white male protagonist, that forms the central action of the commercial. Likely unintended, but still subtly rendered, the idea of blackness here serves as a backdrop to the narrative of Detroit's rebirth, which is a theme that will appear again in chapter 5.

Phoenix Rising?

The "Born of Fire" ad continued to run in its original form as well as cut into thirty- and sixty-second versions throughout the next year. In addition, the marketing team rounded out the "Imported from Detroit" campaign with four more commercials, released over the next year. Each thirty- or sixty-second ad told the story of the rise of a hometown hero, for example in the case of Detroit Lions defensive tackle Ndamukong Suh making a return to his hometown as a proud Detroit player and Chrysler driver. These national spots had the same feel and narrative structure of the original "Born of Fire" ad and showed the rebranded fleet of Chrysler models.

Chrysler followed up the suite of "Born of Fire" inspired spots with a new commercial, which premiered during Super Bowl 2012 and was called "It's Halftime America"; the two-minute spot literally kicked off halftime. Still part of the "Imported from Detroit" campaign, this commercial has not an anonymous everyman as narrator but one of the most iconic figures of American masculinity—Clint Eastwood. As he begins his story suggesting "halftime" as a parable for America, viewers begin to see images of a front porch of a farmhouse covered in morning dew, a bird's-eye view of a city, a waterfront—all stand-ins for any town, anywhere, before the scene shifts to images of people. These people all seem to be everyday Americans—waking up, getting out of bed, and getting ready for a new day. As Eastwood's narration transitions from the idea that this is a pause—a moment to get ready for a second half—he offers up Detroit as the underdog making a comeback. He states, "The people of Detroit know a little something about this. They almost lost everything. But we all pulled together, now Motor City is fighting again." As the dialogue continues, Eastwood's narration weaves a story of discord and division of the past setting a stage for a comeback: "After those trials, we all rallied around what was right, and acted as one. Because that's what we do. We find a way through tough times, and if we can't find a way, then we'll make one." At this point in the narration the same people are arriving to work and driving their kids to school (in their Chrysler vehicle, of course). As Eastwood's narration gains momentum, he continues, "Detroit's showing us it can be done. And, what's true about them is true about all of us," as a fleet of Chrysler vehicles rolls down the production line. The commercial concludes with Eastwood directly addressing the camera: "This country can't be knocked out with one punch. We get right back up again and when we do the world is going to hear the roar of our engines. Yeah, it's halftime America. And, our second half is about to begin." Eastwood then walks out of the frame and fades to a black screen before the "Imported from Detroit" logo appears.

Relying on the narrative of Detroit introduced in the "Born of Fire" commercial, the spin-off ad starring Eastwood is selling a narrative of a second-half comeback for the nation. The commercial, much like the prior year's "Born of Fire," relied on a narrative of Detroit's role as an outsider and its commitment to hard work and its comeback as the ultimate underdog. At work here is an affirmation of Detroit as a phoenix, told by one of America's greatest icons of masculinity and frontier. The reaction to the commercial was mixed as many found the tone too excessive, too solemn, and it was panned by critics, widely seen by many as "jumping the shark," yet it lived on in renewed forms as it was spoofed by *Saturday Night Live, 30 Rock,* and *Second City,* among others.[58] The commercial also faced criticism from politicians, pundits, and the Republican Party for what some believed was an endorsement of both the auto industry bailout and a second term for the Obama administration.[59] However, the commercial's symbolic resonance that the nation, like Detroit, was on the verge of pulling out a win, appealed to many and created an initial favorable reaction.

Through potent imagery, rousing narration, first-person camerawork, and editing more akin to feature films than car advertising, "Born of Fire" offers the rebirth of Detroit as an allegory for the larger rebirth of middle-class America—a self-determined and proud phoenix rising from the ashes of economic downturn. The dramatic transition—from a stagnant, frozen landscape to a fiery landscape of hard work, perseverance, and determination—forms the backbone of the narrative arc of Detroit's contemporary rebirth. While the commercial was hailed as presenting a "new" version of Detroit, its ultimate message, and its masculine tug-on-the-heartstrings appeal, is quite old: "Born of Fire" is nothing if not a symbolic reaffirmation of the American myth of egalitarian access. The success of the ad campaign not only increased interest in the Chrysler brand but merged the contemporary phoenix narrative of Detroit's resurgence with a national narrative of hope in the face of the worst recession since the Great Depression. The "Born of Fire" commercial, about a mythic rise from destruction, embodies a larger shift: from Detroit as the epitome of postindustrial crisis to Detroit as a city of hope, an allegory for industriousness, resilience, and survival against all odds. Chrysler is thus recycling the trope of meritocracy and equality of opportunity in order to sell the commodity. In so doing the commercial sells the story of individual success, made even greater because of adversity.

"Born of Fire" as an example of the branding of Detroit as a regenerative phoenix centers Detroit as a stand-in for the embattled white male workforce and hints at (his) ultimate return to glory, through grit and perseverance, in the wake of an unnamed threat. This depiction situates Detroit—a stand-in for the domestic automobile industry in particular, and the postindustrial U.S. city in general—as a place to locate the enduring American spirit. The achievement of the enormously popular and culturally resonant branding campaign lay in its ability to connect Detroit's story of regeneration as an anthem. While the focus of this chapter is on the Chrysler commercial, this particular bit of cultural ephemera is but one example of the broader rebranding of Detroit. As companies such as a high-end watch maker, Apple, and as described in chapter 5, a specialty grocery chain, utilize the "brand" of Detroit as a symbol to sell their products, the questions of narrative strategy are all the more compelling.[60] In this particular "Imported from Detroit" ad campaign, Chrysler was able to shift the narrative of Detroit (and by extension, its brand) through selling the story of hard work, determination, and comeback through what Raymond Williams calls "the magic of advertising." Furthermore, it is the same corporations and private investors that seek to profit from a branding strategy that uses Detroit's gritty, urban decline as a backdrop to sell their products as unique and innovative.

CHAPTER 4

Flickers of the American Dream

Filming Possibility in Decline

> I'm gonna take you out to where I got hired at in 1968. The Cadillac assembly plant. This plant was huge, all of this was the plant. . . . It was the first job I ever had, you know. It was the first job I ever had.
>
> —George McGregor, *Detropia*

> I can't say this hood is to be blamed. They chose that life, it didn't choose them.
>
> —Queen, *Deforce*

Contemporary Detroit is the film muse of the decade as it has served as both subject and backdrop of at least sixty short and feature-length documentary films produced in or about Detroit from 2008 to 2014.[1] The news reports on Detroit reached a fever pitch in the lead-up to the government bailout of the automobile industry in 2008. This, coupled with the publication of high-profile photographic images in 2010 of the "ruins" of Detroit, stoked interest that boiled over to the documentary film genre as numerous filmmakers sought to conceptualize what happened in Detroit's past, the reality of Detroit's present, and the possibilities for Detroit's future. The Detroit documentary film genre bordered on the point of cliché as Dustin Dwyer, a journalist for Michigan Radio, the local affiliate of National Public Radio, published an article in February 2012 titled "Our How-To Guide for Making a Hardscrabble, Gritty, Post-Industrial Documentary about Detroit."[2] As much as the article is meant to be comical, as evidenced by Dwyer's last line of copy—"Note to Detroit's documentary filmmakers: We kid because we love"—the article is intended to draw attention to the rather formulaic way in which Detroit is being presented in many documentary films. Dwyer breaks down the commonplace template along four main narrative movements, complete with suggestions of pre-scouted locations for shots and archival footage to include. His summation of the genre as encompassed by the "How To" begins with an opening shot of an abandoned building, sets up the historic rise through "Act One: Paris of the Midwest," moves into the city's decline in "Act Two: The Post-Apocalyptic Hell-Scape," before concluding with "Act Three: A Glimmer of Hope." Although Dwyer demurs that he, like me, has not seen all films of the genre, I agree with his lighthearted assessment. As much as the article is meant to be comical, it contains more than an ounce of truth as many films solidify along this rather formulaic narrative of Detroit, which is, as has been shown throughout the book, the narrative of rise, fall, and the possibility of rise again.

What is unique about this time period, beyond the sheer number of films, is the emphasis on moving Detroit's narrative beyond a conception of "postindustrial wasteland" in order to usher in a story of possibility. This chapter turns to the ways in which the myth of the contemporary postindustrial frontier, much like the myth of the historical frontier in American culture, operates not only as a physical place but also as an ideological symbol to suggest the potential of hardworking and determined individuals against all odds.[3] Even as the present is portrayed as bleak, the narrative resolution of Detroit's uncertain future nearly always falls back on a retrenchment of the American idea of success through individual hard work and determination, in spite of hardship.

Centrally, it is the idea that a commitment to individual hard work and faith in the promise of the American Dream that made Detroit a once-great city can operate to make the city great once again. While Detroit was long considered a place to achieve the American Dream, this reputation was demolished by the precipitous declines of the late twentieth century. The trope of the American Dream is now being revived so earnestly, despite the fact that over the last several decades that dream has seemed to *fail so completely* in Detroit. Even as the visual, statistical, and historical evidence all point to the fact that Detroit, and the version of the American Dream it championed, has failed, these documentaries insist on the possibility of revival of this dream. As the most salient illustration of the massive failure of that dream, it makes the premise of rebirth in the city even more striking.

In order to analyze how narratives of past greatness set up a contemporary narrative of possibility against the odds, I look specifically at two documentary films, Daniel Falconer's *Deforce* (2010) and Heidi Ewing and Rachel Grady's *Detropia* (2011). These two films were each specifically chosen from the wide field of documentary films because they are part of the subgenre of Detroit documentary film notable for the metropolitan Detroit roots of its filmmakers.[4] The filmmakers' hometown origin—Daniel Falconer grew up, as I did, in the northern suburbs, and Heidi Ewing is from the western suburbs—has been played up by reviewers and in interviews with the filmmakers.[5] In 2012 the *New York Times* featured a story on hometown documentary portrayals of the city, stating: "Now native filmmakers from the Detroit region are offering their own take on the city's plight, hoping to provide a more nuanced and insightful examination than what outsiders have contributed."[6] Of this subcategory of "native" Detroit documentaries, I chose to analyze these two films for how they simultaneously conform to and stand out from the genre of Detroit documentary film. In both cases Detroit's past greatness looms larger than life—each of the films, like most of the genre, hold tight to the narrative of Detroit's past as a time of prosperity and growth. I chose *Deforce* as one of the films to discuss in this chapter due to its unique framework, which names and analyzes structural racism as a key factor in the decline of Detroit. Often characterized as a film that unflinchingly critiques policies and practices of the city's urban planning, police force, and government corruption, it resolutely links contemporary Detroit's present state of decline to a series of historical actions. Although it received mostly positive reviews where and when it was screened, it was distributed for theatrical release only at film festivals, and it is not widely available for instant streaming.[7] *Detropia* was chosen primarily because it is arguably the most well-known Detroit documentary film. Its nomination for a top prize at the Sundance Film Festival, placement on the short list for the Academy Award Documentary Film nominations, and reviews in highly trafficked online and print news outlets like the *New York Times, Salon, USA Today,* the *New Yorker,* and *Huffington Post* ensured that news of the film reached a wide audience.[8] *Detropia* represents Detroit as a beautiful, tenuous possibility, in the wake of globalization. The two films are quite different in their visions of the city, and yet even these disparate portrayals insist on emphasizing Detroit's past greatness, and ultimately consolidate along lines of neoliberal promise of both past and future through the actions of individuals in the present. Even as these filmic narratives seek to illuminate multiple and interlocking systems of racism, government malfeasance, corporate greed, and failing public services, they all too often default to a benign resolution wherein the structural racism of the past and present is resolved in the representation of Detroit as a frontier of possibility through individual hard work and the sheer determination of neoliberal individualism. In so doing they set up and replicate the triumph of individual determination in the face of great odds, echoing the idea of the triumph of man over obstacle, disciplining a wild frontier into a space of productivity.

The False Hope of Choice in the Neoliberal City

Deforce (2010), directed, coproduced, and cowritten by Daniel Falconer, frames the decline of contemporary Detroit as the manifestation of historical racism. The first two and a half minutes of the film unfold in a disorienting montage of archival news footage, beginning with Franklin Delano Roosevelt's proclamation that "American civilization is in danger" and we are the arsenal of democracy. From this clip, historic newsreel leads the viewers through the story of Detroit's growth and decline, which features a cacophony of overlapping news clips that reference Detroit's misery in the forms of increasing murder and unemployment rates. The overall effect of this opening is simultaneously disorienting in the shift from rise to decline and overwhelming in the sheer amount of news footage it provides to set the story of Detroit's decline. This introductory montage immediately orients the audience to the narrative arc of the film, one that replicates the story of rise and decline. While the film's title is never addressed in the film or in interviews that Falconer gives, the name *Deforce* is likely an assemblage of Detroit and force. And like the French origin of Detroit's own name (as discussed in the conclusion), the signification of "de" lends a suggestion of the origin and sustenance of force in Detroit's story. Even as it begins in this seemingly ubiquitous fashion, *Deforce* makes a pointed departure from standard narratives of Detroit by explicitly asserting in the opening minutes that opportunities for home ownership, jobs, and education were mediated by racially exclusive access and that in turn Detroit's decline has at its center racism and the failure of the city's leadership class. At its core the film's central contention is the idea that racism created opportunities for access to wealth accumulation and home ownership for whites and barriers of access to wealth accumulation and home ownership for African Americans. *Deforce* critiques the normative narrative of white flight that abounds, which was discussed, for example, in chapter 1. The film asserts that Detroit's suburbs were developed not merely because white Detroiters "fled" the city but because of local, state, and federal policies and practices that created incentives for movement to the suburbs, at the literal expense of the city, providing a direct contradiction to the benign narrative of exodus that was detailed in previous chapters. The film explicitly considers the implications of a system wherein access to many of Detroit's suburbs was predicated on access to whiteness. Falconer shows the nostalgic past as simultaneously a time for great opportunity for whites and a time of racist inequality for people of color at work in Detroit's historic development.

This film is, on the one hand, a distinct departure from other contemporary Detroit documentaries because of its complete transparency about the historic and still-persisting forces of racism in the development of the city. On the other hand, it reaffirms Detroit as an example of what the geographer David Wilson defines as the contemporary structure of the U.S. black urban ghetto: a location whose uneven development is strategic, intended to isolate and warehouse those deemed "harmful" to the more profitable effort to privatize and redevelop the urban core.[9] Key to both David Wilson's argument and Ruth Wilson Gilmore's argument of the unevenness of capitalism as discussed in chapter 2 is the insistence that the historical and ongoing unevenness of disaccumulation and accumulation in the United States is linked to race. This is where narratively *Deforce* fails to connect the future to the past. Although the filmmaker does an excellent job of showcasing the historical operation of race and uneven development, in some ways the present-day representation of the city and its residents falls back onto personal solutions for structural problems. In the balance of this section I argue that *Deforce,* and its bold initial assertion of the force of institutional racism in Detroit's decline, ultimately lapses into a sentiment that "ghetto life" is a result of individual choice. This idea is depicted as an update of the "culture of poverty," as discussed in chapter 2, the idea that, as Robin Kelley suggests, the underclass and the ghetto have been constructed by social scientists "as a reservoir of pathologies and bad cultural values."[10] Through filmic conventions and its use of personal stories, *Deforce* reinforces a narrative of contemporary residents as social problems, a community that has been failed by public services and can only be saved by individually driven market-based interventions. *Deforce* insists on the false hope of a market-based, neoliberal solution of "legitimate" work and education to what it reproduces as a culture of poverty problem.

Deforce takes a conventional approach to documentary film, establishing the authority of the film through the use of voice-over narration. The voice-over serves to weave together the pieces of evidence into an overall narrative arc that argues that government mismanagement, corruption, and racism are to blame for Detroit's decline. In addition to narration, the film also utilizes on-screen section titles to provide an overall framework of argument, which also appear in the breakdown of DVD chapters.[11] Documentary film involves a "tacit agreement whereby documentarians are expected to earn the trust of the audience by offering truthful information about their subject."[12] Falconer earns our trust early on through the use of archival film, news reports, photographs, maps, statistical facts, and interviews with experts: historians, professors, archivists, lawyers, and community leaders in Detroit. All are typical parts of constructing a documentary argument, and Falconer relies on these types of sources to make an argument that historically institutional racism resulted in black containment within the central city and made Detroit into what the narrator characterizes as "one big ghetto." In the first sections of the film, which establish Detroit's history of institutional racism, the primary data sources the film relies on—archival images, policy and historical documents, statistics, and legislation—are linked through the voice-over narration and expert interviews. The use of expert interviews in *Deforce* follows the well-established form and methods of camerawork, which is "normally static and self-effacing," positioned to the side of the subject rather than head on, and the interviewees "speak in a somewhat formal tone but without addressing the audience directly."[13] The credibility of the expert is well established both through genre convention as well in the on-screen captions that provide the individual credentials of each interviewee. Although some of the elements of the first half of the film appear in the second half, the data sources of the second half rely primarily on interviews with local Detroit residents shot on the front porch, sidewalk, and adjacent lot to the home of one of the interviewees. While I discuss this element of filmmaking in much greater detail in the next few pages, it is important to note that overall the effect of this difference between the use of evidence of the film is unsettling, particularly in the marked contrast in how it portrays "real Detroiters" and "experts" on screen.

The second half of the film focuses on contemporary Detroit, and the film relies less and less on archival images, data, and voice-over narration and more and more on interviews with a group of about ten black Detroiters ranging in age from about early twenties to late thirties. While all the other interviewees are filmed in the typical style of documentary expert as discussed above, these later interviews are never conceptualized as to how and why these specific Detroiters are included in the film.[14] These young black men and women, who are referred to not as individuals but on the film's website collectively as "Detroit Neighborhood Residents" and in the film credits as the "Dexter crew," a geographic reference to the main street in the neighborhood, serve as the primary data source to contextualize the words of the experts in the second half of the film. This shift in data operates to underscore a larger shift in narrative argument, from historical racism to contemporary culture of poverty. For, in the early section of the film, the story of uneven development of the city and the interlocking forces of institutional racism are well established and corroborated through archival documents, media reports, and a wide variety of academic and community experts. Yet in the second half of the film, the contemporary narrative of continuing poverty for the black underclass that remains is told via the stories of individual choices and firsthand accounts. So in one way while Falconer corrects the presumed invisibility or disappearance of the black residents that are discussed in chapters 2 and 5, the deep-seated poverty seen in the second half of the film loses the macro-level focus and feels very much like a micro-level examination of individual choices.

The idea of a culture of poverty is represented through both the physical landscape and the Detroiters interviewed. The first time the members of the Dexter crew appear on screen as interview subjects occurs midway through the film in the section titled "Living Standards." After the narrator and expert interviewees establish the near absence of city services as a result of the declining tax base, the interviews with the Dexter crew continue through the end of the film as sources of primary data. The introduction of the Dexter crew begins with two interviewees, identified only as "Jig" and "Nod," who stand in a lot next to a decrepit brick house heavily tagged with graffiti. The lot itself is blanketed with twelve-inch-high grass, and the camera films Jig and Nod from about the knee up. This angle captures them surrounded by the lush green of the tall summer grass and a blighted home in the background; most disturbingly, this angle cuts out their lower legs and feet, visually rendering them as immobile.

This type of filming is in marked contrast to the interviews with the expert subjects. The experts are filmed in typical documentary talking-head style where they are shot from the midtorso up, sitting in a chair in a professional-looking office, wearing suit jackets and button-down shirts. The experts are identified by a first and last name, a professional title, and then often a descriptive phrase like "longtime Detroiter," which gives them credibility not only professionally but also as "Detroiters." In contrast, the Dexter crew's interviews all take place outside—in a vacant lot, on a front porch, on the sidewalk—and all of the people are filmed in either T-shirts or tank tops. The shots are set up at a further distance from the interview subject, allowing a view of not only the person speaking but also a backdrop of other people, buildings, or a streetscape in the background. The people featured as part of the Dexter crew are linked through the film to the outside, to nature, and to the environment. In this way, the Dexter crew is positioned as part of the landscape. The experts, on the other hand, are filmed in generic settings that could be placed in any city, anywhere. As such the experts are presented as not only of a different class, professional, and educational background but literally of a different environment, setting up a dichotomy of "expert" Detroiters and "neighborhood" Detroiters.

Against the visual backdrop of blight and grassland, Nod states, "It's bad to other people because they didn't grow up over here, but to us it's just regular, you know what I'm saying, it's just regular." Positioned within a scene of physically decaying structure and following expert interviews suggesting that Detroit is structurally broken are the narrative contexts that Nod seems to be testifying to: the lack of city structures and the "living standards" exemplified by this blighted lot are "just regular," part of the everyday. In this representation of blight and declining city services as part of everyday living, the distinction of what may be "just regular" for the presumed viewers and the neighborhood residents is created. Whereas the experts are featured talking about declining services, ongoing blight, and lack of opportunity for both education and employment as a shameful state of the city, the Dexter crew is featured as living in this decaying atmosphere. The difference in location functions in one way to position the residents and their neighborhood as a spectacle to outsiders in their acceptance of the devastating images of blight as unremarkable, similar to Vergara's *Row Houses on Alfred Street* (Figure 7), which depicts neighborhood residents casually interacting in front of a blighted home (see chapter 2). This representation also serves the narrative function seen throughout the book—the idea that the city has been ill-used by its current occupants—and sets up the city for reclamation by the local and outside elites, corporations, and government, as will be seen fully in chapter 5. Directly following Nod's comment that the blighted lot is "just regular" is a statement from Jig that "it always was a drug area, for sure, for sure." Nod expands upon Jig's statement by saying, "Before our time." This comment does not support structural failures, lack of city services, or decades of institutional racism that impact living standards. The use of first-person voice here shifts the filmic narrative from structural inequities to the neighborhood as a drug area, suggesting a generations-long degeneracy of the community.

The difference in the visual and narrative setup of the Dexter crew is made clearer through interviews where Falconer discusses his relationship to the residents and directorial choices made when filming. He reflected on how he approached and established rapport with the participating Detroit residents in an interview with *BoxOffice:*

> They were actually quite willing. You have to have a native guide, who came in the form of Dr. Luke Bergmann, who you'll probably remember from the movie. . . . We contacted him, and he was the one who brokered that. He introduced me to the residents because he has been living among them for a long time and profiling them and there was a lot of

> trust there. . . . They're not skeptical of me or wondering why I'm putting a camera in their face. They're happy to share their stories. . . . I think for them it was just nice to know that anyone from the outside cared, and we would just let the camera roll and they could talk as they wanted, and then later I could do my thing with it, as opposed to rapid fire questions or anything like that.[15]

The difference in visual and narrative treatment of the residents versus the experts was a large source of discomfort I experienced while first watching the portrayals of the residents in the film, and it grew stronger as I viewed the film again and again. On the one hand, Falconer's film is a hard-hitting look at the historical role of institutional racism and government corruption. But on the other hand, the visual and narrative use of the Dexter crew in the film seemed out of step with this larger argument. In some respects it seemed as if these residents were shown mostly to provide evidence of the long-lasting impacts of the failure of the city. The binary setup palpable in the film of "native informant" and "outside expert" is likely a result of Falconer's own description of the interview process. Ultimately, the focus on the perceived or anticipated difference between Falconer and the Dexter crew based on geography is a theme that emerges not only in the film (in the setup of the city–metropolitan area divide) but also throughout Falconer's own interviews. His representation of himself as "from the outside" and Bergmann as a "native guide" serves as an anthropological binary that sees the "native" as a population to be studied and whose stories and culture can be carried back to the outside. It is here that for me the critique of institutional racism is weakened by Falconer's own unexamined perspective—which is never addressed directly in the film but is palpable throughout in the series of narrative choices he makes.

Falconer has constructed a framework of structural forces as culpable for the decline of the city, built through expert testimony and research statistics that provide evidence to the impacts of overpolicing on poor and urban neighborhoods, the mass incarceration of so many young black men, and the lack of employment and educational opportunities in the city. Falconer follows up the scene featuring Jig and Nod with another example that emphasizes the degradation of the neighborhood by individuals involved in the drug trade. Immediately following their segment is the first appearance of Queen, one of the interviewees the filmmaker spends the most time featuring, discussed in more detail later in this section. In her first appearance, she states, "You know what made me want to move? When my son, he's sixteen now, he sat on the fucking curb and said, 'I'm tired of looking at all these crack heads.'" Queen's statement paired alongside Jig and Nod's historical framing of the neighborhood as a "drug area" constructs their neighborhood not simply as blighted because of declining city services but as a hub of the drug trade, within which all three respondents discuss their participation at later points in the film. While the use here of the residents' voices could serve as another, equally expert point of the view of institutional racism, the structure of the interviews and the differences in filming and construction yield not first-person experts but in many ways serve as a way to perpetuate a transition from structural inequities to the street-level pathologies of drugs and blight as "just regular." While I do not think that this is the intent of the filmmaker, the end result provides a portrayal of the Dexter crew not as expert interviewees but as either victims of a system or poor personal choices, setting up a rationale for outside intervention.

Falconer clearly seeks to unsettle the status quo regarding how American inner cities are approached, stating in an interview that "the inner-city faces severe quality of life issues that are quite different from how most of the country lives."[16] Indeed, he and his coproducer came to the project with "an interest in social issues and quality of life problems facing urban centers."[17] The intention of the film is no less than to highlight the role of racism and government corruption in Detroit's decline, which it does. Yet in many ways Falconer's film reproduces the Detroit/metropolitan Detroit divide that underwrites the narrative of exodus discussed in chapter 1. Even as Falconer is showing *how* that divide was created through structural racism and that the divide resulted in real-life differences in access to jobs, education, and housing, he too falls victim to reconstructing the divide as simultaneously real but false. In an interview with the ActNow Foundation, Falconer reflects:

> But what also surprised me in a very positive way was how when we went into the city and talked to some residents in unsafe neighborhoods it was

> amazing to see how readily my crew, who is mostly suburban and college educated, and these guys who have lived exclusively in the drug trade and have been in and out of jail, how easily we could relate. We got along and laughed. It just became clear to me how much the divisions are kind of manufactured and maintained and don't really have anything to do with an actual difference between us in any way as people.[18]

The quote reflects the complexity of the issue. While the reflection supports the filmmaker's own recognition of his privilege, at the same time he flattens it out. With this idea that the divisions are "manufactured and maintained and don't have anything to do with an actual difference between us," he undermines the perspective of the inequities that institutional racism yields and also makes his just named privilege invisible. With a college education and a life lived not "in and out of jail" but in the "safety" of the suburbs intimated by the position of "going into the city" and its "unsafe neighborhoods," there are many divisions created by social forces. Even as Falconer is attempting here a variation of "we are all just human," the effect actually serves to undermine his own argument that structural factors inhibit the access of young people in Detroit to education and employment due to a corrupt and brutal systemic disregard. In the film's promise to show the continuing impacts of racism in the city, he falls into the trap of the neoliberal city, suggesting that in the end each individual has both the promise and potential to rise above his or her situation, creating a better Detroit through engagement and interaction.

The idea that there are no actual divisions between the presumed viewer and the Dexter crew is the emphasis that takes over the second half of the film. Falconer's argument moves into a perspective that the only solvable problem in impoverished Detroit is fixing individual lives of poverty and criminality. While this is a compassionate goal, the narrative resolution that the film presents is not a change of the structure that has created such an atmosphere but an opportunity for change that rests squarely on the shoulders of individuals through a representation of choice. This is not meant as a critique of individual agency but rather a critique that Falconer falls back into his own trap; through his directorial choices he replicates the idea of the culture of poverty: that poor people continue to be poor because of *their* poor choices, not because of systemic inequities.

The focus on the individual is most clearly emphasized by the representation of being "in the life" as a viable economic opportunity.[19] Even as the city and its neighborhood residents (in contrast to its expert residents) are depicted as extremely poor, respondents and experts talk about the informal economy of the drug trade as a way to make money and as a lucrative enterprise within the city. One of the experts who appears on screen frequently is Dr. Luke Bergmann. Bergmann, the "insider" noted by Falconer above, is a cultural anthropologist who wrote a book on Detroit's drug trade and at the time of filming was a research director at the Detroit Department of Health and Wellness Promotion.[20] In one of the clips from his interview, Bergmann recounts his experiences of what he calls the "physical deprivation and resource deprivation in which so many people in this city are living." Bergmann continues: "I mean I would go into house after house after house with the young people, with whom I might have just gone to Fairlane and dropped three hundred bucks on some shoes.[21] I'd go into their house and there'd be no furniture. You know, and I would almost say that's the norm, no furniture." The idea that there is an underground economy that can support three-hundred-dollar shoes sits alongside the idea that there are Detroiters who choose to purchase these shoes rather than furniture. This trope of personal choice within the structurally inadequate system at work serves to redeploy the narrative of unfit choices or cultural values, what David Wilson refers to as the construction of "consumptive degeneracy" of ghetto residents.[22] While most would agree that shoes are more important than furniture, especially with the vicious cold and snow of Detroit's winters, it is not the "shoes" as a functional necessity that is highlighted here but Bergmann's befuddlement about the three-hundred-dollar shoes. His emphasis is but one example of obsession over the so-called dysfunctional consumption of poor people, practiced by government legislators, social reformers, and academics alike, and their desire to police the consumption of the poor.

Amid the background framework of interlocking structures that cause systemic poverty and the violence of the city's drug trade, Queen's narrative is utilized as a direct testimony to residents' seemingly poor choices in the face of poverty. Queen is likely in her thirties and is presented as likeable, humorous, and "real," as she freely shares her experiences. She reveals to the filmmakers that she got her start in the drug trade in an unspecified role at the age of thirteen. The film doesn't expand on this but rather situates her relationship to the drug trade through her personal experience of tragedy. As Queen talks about the impact of drugs on the neighborhood a text-over appears on screen to inform viewers that "Queen has seen both of her brothers murdered in the neighborhood."[23] Although this interview is spliced with an expert's critique of overpolicing and the excessive criminalization of poor, urban youth as drug offenders, the focus on Queen's personal experience serves to shift the structural framework of racism, poverty, and criminalization to individual choices. As Queen recounts her youngest brother, she recalls, "He said, 'I'll die on Dexter,' and sure enough he died on Dexter. . . . He said no one is ever gonna run him or take him from his hood. And sure enough, my brother was dead in a car on Dexter." She makes clear that he died because of his commitment to the neighborhood, to "the life." Ultimately, she suggests that both of her brothers consciously made the personal decisions that resulted in their deaths. After talking about her brothers' murders, she reflects, "I can't say this hood is to be blamed. They chose that life, it didn't choose them. They loved it, this is what they did." Queen's deceased brothers are evoked not as a critique of the system, poverty, or racism, but to illuminate the idea that being in the life was a choice that her brothers made and loved, which ultimately from the perspective of the film feels like an uncomfortable conclusion. Perhaps the intent of the film is to show that the choice for Queen's brothers, like many of the Dexter crew, is to be in the life or not, that work is work, and Queen's brothers were able to pursue a line of work that they loved and, no matter the dangers, was fulfilling. However, this element of agency that could be read into the scene feels full of futility, supported by the expert interviews in the film that point to the bleakness of poverty and incarceration. Falconer's interview with Queen, just like Bergmann's prior comment above in regard to selective choices in how and where to spend money, serves to contradict his more important argument about the systemic reasons for endemic poverty in the city. In so doing, the violence and deprivation wrought by institutional racism is ultimately rendered as a series of individual choices.

Deforce defaults to a neoliberal narrative of choice, an assumption that the members of the Dexter crew have options and opportunities, an assumption that no matter the poverty there are always multiple paths to take. This is the rhetoric of neoliberal individualism, the idea that if you work hard enough, you will find opportunity and reward. Ultimately, *Deforce* suggests that the promise of the American Dream is delayed, but delayed due to the choices made by each of us. The film in the end embraces the neoliberal version of "magical thinking," constructing hope for the city, as an expert opines, "These people are tough around here, we'll survive." And it is true, no matter how Detroiters are described in any of the various cases in this book, they are done so with a hardscrabble undeniably American "can do" frontier spirit.

In its final turn the film relies on the Dexter crew to suggest the other paths and possibilities and take personal responsibility for choosing those paths. Eato, one of the Dexter crew who primarily serves as a backdrop during the film, has his only line of dialogue when he states, in the last few minutes of the film, "Go to school, go to college. It will pay off in the end if you just dig down deep and grind. Motherfuckers in the streets go and grind, go to school." This gives weight to the idea that street life, just like school, is hard work, but ultimately that the life of the drug trade is not the path to follow; school and education represent the bigger payoff. This is further underscored by Jig's concluding comment that, although at the time of filming he is still actively working in the drug trade, "I got jobs and school in my future; in five years I got to be in a different place, a different path."[24] He suggests that a different path is possible through school and education. This conclusion presents a narrative resolution that is only possible through literal movement from streets to school and that the responsibility to pursue this path is ultimately up to the individual to choose the path to school as opposed to the path into the drug trade. Yet what is lost in these moments is a more brutal reality: even if Jig dedicates himself to education, this choice is not likely to lead him out of the impoverished urban core. In the context of Detroit's failing public schools, lamentable public transportation, and deplorable city services, which the film just spent seventy minutes highlighting, the promise of education as a path to mobility rings empty.

While *Deforce* refuses the narrative of the nostalgic past as a time of uniform opportunity, it presents a resolution of the future through a narrative of neoliberal possibility. The resulting impression is that the "Detroit residents" who are interviewed are seen as personally and individually responsible for their choices. This is in stark contrast to the argument developed in the first half of the film. Ultimately, these first-person interviews operate to suggest that the "culture of poverty" reigns large in Detroit and that a better Detroit will only be possible when neighborhood residents, helped in part by community organizations, make better choices. Even though the film makes a pointed critique of the work of institutional racism, it simultaneously redeploys a culture of poverty problem, ultimately identifying that these members of the Dexter crew will only shift their lives from one of crime, poverty, and drugs to fully contributing members of society through individually making better choices. Indeed, the film's final suggestion is that because racism and corruption have yielded such miserable prospects for young black people in particular, only they can make a change, since the structure itself is so broken.

American Dreaming in the Nostalgic Motor City

The documentary film *Detropia,* directed by Heidi Ewing and Rachel Grady, was filmed in 2010 and 2011 and released at the Sundance Film Festival in January 2012.[25] *Detropia* is centered on loose day-to-day portrayals of its three main subjects: George McGregor, president of UAW Local 22; Tommy Stephens, a retired schoolteacher and owner of the Raven Lounge; and Crystal Starr, a Detroit video blogger. *Detropia* situates Detroit's crisis as an assault on the American Dream wrought by globalization. The filmmakers focus on contemporary corporate malevolence, in juxtaposition to what they suggest as historical corporate benevolence, an overworked emphasis that obscures other factors at play in the economic decline of the city. Rather than a benevolent system that facilitated mobility and access to the American Dream, the much-vaunted rise of corporate capitalism contributed to and was enacted through systems of racism, nativism, classism, and sexism. This can be seen in examples during the boom days of the automotive industry in the early and mid-twentieth century such as Ford Motor Company's sociology department, which operated from 1914 to 1920 to ensure that each worker's personal life met particular standards around comportment, class, behavior, morality, and aspirational citizenship. Only then was the worker eligible for the much-celebrated five-dollar-a-day wage.[26] Even as Ford eventually grew to be "the largest single employer of blacks in the auto industry,"[27] one must also examine Ford's decision in the 1920s to move its assembly from Highland Park to the River Rouge complex in Dearborn. While the intent of movement to the larger area in Dearborn was to develop a manufacturing complex where the complete process from raw material to finished good could be completed, it should also be noted that Dearborn was a notorious "sundown town."[28] Dearborn is known for the unapologetically segregationist stance of its longtime mayor, Orville Hubbard, infamous for his efforts to keep Dearborn white during his tenure from 1942 to 1978.[29] Therefore, even as Ford hired black workers at River Rouge, a main location for employment, Dearborn had a clearly articulated practice of residential exclusion of African Americans. These are but two of many reminders that past corporate benevolence was far from certain for many and was hardly a reliable means to the American Dream. The nostalgic retelling of the past overlooks the institutional racism that undergirds much of Detroit's historical development. But, to be fair, this narrative omission is not unique to Ewing and Grady's film. The danger, however, in glossing over the past is that it erases the inequities embedded in the narrative of "possibility" and romanticizes a long-gone benevolent capitalist system and demonizes the current one, thus refusing to recognize that past and present are not all that separate.

Although Ewing and Grady make a compelling argument about how globalization has wreaked havoc and continues to impact Detroiters' everyday lives, their lack of attention to institutional racism is striking. In the same ways that the City-Data posters (see chapter 1) discuss the rise of Detroit as "not about race," Ewing and Grady similarly never situate the relationship between racial access to suburbs and the decentralization of Detroit-based jobs to the metropolitan Detroit periphery. While, on the one hand, they point to the structural forces that move jobs abroad and increase unemployment in the United States, on the other hand, their emphasis on both a middle-class "ideal" and on individual stories of survival—in spite of the assaults of unemployment and shrinking city services—retrenches a narrative of the neoliberal individual. The film lionizes this ideal of one who achieves success through self-reliance and dogged determination in the characterization of the individual Detroiters it features. In particular, *Detropia* underscores Jodi Melamed's notion of neoliberal multiculturalism, wherein the widely proffered cultural philosophies of the United States celebrate multicultural access to success as a legitimization of neoliberalism, arguing that contemporary capitalism is explicitly not racist.[30] Ewing and Grady's choice to feature two older middle-class African American men and a younger African American woman as archetypal representatives of Detroit enables them to create a narrative that is color-blind; a vision of Detroit in which there is equal access to jobs, education, and housing; and ultimately a nostalgic embrace of the American Dream. The film suggests that access to the dream was obtainable in the past but is not obtainable today for the working class because of corporate greed and government ignorance. It is this fissure between past and present on which the film spends most of its time, highlighting the starkness of the present against the longing for the nostalgic possibilities of the past.

This nonresolved past is best seen in Crystal Starr's opening scene, which simultaneously operates as an embrace of the American Dream and serves as a way to trouble the idea of the past as a uniformly "better time." Crystal Starr, identified by the filmmakers in text-over narration as "a Detroit video blogger," is the first main character introduced, although her narrative is developed the least amount over the course of the film. Instead, she is utilized in the film as the vehicle through which the multiple narratives of the film connect, serving as the street-level eyes and ears of the city.[31] While McGregor and Stephens are the storytellers of the past, it is Starr who serves as a guide to the contemporary city. In fact, it is Starr's silhouette, a fade-in from a larger shot of her against the Detroit skyline, upon which the film's title is imposed in the opening montage.

As much as the filmmakers later link McGregor and Stephens to Detroit by work, Starr's role is not to guide us through her personal path to the American Dream but to conjure Detroit's history from its otherworldly ruins. Just as Stephens and McGregor construct for the viewer a narrative of historic Detroit as a proxy for mobility, Starr's role suggests the reverberations of Detroit's past. From the title screen, Starr is the silhouette, the ghostly figure whose very presence can only be seen in juxtaposition to the illumination of the skyline. Starr's narrative begins as she leads the viewer through an abandoned apartment building in ruin. This scene begins in a harshly lit foyer, where she directly addresses what appears to be a first-generation camera phone: "July 4, 2010, Independence Day, we're going real revolutionary." Already in this setup, her story can be read in opposition to our typical celebrations of "independence"; rather than Fourth of July fireworks or a barbeque, she sets off to explore decaying buildings. The grainy footage from Starr's camera phone records her in the room, as she explains that "we're in a beautiful building."

As she begins to move, the film quality, camerawork, and perspective shifts from Starr as auteur to the filmmakers' shot of her silhouette leading viewers down a hallway, as a carefully framed subject. As she guides us through the building's darkness, she is a shadowy figure, illuminated only by her flashlight and the faint natural light that spills into rooms—presumably from exterior windows—adjacent to the hall she is walking through. As the audience watches her exploring this space, she says, "History is just one of my things, even since grade school. That's a passion. What was there? Who was there?" The dialogue is delivered slowly, matching her pace as she slowly shines her light around, deciding what to pursue or take in next. As she looks at both objects and architecture, she reflects, "These hallways though, I'm trying, I mean I'm picturing this place clean. People walking around and shit happening." The focus in this section is not the actual spaces that Starr is looking at, as the viewers never see the exact beauty or hallways that she is seeing. Unlike other moments of the film that indulge in a view of Detroit as "ruin porn," the camera's focus, trained on her shadowy silhouette, allows us to only see her, not what she sees. We see Starr moving through the ill-lit hallway, a shadowy figure who underscores these passageways as a ghostly space. Near a doorway Starr pauses to play with an intercom system, playfully speaking into it, "Bring that shit on up here girl," and laughing. In this moment the camera frames her upper half with her back to the camera on the left of the screen, the intercom in the center, and to the right is a dirty mirror, in which the camera captures Starr's reflection before she turns to look at her image directly. Although Starr is facing the mirror, her features are still obscured by the dim lighting and layer of dirt on the mirror. In this way, rather than an actual, clearly depicted individual, she is a stand-in, a reflection of all those who were there before. This scene is saturated with creams, browns, and blacks, a sepia-tinted color palette that underscores the historical quality of the image making and frames Crystal Starr as a ghostly guide to the past.

As Starr moves from the interior space of the hallways into an apartment, she transitions from a shadow to a fully legible person, bathed in muted sunlight. The camera captures the view through a large picture window—the glass long gone—which serves to frame a vivid, colorful view of the city, the lush greens of trees and grass, the rich reds of two-story brick structures, and the white low clouds in the distance in stark contrast to the interior, with its muted colors of faded paint and weathered walls. As she moves about the apartment, taking in the beautiful panorama, she looks to the camera and asks, "Can you imagine having breakfast right here? You know what I mean? I mean look at your view, look at your view in the morning. Yeah, I'm gonna go out and conquer the world cause I can damn near see it from right here." Here, Starr's own love for the city and determination in the face of failing public schools and city government that she addresses later in the film strikes us as all the more heartfelt in this moment. Indeed, it is the resoluteness represented here as Starr, even in her full awareness of the city's problems, offers the idea that if one can see it, one can dream it.

The camera takes in a long shot of the vista through the window frame and slowly pans into downtown in the distance, out again, and down to the two-story houses in the neighborhood adjacent to and below the vantage point of the apartment she is in. This is all taken as one uncut shot, visually tying together the downtown center of power and the neighborhood. In this visual representation—although Starr gives voice that the world is outside, just beyond—the visual panning into downtown in the distance serves to situate the center of Detroit's power as so close, yet out of reach. As the camera takes in the beauty and grandeur through the window, Starr says, almost inaudibly, under her breath, what sounds like: "Can't leave, man, I can't fucking leave." What this statement means is unclear; for the duration of the film the prospect of departure is not raised again, nor is it even considered that Starr (or any of the other people in the film) would leave. However, the ambiguity of her statement is revealing. Rather than emphasizing mobility, it is also possible that the visual composition of the shot, and Starr's barely audible utterance, serve as a counterpoint to that narrative of mobility. Although Starr's discussion alludes to going out and conquering this world, she is filmed inside this crumbling room, sitting next to and looking out upon the view, as if ensconced in a lookout tower, high above and removed from the city below. She literally is pictured as removed from the city—both in the contemporary present as well as in her embodiment of the past. This scene, rather than supporting an idea that a conquerable world is right out there, shows instead the literal distance between this place and the downtown center of power. This hint, then—that she cannot leave—is an important subversion to the notion of mobility, to the suggestion that everyone had or has access to this American Dream. That dream is contradicted by her quiet, almost resigned statement: she can't leave. As she sits, gazing out upon the city and smoking, she embraces the ghosts of the past and situates them in the present: "I feel like I was maybe here a little while back. Or I'm older than I really am but I just have this young, this young body and spirit and mind, but I have the memory of this place when it was banging. That's how I feel."[32] Starr's relative youth and position within the film narrative enables her to figure as simultaneously part of the contemporary moment, the ghostly past, and the still-to-be-determined future. The people in the film, even as they cling to hope, do so with the resigned knowledge of the complexity of Detroit's problems.

The past is obliquely framed through a specter of "better times," as much of the main characters' specific biographies are missing. In fact, we only know that Tommy Stephens was a schoolteacher because of a text-over narration when he is first introduced. And for Starr we have no hint of her past from the on-screen depiction. Only George McGregor tells his story, and in many ways his specific biographical example—growing up poor and rising to the middle class via access to a "good job"—serves as proof of the reality of multiracial access to the American Dream, echoing the sentiment expressed in the "Born of Fire" commercial discussed in chapter 3. Well into his sixties, McGregor, a UAW local president, has worked in the auto industry for over forty years.

George McGregor initially appears in the first ten minutes of the film as it transitions from the past that Starr's opening sequence describes into the contemporary city. The scene moves from historic footage of a vintage car commercial to a contemporary moment in an establishing sequence that positions the camera as a proxy for the viewers, who sit alongside McGregor in the front seat of a car looking through the windshield. Before he is introduced, the camera rapidly cuts from the street in front to a close shot of McGregor's head and chest before focusing on a close-up of his forearm and hand casually holding the steering wheel—the Cadillac symbol prominently displayed in the center of the wheel. The camera settles back to the man behind the wheel as he explains, "I'm gonna take you out to where I got hired at in 1968. The Cadillac assembly plant." The quick cuts between McGregor's profile and the interior of the car and the scene out the window tie together the car as a commodity and the man as an extension of the car as both autoworker and consumer. In 1968 McGregor got his first job in Detroit, assembling Cadillacs; now he drives a Cadillac. It is from his luxury vehicle that he takes viewers on a tour of his laboring past, literally moving around the city, showing the now-defunct places from which he made his living. McGregor points out what used to be the reach of the plant. From within the moving car the plant itself is not visible; the visual absence suggests that it is no longer present, even as a ruin. Gesturing toward a lot that now serves as storage space for dumpsters, he states, "This plant was huge, all of this was the plant." As he points this out, he remarks somewhat forlornly, "It was the first job I ever had, you know. It was the first job I ever had." It is not until this statement that text-over on-screen narration tells the viewers that their guide is George McGregor, president of Local 22, UAW. Heavy with symbolism, the text appears as McGregor is driving down a freeway. Filmed from a passenger's seat point of view, the shot captures McGregor from the chest up in the foreground with oncoming traffic zooming in the opposite direction in the background. He is literally moving in the wrong direction, against the flow of traffic that is rapidly passing him, a visual hint that ultimately this way of life is outmoded and moving in the wrong direction.

As McGregor continues his tour, he reminisces about his first paycheck from the Cadillac assembly plant; even though it only covered his first three days of work, it "made my old paycheck in Tennessee look like I don't know what." Detroit's past, it is clear, was bountiful, and hard work could bring abundant economic achievement. McGregor's tour also shows the prior fullness of the neighborhoods that ringed the factory. In addition to showing the places where he used to work, his tour reveals the close proximity of the factory to neighborhoods, showing homes and businesses that abut the entrances and lots of factory complexes. As he drives the city streets, he points out places of leisure as well as places of work. Gesturing toward a two-story brick building, he recalls, "This is one of the hotels we used to hang out in at night." Clearly finding joy in these memories of the past, he chuckles and says gleefully, "It was fun. Big fun, yeah!" The message is subtle, but clear—the work in Detroit that offered paychecks that made Southern pay "look like I don't even know what" enabled a life to support not only the basics but also leisure. McGregor's story mirrors that common Detroit narrative, which has been heard throughout the book: the city was a location of economic opportunity, open and available to anyone who could put in a hard day's work. McGregor's version is especially resonant as it dovetails with the popular narrative of the Great Migration.[33]

While McGregor's fond retelling of a nostalgic past is upheld throughout the film, the larger context into which he migrated is conspicuously absent. McGregor tells viewers that he moved to Detroit in 1968, a time period that historians mark as the tail end of the Second Great Migration and that at least older viewers may remember as the height of a decade of urban unrest, marked by rebellions and rioting in cities around the country.[34] McGregor migrated to Detroit the year after the 1967 rebellion, the same year in which the Kerner Commission issued its report stating that one of the primary causes of rebellions in Detroit and other urban centers around the country was white racism in housing, education, jobs, and government, and declared its infamous pronouncement, "Our nation is moving toward two societies, one black, one white—separate and unequal." Ewing and Grady omit here the sociohistoric context of McGregor's movement to the city, not addressing the riot until nearly sixty minutes later. Notably, the later mention consists only of archival news footage, complete with their original sound bites to offer context. None of the film's subjects mentions this event at all, and the sixty-second montage of footage seems almost obligatory rather than narratively important. Instead, the filmmakers focus on the time of McGregor's move to Detroit in the late 1960s as one of high mobility—both economically as well as physically for McGregor, and presumably others like him, as he attained economic security as well as pleasure through work in the factories of Detroit.

In McGregor's tour, the past is represented as wholly positive rather than burdened by the city's overcrowded and dilapidated housing; racist restrictions to newer suburban housing, jobs, and education; and a manufacturing industry already well on its path of decentralizing production to surrounding metropolitan Detroit.

Therefore, George McGregor's story functions as a parable for the death of the American Dream. The use of personal narratives of Detroit's heyday and the idealized past is an important undercurrent in this and nearly every Detroit-centered documentary. Historical Detroit is depicted as a space of mobility and contemporary Detroit as one of immobility—linked to the rise and fall of the automobile industry. Yet the cracks in this dichotomy are visible in McGregor's own narrative. At the same time the filmmakers construct McGregor's way of life as disappearing, his role as a mobile subject driving the landscape in a new Cadillac suggests a rupture in an overly simplistic idea of the demise of the industry. It is these fissures in the narrative that haunt Detroit's past and present alike. As the camera pans empty lots and still, silent factories outside the passenger window of the car, McGregor states, "Shit, after the plant left, the neighborhood left." The car drives past what seems like an endless expanse of empty lots of industrial parks in the foreground—two-story houses in various states of occupancy and a spattering of parked cars are in the background, literally next to the grounds of the industrial lot, supporting the sense that the neighborhoods sprung up to meet the needs of the plants and workers, and that much of the vibrancy and population has departed as well. McGregor points out the American Axle plant: "See how large it is, just to build axles. All of this is empty. Yeah, they build a new plant in Mexico and took all the work to Mexico. Yeah, that's where it's at." McGregor's story operates to not only show the heights of the physical city but also suggest the richness of life facilitated by work—bustling neighborhoods, clubs, and leisure spaces.

McGregor's tour of his (and Detroit's) history drives viewers through the nostalgic past into a parking lot of the present. The car comes to a stop and the camera pans across an awning that reads: "A Stronger America" and then "We Built This City: UAW Local 22." The camera moves inside, in high contrast to the outdoor landscapes and streets whizzing by through the passenger window, to a UAW meeting, where a group of about twenty-five middle-aged men and a couple of women are seated around tables in a gymnasium listening as McGregor gives his report to the assembled union members. The membership listens in total silence as McGregor presents the proposed new contract from the American Axle management. The information is depressing and the members stonily sit, hands in front of their mouths, shaking their heads in disbelief as McGregor, who prefaced his comments with "This is the most difficult management I've ever worked with. . . . You're gonna get mad, I can tell you that," begins to tell his members that the company proposed wage cuts anywhere from $0.50 to $3.35 per hour for existing workers and a regression to a starting wage of $10.00 for new workers. He recounts how he protested the proposed wage cuts during negotiations, and how management responded, "I don't care about your guys having a livable wage." One of the members asks aloud, "How do you think we're going to feel everyday going into work?" He pauses as others nod their heads in agreement and then answers his own question by stating, "They don't care. That's the biggest problem." This scene, on the heels of McGregor's reminiscing about the past, seems to suggest that the past was not only a time of economic prosperity but also a time when corporations cared about workers. This scene is one of the saddest in the film; we see the members visibly upset by the situation, not full of rage or exploding in anger but expressing a quiet condemnation, backed into a corner, stunned into a near silence. Ultimately, the membership votes to not take a vote on American Axle's proposal, taking a unanimous stand against the proposal as "humiliating." The text-over narration next reveals that the plant was eventually closed, implying that everyone just seen is now out of a job.[35] The meeting also underscores the idea that this way of life is indeed dying out. While most of the membership represented was not as old as McGregor, they are as a whole well into middle age.

The film portrays McGregor and Tommy Stephens (whose bar seems a haven for aging and retired autoworkers) as midlevel leaders of industries whose futures are precarious because of the disappearance of auto industry jobs under the specter of globalization. The filmmakers seem to ascribe everything to do with Detroit's economic decline to globalization and the myopic vision of the American auto industry. In a particularly pointed scene where Tommy Stephens goes to the North America International

Auto Show, held every January in Detroit, the twin threats of globalization and myopia are on full display. Stephens attends the show, like many Detroiters, interested in seeing the new automobile models on display. He is particularly excited to see the electric-powered Chevrolet Volt, given the proximity of his blues club to the General Motors Detroit Hamtramack Assembly Plant where it is built. Stephens asks questions to the representative on hand about battery and charging life and also about the possibility for new technology. Afterward he visits a booth for the solar-powered BYD car. After visiting the booth and learning from BYD's representative that the car is manufactured in China, and soon concluding that it is a direct competitor to the Chevrolet Volt, he is floored by the starting price. The BYD has a $28,000 starting price in comparison to the Volt's $41,000 entry point. Stephens then goes back to the Volt display and asks the Chevrolet representative: "What are we going to do about that BYD over there, that Chinese electric car? Have you seen it? The Chinese electric car, it runs more than this and it costs twenty grand!" The representative and the other onlookers are defensive of the Volt, stating that it is a "nicer car," that Stephens is comparing "apples to oranges." Stephens rebuts with "Can I take you back to the sixties and talk about Honda for a moment? Don't you remember when nobody would buy Honda?" The representative and the other onlookers continue to defend the Volt, and Stephens mutters to his wife as they walk away from the Volt display that "we got our heads in the sand again." He is clearly frustrated, and his wife tells him to "leave it alone." But the points that he raises, about the myopia of Detroit automakers in not seeing the bigger picture, writing off its competition without regard to the actual market, are made. As much as Stephens is rooting for the industry to come back so that his club will come back, he is visibly frustrated with the shortsightedness of the decision makers.

The easy binary that the film sets up through Stephens between Detroit and China as global other is complicated later in the film when a scene shows Stephens watching a news report that announces General Motors is moving the research and development platform for its electric vehicles to Shanghai. This is but a small hint of the interconnection between the regional, state, national, and global system of automobile manufacturing. This singular narrative of globalization, while likely prudent for a ninety-minute film, fails to analyze where else in the region and nation as well as the world these jobs have shifted and why. This, however, is rather pro forma for the Detroit documentary genre as a whole—which typically situates Detroit's early twentieth-century rise alongside immigration and migration into the city to work in a thriving auto industry and its decline as synonymous with a mass evacuation of the city due to global automotive competition, as discussed in chapter 3. As described previously, this overemphasis on the movement of individuals and of their jobs envisions Detroit as a disconnected island. That view fails to situate the growth not only of the global industry but of metropolitan Detroit as a whole (and the institutional racism and government financing that contributed to it). Instead, a wider view of global capitalism would situate Detroit as but one location of a network of communities, from southeast Michigan to Mexico, from Kentucky to Southeast Asia, from China to Canada, where highly mobile corporations rely on government incentives and a surplus of continually devalued labor ever ready to accommodate their relocation.

The pivot on which this film is premised—that Detroit embodies the beginning, the end, and a new possibility of the American Dream—is nowhere more clearly expressed than toward the end of the film. *Detropia* turns to the "creative class" as a continuation of a cycle introduced by McGregor—of people moving to Detroit for opportunity. In the last twenty minutes of the film, viewers are introduced to Steve and Dorota Coy, a young, white, wife and husband performance and visual arts team, the Hygienic Dress League, whose work satirizes global corporations.[36] The camera records the Coys performing an art piece at the side of a freeway and then as the couple sets up and photographs their own performance piece in the middle of a snow-covered vacant lot. After this visual introduction to their work, Steve Coy tells their migration story to the camera: he and Dorota chose to move here because "we knew that Detroit had an abundance of space and old warehouses." As he unpacks groceries and cleaning supplies in his kitchen, he shares that they recently bought their "amazing loft" and are still able to also keep their art studio. He explains, "Detroit is constantly amazing me. I feel like it's reevaluating what the value of things are." He comments on what he sees as the city's affordability and notes that elsewhere, "I would never be able to own a home as an artist." The interview with Coy ends with his statement, "We can experiment here. Because if we fail, we haven't really fallen anywhere," suggesting that at the same time Detroit is amazing, it is simultaneously a nowhere, a place to experiment. This speculative statement underscores the evocation of Detroit as a frontier—if you fail, your failure doesn't matter much because it isn't anywhere significant, but at the same time the potential and possibility for success are what motivate the movement. For these residents, today's Detroit *is* a location of possibility (as seen in the film and discussed further in the next chapter), a playground wherein the neoliberal rhetoric of hard work and attainment of success is fueled by a creative hunger. Heidi Ewing speaks to the complexity of the new population in an interview:

> We could have built our whole film out of, like, those four blocks of downtown, and we definitely decided not to. . . . As for the all-hailed artists, I'm glad they're coming and all, but you know what? They're opening expensive restaurants and coffee shops, and they all frequent each other's businesses. Most Detroiters are being left out of that economy. . . . There's got to be some kind of communication between these groups. A lot of these people arriving are like, "This is Dodge City, man! I can do whatever the hell I want! It's a blank slate!" Well, Detroit is not a blank slate. That colonizer's attitude? You guys should tone that down, because there are people who've lived there a long time.[37]

In the film Ewing and Grady subtly draw out these complexities, that for longtime residents—working class, primarily black—the American Dream is no longer sustainable, that the reliance on the auto industry to "provide jobs" makes Detroit workers obsolete. In so doing, the film provides a critiquc of the new arrivals in the face of Detroit's ongoing difficulties.

However, the narrative framework of the film situates the Coys and other new arrivals as bookends for the prior stories. It is an image of the Coys—in their performance costume of a suit for Steve, a fur coat for Dorota, and gold-painted gas masks and eye goggles for both—that adorns the movie poster and DVD cover for the film. The film's narrative resolution then is not the story told by Crystal Starr, George McGregor, or Tommy Stephens, but of these new arrivals. Even as the Coys' move to

Detroit in some ways echoes George McGregor's story—the idea that the young can come to Detroit and forge a path; that hard work will be enough, financial reward can be had, and the American Dream of home ownership and upward mobility is achievable—the choice to symbolize the future of Detroit through the "all-hailed artists" is significant. The other stories that form the background of the film—the town hall meeting featuring testimonies of what cuts to city bus service would mean; the ill-formed, government-led proposal to "right-size the city"; the group of young "scrappers" who literally make ends meet by disassembling old homes, factories, and businesses to sell the steel and copper that they scavenge—make it clear that Detroit as mobility, that Detroit as a frontier of opportunity, is a fallacy for most Detroiters. This side of Detroit—where everyday people are working hard but barely getting by—haunts the narrative of mobility that the film's main characters represent. The film's name, *Detropia,* is described as a portmanteau of *Detroit* and *utopia* inspired by a sign on an abandoned auto parts building. The irony intended by the tagger who created the "utopia" sign is not lost on the filmmakers or viewers, and some suggest the title more accurately represents a portmanteau of *Detroit* and *dystopia.* Yet the hints of the unresolved dichotomy of utopia/dystopia permeate the film through its representation of its old and new residents.

Detroit as a Frontier of Possibility

It seems, from these films, that Detroit's future is possible, but for a select few and only through a narrative of hard work and reinvestment. In this chapter and as detailed throughout the book, the narrative of success through individualism, hard work, and determination seeks to undermine the structural forces, both those of the past and of today, at work in the city. In so doing the notion of Detroit as a place of open access and potential for middle-class achievement, as evidenced by the historical narrative of Detroit as a city of working-class mobility, is redeployed and continually produced. Ultimately, each of the films suggests that Detroit's future is at a precipice—where change at the city or governmental level is impossible—and that the hard work and determination of Detroiters themselves are the only solution to turning the city around. Yet for many longtime Detroiters, represented by the Dexter crew in *Deforce* and most of the everyday people featured in *Detropia,* the possibility of the future seems an empty promise. For Detroit's poor, working-class, and black residents, the future seems bleak.

In many ways, then, the films of Falconer and Ewing and Grady each set up Detroit as simultaneously empty *and* ready for intervention by outsiders, constructing it as a manifestation of the neoliberal city, ready for investment after decades of decline and disinvestment. The productions here ironically suggest that Detroit—precisely because of its failure of the American Dream—is an ideal site for the twenty-first-century version of that dream to take place. The fact that this can happen, that the past can be extolled as a time of possibility, even as that possibility crashed and burned, is one of the most fascinating continuing myths of Detroit, which will be explored more fully in the next and final chapter. Yet this construction is essential in the representation of Detroit as a frontier, de-occupied of productive systems and ready for development.

CHAPTER 5

Feeding Detroit's Rise

Provisions for Urban Pioneers

> Detroit may be bankrupt, but at least it has a Whole Foods.
>
> —Annie Gasparro, *Wall Street Journal*

> I love Detroit. . . . I think it's one of the most beautiful cities in America—still. The same incompetence and neglect that led to its current state of affairs has, at least, left us with a cityscape that even now, taunts us with the memories of our once-outsized dreams.
>
> I love Detroiters. You've got to have a sense of humor to live in a city so relentlessly fucked. You've got to be tough—and occasionally even devious. And Detroiters are funny, tough—and supreme improvisers.
>
> —Anthony Bourdain

On November 10, 2013, CNN aired the finale of the second season of Anthony Bourdain's television show *Parts Unknown.* As a gregarious and adventurous celebrity chef, Bourdain has become known in recent years for his culinary tourism shows, *No Reservations* and *Parts Unknown.* In these shows he features unusual and exotic foods in untraveled places, or finds similarly unusual foods or dining experiences even in places his audience knows well, bringing into our living rooms a sense of adventure. For the season 2 finale, he chose Detroit. The first ten minutes of the Detroit episode show not a scrap of food or even talk of food. Instead, the episode takes what we can now recognize as a standard narrative approach to the city. The camera opens on Bourdain and his local guide, the Detroit-based journalist and memoirist Charlie LeDuff, standing in a field of tall summer grasses. It is July. We see Bourdain and LeDuff in a prairie-type landscape, yet the frames are just wide enough to catch the spires of downtown buildings in the distance, the lights of Comerica Park and the roof of Ford Field in the foreground. In a 180-degree pan of the location, the camera lingers on a clearly blighted Brush Park mansion, echoing Vergara's images from fifteen years earlier of this neighborhood's magnificent decline. Of interest here is the fact that the camera does not pan north. If it did, it would have captured the rash of building and development in Midtown Detroit, including the brand new Whole Foods Market that opened the month prior to Bourdain's visit, less than half a mile from the location where Bourdain and LeDuff stand.

These first ten minutes of the episode, unbroken by commercials, start with historic B-roll footage of Detroit in its 1950s heyday, busy downtown city streets and cars zooming down newly built expressways, workers on the line in a factory—the types of images that are featured in the Detroit documentaries discussed in chapter 4, the types that situate Detroit's past as the highly productive "Motor City." After these sequences, accompanied by a voice-over from Bourdain that paints the all-too-familiar picture of Detroit as ruined, the camera turns to blight. As Bourdain is guided through the enormous ruins of the Packard Automotive Plant, he draws the contrast from its 1903 origins as "the most advanced facility of its kind, anywhere in the world" to its utter destruction and ruin. At times he borders on Vergara's proposal of saving ruins for ruins' sake. His stories, which by 2013 sound almost overdone in their familiarity, are made more interesting by the fact that he is so self-aware that he is indulging in what is now a trite representation of the city. In a Tumblr post, a part of the prerelease marketing of the episode, Bourdain acknowledges his intentional manufacturing of a particular image of the city, stating: "I, too, I'm afraid, am guilty of wallowing in ruin porn, of making sure we pointed our cameras, lingered even, in the waist high grass, overgrown gardens, abandoned mansions, crumbling towers, denuded neighborhoods of what was once an all powerful metropolis, the engine of capitalism."[1] For Bourdain, like many others, the reason Detroit is beautiful is because it has defied the expectation that old buildings get razed and redeveloped. Rather, Detroit crumbles, and thus looks like nowhere else in the United States. These images of Detroit set up the narrative of the city, similar to Vergara's vision of Detroit as abandoned and blighted yet *fertile* ground for both prairie grasses and diehard Detroiters, and take up the entire first quarter of the show.[2] Bourdain doesn't start eating or even talking about food until eleven minutes into the episode. The food that Bourdain eats and businesses that he patronizes are framed through the B-roll tale of the introduction, which is also emphasized through his Tumblr post: Detroit is like nowhere else. Both the landscape and the people are lovable and authentic in their beauty, humor, and toughness. Bourdain presents the city and its denizens as unequivocally unique and authentically Detroit.[3]

Although Bourdain doesn't mention neoliberal urban growth specifically, these tensions underlie the stories of the episode. Bourdain's take on the city, like so many of the stories seen in this book, encapsulates the tension of neoliberal urban growth—wherein the public sector is increasingly run like the private marketplace, where private capital large and small sets the pace, and where formerly public services like schools and infrastructure are increasingly privatized, as discussed in his conversation over burgers and drinks with the longtime political strategist Adolpho Mongo. By scripting the new development of Detroit against the backdrop of bankruptcy and large-scale public failure, investment is uniformly seen as the savior, the missing ingredient that will facilitate a renaissance of both culture and population. Bourdain plays heavily on the "Detroitness" of the people and businesses, celebrating Detroiters' hardiness and entrepreneurial spirit. He visits two establishments run out of private homes, the first Greedy Greg's and the second a *pupusería* with no sign or advertising that relies on customers by word of mouth. When he visits the *pupusería* he asks his guides where the lines of foodies are, and wonders in both locations how the modest restaurants can further monetize their brand and grow into lines-out-the-door establishments. Midway through the episode his somewhat sardonic tone addresses viewers in a voice-over: "At this point, you may be asking, what about all the cool stuff I hear about Detroit? The vibrant, new, do-it-yourself culture of urban renaissance, young entrepreneurs, artists, transforming the city one block at a time. Where's that?" And the next scene cuts to Bourdain having dinner at a pop-up fine-dining restaurant run by a New York–trained chef who wants to bring Michelin-level dining to Detroit. Here again the tensions between the hip "new Detroit" and the storied authentic "old Detroit" emerge. Even as Bourdain is ambivalent at best in the episode about the "new Detroit," the reality is that his show is featuring the city in this narrative light of hopeful resilience because it sells. His action-packed narrative is, at first glance, a new look at Detroit, verifiably "parts unknown." Yet even as Bourdain's tour offers "unknown" locations, moving beyond the typical Detroit itinerary, the narrative he situates these locations into relies on the same old narrative about Detroit that undergirds nearly every contemporary feature on the city: industrial rise, location of immigration and great migration, corruption, abandonment, ruin, and hope. Because of the city's precipitous decline and disinvestment during the late twentieth century, development of all kind is almost unilaterally considered "good."

This chapter's intent is to look closely at narratives of Detroit's rise in order to understand how each of the themes explored thus far in each chapter of the book—exodus, ruin, rebirth, and possibility—work together to undergird a narrative of rise. The first two chapters of the book showed how the narrative of decline emerged, and chapters 3 and 4 explored the persistence of the narrative of Detroit's possibility and determination in the face of that decline. This chapter brings these threads together, to reveal today's manifestation of Detroit as a frontier of economic possibility. I argue here that the narrative of a Detroit ripe for rise relies on a shifting vision of the city as a valuable location of development. The notion of development, at the heart of this tale, is a deceptively complex concept. At the center of the concept is the idea of growth and change as inherently good; when applied to Detroit, the urge "to develop" a city that by all accounts has reached rock bottom is frequently seen as an act of charity. Or maybe not, as the billionaire investor Warren Buffett said in an interview in advance of his keynote address at the invitation-only September 2014 "Detroit Homecoming" conference: "We're ready to buy a business here tomorrow. Every city has issues . . . that's the time to buy."[4] Indeed, Buffett elaborated on this, comparing Detroit to New York, referencing New York's 1970s financial crisis and stating, "Investment was paralyzed. Look at it today. Great cities will remain great as long as they tackle problems." Tellingly, if we look to Miriam Greenberg's study of how New York City was branded in the 1970s "to sell the city's post-industrial and neoliberal program of economic development,"[5] the parallels are potentially all the more startling. Greenberg's study reveals the effectiveness of New York's multipronged branding campaigns in bringing both private investment and tourism dollars to a city in crisis, yet also highlights the "highly unequal socio-economic reality" that the branding concealed and whose effectiveness on increasing investment further heightened.

Development in Detroit, like development in cities across the world, brings all sorts of benefits and drawbacks. However, the mainstream narrative of development in Detroit is primarily told as a story of celebration and progress. Like Greenberg's study of New York where "the bulk of the 'rebound' was driven and enjoyed by local elites, out-of-towners, and recent transplants" mobilizing a "new economy" that has numerous benefits and success stories for these investors, it has a deleterious impact for those who are outside of these beneficiaries.[6] I am most interested in how Detroit's rise is scripted as a celebration of development by those marshaling this "new economy," using as its backdrop the poverty and disinvestment of the "old economy." And, importantly for this book, I look at the ways in which race operates as a signifier of both an authentic past and a promising future in these iterations. Racial coding is central to these narratives, and the rise again of Detroit simultaneously builds upon and distances itself from the city's blackness. I suggest here that even as local elites, recent transplants, and new investors celebrate Detroit's twenty-first-century rise as "not about race," the narratives of development highlight Detroit's history through a clearly racialized lens. Indeed, the representational blackness of the city is often used to signify Detroit's "authenticity" at the same time that the increasing pockets of whites in residential neighborhoods is used to signify Detroit's growth.

In constructing the city as a postindustrial frontier, one that is ripe for investment, it is necessary to construct the deficiency of the city as changeable. Its problems are thus essential for this narrative, as long as they can be framed as fixable. It is the idea of Detroit as a problem to be solved, in other words, that facilitates the opportunity—and the motivation—for development. The story of development is most often conceptualized as "making change" and "doing good" for the community rather than simply financial gain. This presumption relies on both the idea of the empty and underperforming city as well as the idea that old Detroit is being replaced by a new and improved Detroit. While Detroit of the 1990s was, as Vergara pronounced, "a skyscraper graveyard," those very same buildings of Detroit's downtown are the building blocks of the city's growth just two decades later. Detroit has in the last few years emerged as a "new Brooklyn," a hip place to live, work, and invest. The tortured saga of the city's bankruptcy, alongside persistent stories about ruined neighborhoods, spreading blight, and a wide-scale water shutoff, now sit side by side with a very different narrative: Detroit as destination. One of the ways Detroit has emerged as an economic frontier, a place of rise, is through its authentic appeal. The draw for many newcomers is the idea that, as Bourdain states: "Detroit didn't (or couldn't) go on the usual idiot building spree, tearing down old buildings and paving over city center as 'pedestrian malls,' ruining the city's character. . . . Detroit looks like nowhere else. Detroit looks like motherfuckin' Detroit. As it should."[7] Indeed, much of the fascination with Detroit as a valuable twenty-first-century location is in the reclamation and repurposing of its twentieth-century cultural history evident in its built environment and population growth. This chapter analyzes the stories of rise against the backdrop of exodus, ruin, rebirth, and possibility. In particular, I analyze the idea of "hunger"—both as a lack of and as a desire for—as a framework that underwrites the development of twenty-first-century Detroit.

Quickening the Appetite: Cool Kids in the City

In July 2014 the *New York Times Magazine* ran a story by Ben Austen titled "Post Post-Apocalyptic Detroit," with a cover image that featured in bold typeface the words "Detroit, through Rose-Colored Glasses."[8] The cover presented a photograph—taken by Andrew Moore, part of the new cohort of Detroit photographers discussed in chapter 2—of a modern and thriving downtown, which was seen through an obviously rosy, warm-hued filter. The result was a marked contrast to the visual representation of Detroit as a blighted, decayed landscape, the ubiquitous image of the ruined city for at least the prior twenty-five years. Instead it presents a vision of downtown Detroit's occupancy—skyscrapers and office buildings with prominent corporate names and logos atop their roofs, cars and people dotting the street, the neatly landscaped Campus Martius Park at the center of the image. The story, part of a conversation both national and local about Detroit's future, which has spiked amid Detroit's public bankruptcy filings, centers on the possibility of a promising future spearheaded by innovative and determined investors. The most visible investor is Dan Gilbert, the hometown billionaire most prominently behind Detroit's recent development in terms of both financial investments and boosterism; indeed, it was he who interviewed Warren Buffett on stage during the 2014 "Detroit Homecoming" conference.

Dan Gilbert was born in Detroit and raised in metropolitan Detroit; his father and grandfather, both born-and-raised Detroiters, owned and operated a bar in the city.[9] Gilbert made his fortune in the mortgage industry. His initial venture, Rock Financial, grew as a mortgage lender, and its development of online mortgages caught the eye of Intuit, which eventually purchased the company, renaming the product "Quicken Loans." As the company grew, with Gilbert still at its helm, he purchased Quicken back from Intuit in the early 2000s and remains its CEO. He also is a sports fan and owns the NBA's Cleveland Cavaliers and a handful of minor league sports teams, in addition to four casinos, real estate, and dozens of smaller company offshoots.[10] One of Gilbert's most recent investments, and most public, is Detroit itself.

Gilbert's goal, though, is not only to buy property, but to invest in the rebuilding of Detroit.[11] Gilbert is one of the biggest proponents of Detroit's "potential," largely symbolized by his decision to move Quicken's headquarters and its employees from metropolitan Detroit to downtown Detroit in 2010. Gilbert and his company, Rock Ventures, have proudly disclosed its holdings in Detroit; as of July 9, 2014, they consisted of "$1.3 Billion+ invested in Detroit" and "9 million+ square feet" across its "60+ properties owned."[12] What is mind-boggling is that Gilbert's investments have primarily occurred in the short span of five years since his 2009 announcement that Quicken would relocate its offices to downtown Detroit.[13] That is over 1.3 billion dollars in five years, an astonishing amount of money by any count. Gilbert's investment strategy in Detroit is to fill downtown with his employees, as well as with housing and restaurants and other lifestyle amenities that in the end will attract other investors and consumers and ultimately provide a growing and economically beneficial demand for downtown Detroit.

Gilbert's investment plan, and the growth he forecasts, relies not only on what Sharon Zukin identifies as the "traditional" economic factors of land, labor, and economy but also on the symbolic economy, "the intertwining of cultural symbols and entrepreneurial capital."[14] If Detroit's bankruptcy is the background of this story, then young, educated professionals and the businesses they run and patronize are in the foreground, the core demographic signifiers of the symbolic economy. As will be seen, the relationship between the seemingly incongruous financial tensions of bankruptcy and private investment hinge on the symbolic economy, exemplified by the movement of young people and businesses into Detroit's urban core. I argue that this shifting demographic profile, and its oft-touted manifestations—cool young urbanites and their DIY businesses—serve as the rationale for why Detroit is a "good" investment. The narrative of Detroit's rise relies on the symbolic economy—the cultural symbols that innovative and creative people bring to any city *and* entrepreneurial capital. Many would argue that Detroit is long on great cultural symbols; what has often been less readily available is entrepreneurial capital. Indeed, one of Detroit's most famous examples of success in the symbolic economy, Motown Records, was reliant not only on the immense talent of its stars, songwriters, and musicians but also on the innovation in both the automated production of music *and* the entrepreneurial capital that the Gordy family was able to collectively invest early on to fund the formation of the company.[15] For so long capital has been missing—both for small as well as large businesses—as banks and funders deemed Detroit "too risky" for investment, but since the mid-2000s, Detroit, slowly but surely, has been seen as a place to invest, a place to take a chance and stake a claim. I argue that this shift is explicitly tied to a narrative that white investment is increasing in primarily black Detroit. The same logics that financed racialized investment that enabled white suburbanization (see chapter 1) and deemed primarily black Detroit as "too risky" for investment is now disposed to suggest that Detroit is "ready" for investment once again based on the movement of white residents and businesses to Detroit.

Detroit, many now argue, is no longer just a speculative investment. It is a boomtown. Ben Austen recently placed downtown's residential real estate at 99 percent occupied and office space vacancies at just 11 percent, "the lowest rate in decades."[16] While Gilbert is by no means the only investor in downtown Detroit, he is at this juncture the most prominent in his swift movement back into the city. In the five years from the July 2009 announcement that Quicken would move to downtown to July 2014, there were over twelve thousand "team members" of Rock Ventures companies working in Detroit.[17] In May 2014 the company had sufficient infrastructure that "Quicken Loans and its Family of Companies hire[d] more than 1,000 paid summer interns to spend the summer living, working and playing in Detroit."[18] Gilbert's strategy is to invest in the city and to grow its symbolic economy. Lately, even as Gilbert continues to invest in real estate, his Detroit portfolio now also includes a number of restaurants, gastropubs and bars, as well as a yoga studio.

Gilbert is not only bringing companies to downtown, he is intent on bringing people to downtown. Gilbert said in an interview that part of building Detroit is attracting the type of "new Detroiter" that he wants as part of his corporate developments: "If you want to attract the kind of brains to grow your business . . . you need a strong urban core. It's no secret that people in their 20s and 30s want to be in a vibrant, exciting, urban core. We're not going to get those people if we're in a nice building in the suburbs."[19] This idea, however, is that the strategy of growth, both for Gilbert's businesses and real estate holdings, is dependent on attracting a particular type of demographic. He is looking to bring in a young and educated workforce and to do so he is investing heavily in building a city to attract this population. Implicitly, then, this suggests that there is not a young and educated workforce already in Detroit. If we read this description of the "kind of brains" that Gilbert and others want to attract against the "kinds of brains" we know to be in the city, as featured in *Deforce* and *Detropia,* the stark difference between this new and old Detroit becomes all the more clear. As Greenberg pointed out in her 1970s case study of New York City, an approach of "urban economic development combining intensive media and marketing with neoliberal restructuring" led by a powerful coalition of financial and real estate elites, media and culture industries, and government-prioritized marketing indeed resulted in a rebound of New York's image and financial crisis, but at the expense of the working class and poor.[20] This is already apparent in the developments in Detroit. As will be seen throughout this chapter, so much of the "new Detroit" is indeed for the "new Detroiter." Therefore, even as Detroit as a whole, a city signified by working-class blackness and post-industrial authenticity, is commodified to sell the city, the city's rise is built for and with the intent of a demographically shifting—whiter and more educated—Detroit.

What is apparent in the investments of Dan Gilbert, and in the continuing development of this area, is the influx of businesses that meet and serve the needs of a highly desired population of a young, educated, and, in Detroit, increasingly white population. Gilbert's investments are concentrated in an area of the city identified in promotional and investment material as "Greater Downtown." Geographically, Greater Downtown encompasses downtown, the historic center of the city that begins at the riverfront, expands east along the riverfront through Rivertown to Belle Isle, and west through Corktown. The area moves north though the entertainment and stadium district that connects to Midtown, anchored by Wayne State University and the Detroit Institute of Arts, to Techtown and New Center. This area follows the immediate contours of Woodward Avenue north–south and the riverfront along the southern edge. This area, at 7.2 square miles, is just a little more than 5 percent of the entire geographical footprint of the city. Indeed, the focus of the "7.2 SQ MI" report, a February 2013 report released by a consortium of private business and nonprofit groups, hinges on a portrayal of Greater Downtown as embodying this population shift to younger, more educated, and increasingly white residents.[21] According to the report, which relies heavily on data from Census 2000 and 2010, although the overall population of the city, including the Greater Downtown area, is continuing to decline, the document focuses on and sees as an indicator of change particular types of *increases* in the area's demographics. This is the central argument: that even as Detroit's literal population is growing smaller, the celebrated increase is that certain groups of the population are increasing. It is branding magic—even as the number of people in Detroit is declining, the report makes an argument that the city is on the rise. This narrative of growth has been central to scripting Detroit's rebound.

The report highlights the population gain in Greater Downtown of eighteen- to thirty-four-year-olds. Although it is clear from the data that the thirty-five- to fifty-four-year-olds and the fifty-five-plus-year-olds are together over 50 percent of the population, the report as a whole focuses nearly exclusively on the eighteen- to thirty-four-year-old population, to the exclusion of those younger or older.[22] Also important to the representation of the changing demographic is the idea that the population of Greater Detroit is young *and* college educated. The highlighting of this data is notable because the statistics on the college-educated population are only focused on young people, as is evident in the title of the page "Young & College-Educated."[23] It shows the statistics of the Greater Downtown area *only* for twenty-five- to thirty-four-year-olds, which is presented in a way that is confusing but is intended ultimately to highlight that as an overall percentage of the population, this demographic of residents of Greater Downtown is more highly educated than the city, state, and national population at large.[24]

More than simply young and college educated, the report explicitly emphasizes the Greater Downtown area as increasingly white. The report sums up the racial makeup of the area as follows:

> Greater Downtown continues to be racially diverse, with black residents accounting for the racial majority (68%). Between 2000 and 2010, the black population **declined**, the white population **increased**, and Asian and Hispanic populations **remained steady**.[25]

What is of interest for my analysis is the way in which the report emphasizes the increase of the white population and the decline of the black population through bolded typeface. Throughout the report, the details that are furnished in bold type are all aspects of Greater Downtown that are growing or increasing, and deemed a positive addition to a developing area. In this case the report is most concerned not that population as a total is increasing (it is not) but that the percentage of white people is increasing. The bolded text puts forth a distinction of more white people; an increase of 3 percent is the information of note in an accompanying graph, along with its corollary of a 5 percent decrease of the black population. The non-too-subtle message: this area is becoming less black and is significantly less black than Detroit as a whole. In this report the revitalization and flow of private capital is predicated upon the literal, and data-backed, disappearance of black bodies. It is the continuation of the logic expressed in chapter 1, that Detroit spiraled into decline because of a shift in population from white to black. Here, the report plays on the prior narrative of Detroit's fall to suggest that its rise will be possible when the population shift reverses and the balance is tipped back toward a decrease of black people. A similar message is conveyed with the report's use of statistics around native-born and foreign-born populations. The report conveys that the population in Greater Downtown has a higher percentage of foreign-born residents at 8 percent in Greater Downtown, 5 percent in Detroit as a whole, 6 percent in Michigan, and 12 percent in the United States.[26] The takeaway is that this area is *different* because it is whiter, more foreign-born, and less black than the rest of Detroit. Ultimately the document emphasizes the Greater Downtown area as different from the city of Detroit as a whole as it is whiter, younger, and more educated.[27] Thus, Greater Downtown is celebrated as a symbol of good investment precisely because it is less poor, less old, less black, and more educated. This is not to suggest that the movement of whites into Greater Detroit is in and of itself a problem or that new building and increased development is a uniformly bad thing. Rather, I am interested in the ways that this new population is discursively represented as an improvement over the old population, which seems to underscore a more pernicious sentiment: that Detroit's rise again can only happen because the Detroit that currently exists can, and should, be replaced by one that is younger, more educated, and whiter.

The focus of the "7.2 SQ MI" report on shifting demographics is not a Detroit anomaly; rather, it highlights a reversal of a population shift that has been a publicly voiced concern of Rust Belt states, including Michigan, since at least the year 2000. Multiple Michigan governors, for example, have expressed concern over what is perceived as a statewide "brain drain," in the form of young educated people leaving the state and a dearth of young educated people moving into the state.[28] In response, a number of politicians and economic development groups have sought to create what former governor Jennifer Granholm in 2003 called "Cool Cities," with the goal of bringing young people back to Michigan cities. The Cool Cities Initiative in Michigan with its emphasis on "talent, innovation, diversity, and environment" owed much conceptually to Richard Florida's "creative class" concept.[29] And like Florida's concept, although it created a lot of buzz, Cool Cities did not fundamentally change or shift demographic patterns.[30] However, what Cool Cities and the creative class signal is the ideal consumer of a city space. In these types of plans developers, corporations, small business owners, cultural institutions, and the city will grow if—and perhaps only if—they can attract this desired population.

Although the introduction to the "7.2 SQ MI" report states that this is a "data story," in an attempt to situate the findings as a purely quantitative snapshot, the story reveals a very specific qualitative story. In order to situate the 7.2 square miles of greater downtown as a potential for investment,[31] the document creates a social distance from the other 94.8 percent of the city. In reading through the "data story" of the report, it becomes abundantly clear that the "celebration of progress," "continued challenges," and "potential opportunity"[32] that Greater Downtown represents is contingent on the rise of a "new Detroiter," which in effect devalues those who are not young, not college educated, and not white. The problems with this sentiment are numerous: it ignores the contributions of Detroit's longtime population, it feels like a reboot of failed urban renewal policies of the 1950s and the 1970s, and, most dangerous of all, it continues a cycle of private and public investment underwritten by racism and classism. In addition to these problems, this celebration of a "new Detroiter" is also laced with irony, because so much of the appeal of the "new Detroit" is built on the back of "old Detroit," as will become clear in the next two sections.

Destination Detroit: Feeding the Urban Pioneers

In June 2012 *Food & Wine,* a monthly magazine published by Time Inc., ran an eight-page story and photo essay about Detroit with the title "Soul Food for a Hungry City." The images showcased a one-block stretch of Michigan Avenue in the Corktown neighborhood of Detroit. The subhead of the *Food & Wine* article reads: "In Detroit, a city where bad news has long outweighed good, a group of young urban pioneers is bringing the community together around excellent barbecue and fabulous coffee and cocktails."[33] The article goes on to outline a food-specific articulation of the redevelopment of Detroit: a blighted neighborhood, long in the shadow of the hulking ruin of the Michigan Central Station, revived by entrepreneurs who opened a restaurant, coffee bar, and cocktail lounge. And since *Food & Wine* is, after all, a magazine about food and wine, images of beautifully prepared soul food, recipes, and photos of hip, young, and almost entirely white people eating and drinking fill the majority of the rest of the eight-page spread. In both the text and images, Zukin's notion of the symbolic economy is in full view—more than barbeque, coffee, and cocktails, the profile of the entrepreneurs and the customers represents the cultural symbols and capital that make these businesses thrive. The sidebars of the article provide a tour of the block as well as "picks" of locations to visit in Detroit. This article screams: Detroit is on the rise and these "young urban pioneers" are at the center of it. I see in the contemporary development of this particular neighborhood a symbiosis between its historic and continuing importance as a destination.

What these "pioneers" have zeroed in on is the logic of frontier development—historically, the boomtowns of the west grew as they became way stations, hubs of transfers, or destinations based on proximity to the railroad. This system of locomotion provided a rationale for stopping in what seemed like a potentially endless expanse of wide open space. And in Detroit, this block of Corktown served as a way station historically for the railroad industry and has proven to fill that role once again for the ruin tourism industry. Located west of downtown, Corktown is considered Detroit's oldest surviving historic neighborhood. The neighborhood's name is an homage to County Cork, Ireland, and harkens back to the Irish immigrants who established a community here in the mid-1840s. The neighborhood is also home of two of Detroit's most recognizable landmarks: the site of the now-razed Tiger Stadium and Michigan Central Station. Tiger Stadium closed after the 1999 season. Demolition of the stadium began in 2008 and was completed in 2009. This location, at the corner of Michigan and Trumbull in Corktown, continuously served as a baseball field for the ball club that became the Detroit Tigers from the construction of Bennett Park in 1895 until the closure of Tiger Stadium in 1999. The now-vacant field is a location of pilgrimage for baseball enthusiasts, historians, and Detroiters alike. In the years since its demolition, the field has been used as a park and volunteers maintain the field for people to play pick-up games of baseball and softball. In December 2014 the lot was formally approved for redevelopment. As of February 2015 the realty group that the city has approved to redevelop the lot is planning to raise 10 percent of the equity needed for the project through crowdfunding.[34]

The other, even more famous, neighborhood landmark is Michigan Central Station, also known as the Michigan Central Depot, which served as Detroit's main passenger train station from 1913 to 1988. The building, a stunning example of Beaux-Arts architecture designed by the same architectural team as New York City's Grand Central Station, is one of Detroit's most well-known structures, both for the countless images that have been produced highlighting its physical decay and its historic role. From 1913 through its peak use in the 1940s and ultimate closure in 1988, countless people arrived and departed Detroit through this station. During the station's heyday, when passengers arrived they would pass through the front doors and find themselves in Roosevelt Park, the front yard of the station in the heart of Corktown.[35] John Dancy, head of the Detroit Urban League for forty-two years, from 1918 to 1960, recalled that in his early years, "I got into the habit of meeting many of the trains just as a matter of routine. Each afternoon I would go to the Michigan Central station to meet one or both of the trains from Cincinnati."[36] In meeting the trains, Dancy would be there to offer black migrants assistance on where to go for housing, shelter, or job opportunities. Others have written about members of the Detroit Urban League meeting the trains "thrice daily" at Michigan Central Station in order to steer the migrants toward opportunities and to begin part of the Urban League's work in socializing new migrants to the city.[37] Not every Detroit newcomer had such a formal welcoming committee, but each of the many who passed through the doors became one of the thousands who had reached their final destination: Detroit. Michigan Central Station served as the gateway for an untold number of migrants seeking opportunities in this promised land of jobs and opportunity.

I draw out the historical role of the train station, and to a lesser but significant degree the ball field, to tease out the contemporary role of these locations in building and sustaining the twenty-first-century incarnation of the neighborhood. In both the past and present the location of Michigan Central Station is of supreme importance. In the present day, if you have seen an image of Detroit's blight I guarantee that you have seen an image of the train station. Indeed, the shadow of Michigan Central Station is everywhere. Camilo Vergara features the train station in a single image in *The New American Ghetto* and devotes four pages to the shuttered train station in *American Ruin.*[38] The Michigan Central Station is featured in both *Deforce* and *Detropia* as it is in nearly any documentary or visually based story about Detroit. Although the Chrysler commercial does not show the train station and for the most part avoids the more typical ruin photography, the idea of blight is invoked in the opening imagery, and the American flag it features is from the still-standing centerfield flagpole of the demolished Tiger Stadium. However, what is not seen in the widespread images of Corktown's more famous symbols of decline is the sense of the neighborhood at large. In particular, this colorful stretch of storefronts along Michigan Avenue, and its feature as ground zero of Detroit's emerging creative class with its cluster of restaurants, a cafe, and a cocktail bar, is very much connected to these two structures of old Detroit's past. And perhaps unsurprisingly this stretch of development is the "Greater" in the Greater Downtown name, given its location one and a half miles from downtown. In this one location you can get a sense of the proximity of Tiger Stadium and the train station—approximately three-quarters of a mile away from one another. And right along this same thoroughfare, in between these two landmarks, are the businesses featured in the *Food & Wine* article. I position these together to give a fuller sense of Corktown as simultaneously not just development and not just blight, and offer the complexity of the neighborhood's landscape to suggest that blight itself drove the development of this particular section of Michigan Avenue. As the interest in Detroit's abandoned train station increased so too did tourist traffic along the primary path from downtown to Michigan Central Station along Michigan Avenue. Even as stories abound about Detroit celebrating its rise or its inglorious fall, the nuance is that these spaces are often right next to one another, revealing the slow but steady way in which the past decline serves to fuel the contemporary rise.

The national notice of Corktown's revitalization was confirmed in June 2012 when not just *Food & Wine* but also *Bon Appétit,* a monthly magazine published by Condé Nast, included stories about visiting Corktown in its online and print editions.[39] *Bon Appétit* weighed in with "5 Spots to Hit in Corktown, Detroit's Coolest Nabe." The feature in *Bon Appétit* was not even a full-page article, just a brief snippet on the magazine's monthly roundup of what is "going on" in food. It too mentioned the exact same places, along this one-block stretch of Michigan Avenue. The teaser to this story, as well as the *Food & Wine* story, not only weighs in on where to eat but provides a revealing look at what exactly these new businesses are serving up. *Bon Appétit* begins their feature titled "*Detroit?* Yes, Detroit" with a question: "Need a good reason to visit Detroit? Here are five spots that have made the emerging Corktown neighborhood a destination for the city's hungry creative class." Both of these articles capture the shift of Detroit from a place that for decades outsiders were told to avoid to a trending destination to hunger for.

The anchor to the twenty-first-century commercial revitalization along this stretch of Michigan Avenue is the much-touted Slows BarBQ. Opened in 2005, the restaurant specializes in contemporary soul food featuring smoked meats, homemade sauces, and traditional sides. More than a menu that was familiar to the many Detroiters with Southern roots, and a nod to the national trend in comfort cuisine, the restaurant brought a new concept of urban dining to Detroit. Slows blends upscale casual and cool with its dining room, built with richly reclaimed wood, an open floor plan, and a sizable bar at its center that features an enviable rotating list of craft beers on tap. Amid the frenzy of press buzz following the restaurant's opening and growing reputation, wait times neared four hours.[40] With features in magazines, on cooking shows,[41] and on travel blogs, Slows BarBQ has succeeded well beyond the predictions of the owners and public alike, turning into a destination for national and international tourists.

The title of the *Food & Wine* article, "Soul Food for a Hungry City," is both a nod to the dining concept behind Slows BarBQ and a way to represent a particular racial and classed authenticity of Detroit. "Soul food" has a particular regional and racial legacy.[42] As other scholars have established, the institution of slavery itself produced a specific type of food culture, much of which is captured in contemporary renderings of soul food.[43] Additionally, much of what may be deemed historical "Southern" (white) regional cuisine as recorded in cookbooks and newspapers from the nineteenth and twentieth century originates in recipes developed and created by black slaves and later black domestics.[44] However, soul food, even as it is part of Southern cuisine, is deployed as a particularly racialized marker of black food and food culture. Soul food then serves as a code, harkening back to the Great Migration, which brought Southern food cultures to Northern cities en masse. The idea of migration intimated in the food concept is carried through to the chugging train logo of Slows BarBQ. Michigan Central Station as idea and as hulking landmark is palpable. Although the décor is not explicitly a depot theme, the history of this landmark is in the fabric of the restaurant. Slows and the coffee shop, cocktail lounge, wine bar, and multiple restaurants that have joined it in the last decade play on the continued concept of Corktown as the place to welcome visitors to Detroit's Michigan Central Station. Because of its spectacular ruin, the train station remains a point of destination and arrival for people from far and wide.

Race, class, and culture all feature in the articles through the naming of the clientele as "urban pioneers" and "creative class" and showcase that their presence signals a rising Detroit. The last page of the *Food & Wine* article features a full-page image of an almond cake with lemon and crème fraiche glaze and a lone pull quote that reads: "New York City didn't need another coffee bar . . . Detroit did." In many ways, this quote exemplifies the momentum around Detroit's emergence in the larger cultural narrative that it is simultaneously "cool" but also *needy* and *hungry* for more. In both cases "need" and "hunger" are used not in a literal sense; rather, they play on the tension between actual hunger and the desires of the creative class. I want to draw attention to the use of "hunger" as a shorthand for a desire felt by a particular group of consumers. As national depictions show Detroit as a boomtown with opportunity for anyone with a dream and desire, they simultaneously suggest that other Detroiters by omission were not "hungry" for growth, innovation, and development. Not only is this not true, but the cruel irony here is that for so long many Detroiters have lived with a backdrop of a very different kind of hunger. As of 2011, one out of every three Detroit residents lived below the poverty line, and thus many Detroiters were verifiably hungry, living in the grips of food insecurity.[45] In this way the simultaneity of the new "hungry" creative class and the old "hungry" working class in Detroit reveals the complexity of the city. And as discussed in the next section, these multiple definitions of "hunger" are deployed as a rationale for a corporate strategy of development.

Proud to Be Here: "Detroit" as a Corporate Strategy

In July 2011 Whole Foods Market announced a plan to open a store on the corner of Mack and Woodward Avenues in the Midtown neighborhood of Detroit, not surprisingly located within the "Greater Downtown" development area.[46] The news sent a ripple of headlines throughout the country. The actual opening of the store two years later yielded an outpouring of local and national media coverage of the event in stories from *Forbes* to National Public Radio.[47] While metropolitan Detroit already had five existing Whole Foods locations prior to the addition of the Detroit store, all of these stores were located in affluent outlying suburbs.[48] What garnered the widespread media attention was not that a Whole Foods was opening but that it was opening in Detroit. In the symbolic economy, the presence of a Whole Foods Market in Detroit challenged both the image of the grocery chain and the image of Detroit.[49] Whole Foods Market was founded as a single store in 1980 in Austin, Texas, and has since grown into an international "retailer of natural and organic foods," and as of September 2014 operated 399 stores in the United States, Canada, and the United Kingdom.[50] Colloquially referred to as "whole paycheck," Whole Foods Market has established a reputation as catering to an upscale, "yuppie" clientele. As important, their brand relies on the characterization of the store not just as a grocery store but rather as "a lifestyle chain," an example of what Michael Serazio calls "ethos groceries," which he argues "offer the consumer the chance to be simultaneously radical and bourgeois; to be absolved of moral ambivalence about personal wealth and elite status."[51] At the core is the idea that by buying banal everyday objects that have been certified as "good"—organic, whole, natural, fair trade—the middle-class consumer can do good, through good consumption.[52] This is the corporate ethos of "doing good" that the store relied on in its announcement of its new store in Detroit.

The co-CEO of Whole Foods, Walter Robb, expanded the idea of "doing good" not only through consumption but through community engagement by positioning the new store as part of an overall corporate strategy to combat elitism and racism. Robb was quoted in advance of the store opening as saying, "We've tried to put the community first in this effort. . . . I know that we're learning as much as we're giving. Not only are we going after the affordability and the accessibility. . . . Because we're going after elitism, we're going after racism. Detroit's 90 percent African-American."[53] What is of interest is the projection by Robb of the Detroit store as a tool to combat elitism and racism simply by *being* in Detroit. It is telling that Robb's statistic is significantly overstated; Detroit's population as a whole was not "90 percent African-American" but 82.7 percent

African American, lending a much closer rounded number of 80, 83, or 85 percent.[54] Either way, what is important here is Robb's recall and use of Detroit's *blackness* as its key narrative to rationalize how *being here* will combat racism. At the core of this section is not a critique of Whole Foods itself; in full disclosure, I am a longtime customer of this corporation.[55] Rather, I am invested in analyzing the ways in which the corporation's statements about "Detroit," and in particular "Detroit" as a code for "blackness," is a branding strategy to sell itself as a kind and ethical grocery store.

The strategic announcement and development of a store in Detroit, a location of literal and represented majority black and working-class populace, is key to shifting the perception of Whole Foods Market. The Detroit store was the first to open as part of its overall low-income development strategy that is being played out in neighborhoods across the country.[56] Whole Foods Market is aggressively expanding, from a November 2014 estimated 400 stores to a goal of 1,200 stores.[57] Given the company's market saturation in its traditional locations of already affluent communities, its newest strategy is locating in neighborhoods not "traditionally" seen as the store's target demographic in order to continue its corporate expansion. These new stores, like the Detroit store, are considerably smaller than Whole Foods Market's traditional footprint of fifty thousand to seventy thousand square feet.[58] (Detroit's location checks in at twenty thousand square feet.) The Detroit store is part of an overall expansion strategy, and an early test case for its vast "smaller and urban" expansion plan.[59] That terminology, widely used by the company, is a thinly veiled reference to stores located not in already affluent neighborhoods but in "up and coming" neighborhoods. As part of gaining momentum in its expansions, Whole Foods Market references the Midtown Detroit store and its success as the first example of the smaller, urban store.[60] Although the company has not publicly released official figures, Robb has said multiple times, in regard to the Detroit store, "We're in a far better place than I thought we would be. It's far above our modest projections."[61] The store's success, in one of the most derided cities in the country, an icon of urban poverty, is a great marketing tool for continuing expansion. Indeed, the store has been so successful that Whole Foods announced in September 2014 that it was considering locations to open a second Detroit store.[62]

The corporation's effort, let's be clear, was clever, in that they were able to rely on an existing and widespread narrative of Detroit as a "hungry" city. One of the longest-standing urban myths about Detroit is that there "are no grocery stores in Detroit." Although this myth has been debunked numerous times, it is often quoted.[63] However, the designation of Detroit as a "food desert" is often played up, and even though Robb acknowledges that the label is "an insulting term," the concept was frequently mentioned in conjunction with the announcement of the Detroit Whole Foods store.[64] Even though the scholarly literature has established that *food desert* is a term that is ill defined at best, the concept is based on the approximate distance to a supermarket or a business that sells food.[65] The research report "Characteristics and Influential Factors of Food Deserts," published by the U.S. Department of Agriculture, Treasury, and Health and Human Services, is similarly vague in defining a food desert, suggesting that the term refers to "areas in the United States where people have limited access to a variety of healthy and affordable food. . . . These regions of the country often feature large proportions of households with low incomes, inadequate access to transportation, and a limited number of food retailers providing fresh produce and healthy groceries for affordable prices."[66] In this report, individual census tracts qualify for this designation when they meet a low-income *and* a low-access measure.[67] According to this measure, in Detroit, only twenty of its nearly three hundred census tracts are deemed food deserts.[68] While still a significant number, it makes the overall statement "Detroit is a food desert" seem particularly disingenuous. Admittedly though, access to grocery stores can be sparse. A 2011 report counted 115 grocery stores and markets within Detroit city limits.[69] However, stores are not distributed evenly across the city's 139 square miles and, for example, the concentration of the food desert status in the far west side neighborhoods of Brightmoor and Warrendale speaks to the concentration of stores in other neighborhoods.[70]

The Whole Foods Market Midtown Detroit store has several obvious benefits: it adds a national chain grocery store to the city and is another retailer of the SNAP program (the name of the government food stamp program since 2008).[71] It also fills a gap for a higher-end grocer in the city of Detroit. However, its location in Midtown, one of the most densely populated, wealthy, and central neighborhoods of Greater Downtown, does not necessarily mean that it meets the immediate needs of Detroit's hungriest residents. Whole Foods did not publicly release figures for its Midtown store but did say that its SNAP sales were "five or six times the chain's average."[72] Based on her research, the journalist Tracie McMillan estimates that "5 to 12 percent of Whole Foods' Detroit sales are from SNAP."[73] While this suggests the Detroit store does in fact attract a less affluent clientele than the Whole Foods national demographic, McMillan surmises that "since 38 percent of Detroit residents make use of the SNAP program, this estimate suggests the store isn't reaching a cross section of the city, but a targeted, upper-income niche."[74] Given the store's location in Midtown, this makes perfect sense. Yet rather than fighting elitism and racism, in many ways the store seems to be attracting more of the same customers it has in its other locations, with a small section of the hungriest Detroiters. Therefore, the self-promotion of the store as going after these tough social issues falls flat and seems much more like public relations spin.

Whole Foods has made a concerted effort in its Detroit store not only to feature local products (which is common in all its locations) but also to highlight its location. From the mural that greets customers at the entrance with the revived 1970s Detroit slogan "Say Nice Things about Detroit" to the signage that states "Detroit: Proud to be Here" atop a timeline of Whole Foods' corporate history, to the classic Motown music

Figure 9. Midtown Whole Foods produce wall. Photo by John Williams, August 2014. Reproduced with permission from John Williams.

45 records that top each of the checkout lanes, the corporation has made the Detroit store as "Detroit" as possible. Indeed, the store has devoted an entire wall in its produce section to an image telling customers, "We Love Keeping It Local," which sits atop a map of a downtown street grid as shown in Figure 9.

Even with the slogan "We Love Keeping It Local" and a corporate strategy to feature some local vendors and products in all of its locations, Whole Foods is clearly not a small, local upstart but a multinational corporation. In fact, its vast reach was cited as an advantage in much of the media coverage of the store's opening: one of the reasons the opening was seen as news is that a national chain grocery store entered Detroit. The store tirelessly emphasizes its brand as ethical, and emphasizes the need for good, wholesome food. While this is not uncommon to its other locations, in reference to this particular location Walter Robb has been quick to point out, "In Detroit, I see thousands of communities across the United States that don't have fresh healthy food."[75] Therefore, the work of the Detroit location is not simply profits but to provide "fresh healthy food"—in direct juxtaposition to the unnamed bad food long associated not just with Detroit but with poor communities around the country. As a result, the store itself, and the rationale for its development, is seen as benevolent, and a key part of "making it better" for Detroit and communities like Detroit more generally.

This rationale for investment is important given the amount of public money that went into the funding structure that the development relied upon. The development of the store is a result of a partnership between private and public development at the local and state level. The financing structure of the development relied on private capital as well as public money. According to the *Wall Street Journal,* the financing for the store came from a variety of sources: "The $12.9 million Whole Foods store was financed with $6.1 million in private equity from Ram Developers and Whole Foods. Ram contributed 1.9 acres of land for the store valued at about $1 million. . . . The remaining $5.8 million came from state and local grants and the sale of tax credits tied to the project."[76] Indeed, this is the model of development with joint ventures between private corporations, corporate brokers, and public entities rather than individual investors that Jason Hackworth cites as a key element of contemporary neoliberal urbanism.[77] In prior conceptions, corporate participation signified "maturation of gentrification in individual neighborhoods," but now, Hackworth concedes, "firms are increasingly the first to invest and redevelop property for more affluent users."[78] Although Whole Foods made the commitment to expand its brand to include a Detroit store, the potential financial risk was spread throughout a public–private partnership, with the taxpayers of Detroit, and Michigan as a whole, footing a portion of the investment. And ultimately the public money spent to develop this store is a primary example of the neoliberal growth model that fuels uneven impacts of development—the corporate and local elites stand to gain much, wherein the public as a whole will benefit very little or perhaps not at all. The epigraph by the journalist Annie Gasparro that opens this chapter pithily sums up the heart of tensions in the city's growth: "Detroit may be bankrupt, but at least it has a Whole Foods."[79]

Given the rising real estate market demand of Greater Downtown and the increasing concentration of affluent residents and businesses, Whole Foods' decision to locate in Midtown makes a lot of sense.[80] In comparison to other store locations, the store is much smaller with fewer products, yet each time I visit the store is full of shoppers. Every time I have shopped at this location it is bustling, busy, and the parking lot is always full. There are those affiliated with the Detroit Medical Center and Wayne State University, identified by the employee badges they wear; young professionals, including myself; and many people outside the "typical" Whole Foods demographic, including high school and college-aged people, the elderly, the differently abled, and in general people who seemingly represent many walks of life (as much as one can expect to do so in a visit to a grocery store). The market now is serving multiple populations and is visibly one of the least racially segregated spaces in not only Detroit but also metropolitan Detroit. Whole Foods seems genuinely Proud to Be Here, and sincere in its desire to be part of Detroit. The opening of the store in Detroit is much more complex because of the huge amount of PR and marketing generated by the company in relationship to the store as well as the millions of public dollars that underwrote its development. If, for example, Robb himself did not raise the claim that Whole Foods, by being in Detroit, is battling racism and elitism, I don't think that one store or one corporate brand would be expected to do so. But in the invocation of this claim the brand must do much more than simply show up and be present in order to make this claim a reality. Part of the complexity is in the store's self-conscious framing of itself for a Detroit market and of the framing of Detroit for a wider audience. For example, the national narrative of Whole Foods "doing good" in Detroit speaks to a far larger audience than simply the Midtown Detroit consumer; it sends a national message about the company's benevolence. Additionally, and perhaps this is more to the point of the twenty-first-century appeal of Detroit, the "comeback" of Detroit also serves a narrative function of racial reconciliation and healing through evidence of a multiracial middle-class consumer base coming together to eat good and do good for the community at large. In this vision of Detroit, all are welcome, and celebrated—as long as you can afford it.

Just Deserts or Just Desserts?

Americans are currently inundated by stories from the mainstream media that Detroit is possible now. The idea that Detroit is an attractive space, first to visit and then to live, requires not only a shift in perception but also a shift in infrastructure. Even as the population continues its decline, the notion that *some* people are moving to the city is key to the narrative of growth. In a marked shift from the still-prevalent idea of Detroit as crime-ridden and scary—seen in everything from the City-Data forum to the representation of the drug trade in documentary films—the notion of Detroit as livable for a wider (read: whiter) population both upends and confirms every story explored thus far.

Yet the "celebration" of Detroit's comeback needs to be examined. It cannot move forward like something preordained; it cannot be accepted without hesitation. Much as the reality of institutional racism, however veiled, underscores Detroit's decline, so too should this ugly reality undergird its rise. Development is indeed desirable for many longtime residents; yet in the enthusiastic stories of Detroit's revival, we must also heed the concern of Glenn Ross, a longtime Detroiter: "This place needs a lot of change and I give them a lot of credit for investing and wanting to make it happen. . . . But so many people are concerned whether they will still be able to afford it once it changes."[81] For so long Detroit was seen as a place to ignore, or a place to make jokes about its dysfunction from afar. Now the fears of gentrification, felt by residents in "up and coming" neighborhoods all over the country, are palpable in Detroit, indeed making it a "new Brooklyn." To urban planners, development gestures toward growth—buildings, roads, transportation—at the same time it also signals its antonym, a parcel or location that is latent, dormant, under- or undeveloped. As Detroit's rise is scripted by the media, boosters, and investors, the recycling of the trope of a beautiful wasteland—the underdeveloped frontier—serves as the backdrop to all these stories.

I am by no means suggesting that development is a unilaterally bad thing; indeed, the development of a public transit plan to serve Detroit and its metropolitan region is the type of development that would greatly improve the quality of life for *all* of us. But development is almost always approached with ideas of places or locations that are deemed ripe for development or in need of development not necessarily for the benefit of locations or populations but for the benefit of profit. This chapter is about how urban development, and in particular the ways in which development in a city that is primarily black and poor, is situated as a unilateral improvement. I am not suggesting here that Detroit's infrastructure, city governance, and maintenance are not in need of improvement—they most definitely are. However, what is of concern is the idea that places that are populated by primarily working-class and poor people of color are nearly always seen as underdeveloped or poorly developed.[82] And far too often, as Greenberg's study of New York City reveals, the impact of the resulting economic investment from branding a city in crisis as a city on the rise all too often results in the displacement of the poor and working class. As much as Detroit's present representation is shifting, the question of Detroit—its past, its present, and its future—remains intimately bound. Turning toward the conclusion, the battle over the control of the soul of the city and the resource that has long made Detroit an important geographic location—the Detroit River—remains central to its future.

CONCLUSION

The Strait

A Tale of Two Cities

> This country, so temperate, so fertile and so beautiful that it may justly be called the earthly paradise of North America, deserves all the care of the King to keep it up and to attract inhabitants to it.
>
> —Antoine Laumet de la Mothe Cadillac

> Come realize water's true potential. Dive in to the waters of Pure Michigan.
>
> —Tim Allen, "Pure Michigan" tourism ad

Although the story of Detroit is frequently told as one of fire—a city built from the forge of industry—the story of Detroit is also one of water. As much as twentieth-century Detroit grew through the fire of the factories, the elemental force producing the energy needed for transformation—smelting iron ore into iron, iron into steel, steel into automobiles—is only possible because of water. "Detroit" is French for "strait," a geographical term indicating a narrow waterway that connects two bodies of water. The contemporary spelling reveals the historic influence of the French who named this place *Détroit* in the late seventeenth century, in reference to the waterway, known today as the Detroit River, that provides a connection between Lake Huron and Lake Erie and serves as an international border to Canada. However, the historic pronunciation of the name, in French, "day-TWAH,"[1] is barely inflected in the contemporary standard English pronunciation of "duh-TROIT" or "DEE-troit." Even as Detroit's French history, palpable in street names like Gratiot, Beaubien, and Livernois (the Detroit pronunciation of Gratiot as "grah-SHIT" gets out-of-towners every time), has mostly disappeared from everyday recognition, the city's name and the waterway from which it comes have always served as a defining part of the city. Before *Détroit* the Anishinabeg Native Americans called this area "Bending River." For several hundred years the location was used as a meeting ground where the Anishinabeg tribes—Ojibwa (Chippewa), Ottawa, Potawatomi—came together along with the Wyandot, Iroquois, Fox, Miami, and Sauk to trade, fish, hunt, and meet with one another.[2] Later it was an important settlement and fort for the fur trade between Native Americans and the French.[3] Bending River served as a gathering place that was easily accessible by water and by land. Indeed, the main thoroughfares of the city today—Woodward, Gratiot, Grand River, and Michigan Avenue—follow the established contours of Native American routes that lead to and from the Detroit River, overland trails that connect the Great Lakes region and begin in present-day Illinois, Indiana, Ohio, Pennsylvania, and New York.[4] Detroit's promise then, as now, is dependent on its proximity to water.

As the stark divide between old Detroit and new Detroit seems to increasingly diverge in Detroit's representation as a postindustrial frontier, the work that has been done here, to analyze the role of cultural narratives as locations of racial formation in Detroit's past, present, and future, is all the more important. The way the world is seen emerges from a cacophony of stories, and in today's modes of storytelling that means car commercials, conversations among anonymous posters on an Internet forum, and magazine articles about urban pioneers. Thus they must be taken seriously, for what they say about the past, what they say about the present, and what they portend of the future. Throughout *Beautiful Wasteland* I have undertaken the task of delineating the role of popular narratives as locations of racial formation. In this way the everyday stories of place are the sites where one can most convincingly see the legacies and continuation of the racialization of place, even as legislated history and national narratives would claim that "racism is over." The stories examined here about Detroit create, reaffirm, recycle, and upcycle narratives of the city's past, present, and future. These are but a snapshot, showing just a slice of the many narratives of the city and the simultaneous universality and uniqueness each story represents.

The book began with an analysis of the story of exodus from the dangerous, crime-ridden, and increasingly black city of the late twentieth century and its complete ruin by the 1990s. The narrative moved then into the depictions of the city, even in the face of decline, as a location of rebirth and possibility before ultimately analyzing the rise of the twenty-first-century city. Pronouncements of rebirth, while seductive in their rendering, are very poor at concealing the decades-long disinvestment that lies beneath. While the much-hyped twenty-first-century story of Detroit as a postindustrial frontier suggests a new movement in the city's well-established narrative, I suggest here that this uncritical celebration of Detroit relies on an intentional perspective of seeing and not-seeing old Detroit. This book serves to pinpoint, then, the reality that even as the contemporary popular narrative would lead outsiders to believe that Detroit is the "it" location for new business development and DIY rebirth—a city that can be rebuilt one craft cocktail and entrepreneur at a time—Detroit's past, the long decades of willful disinvestment and racially incentivized departure of population, corporate tax base, and government corruption, are just below the surface of these narratives. The book urges readers to take a moment before heralding the rise of the city and illuminate what the new narratives continue to make invisible. Much as the narrative of Detroit as a location of super-cool old buildings and the American Dream revived persist, this book asks for a moment of pause in the unfurling of Detroit's present and future. We must take stock of the stories told about where we have been, where we are now, and think long and hard about how we imagine the future in this moment of growth.

Readers have arrived here, at the conclusion, with a sense of how contemporary Detroit is seen now, a reimagining of how Antoine Laumet de la Mothe Cadillac saw it in 1702: a beautiful and fertile land aside a waterway of paramount importance, a place to draw new inhabitants to. Detroit is the largest city in Michigan, a state that derives *its* name from the Chippewa words *Michi* (great/large) and *Gama* (lake), which signals the importance of water in the geographic legacy of the state as a whole. Michigan is a state formed of two peninsulas, bordered by four of the five Great Lakes, which as a whole comprise 21 percent of the world's freshwater and 84 percent of North America's surface freshwater.[5] More than three centuries after Cadillac's report to Paris outlined the beauty and fertility of the land adjacent to the river, Detroit's relationship to water remains a key issue.

Here then we come full circle—the beautiful wasteland, the hopeful possibility of the city, and the presumed exodus of the poor and working class if development succeeds. Detroit in the second decade of the twenty-first century is constructed by many as a place of beauty and possibility, in need of discipline. This narrative can be seen prominently in the water crisis that played out in the city of Detroit in 2014 and emerged as a resounding global narrative about the divisions between "new Detroit" and "old Detroit." In the spring of 2014, the Detroit Water and Sewerage Department began shutting off water to customers deemed "delinquent" on payment. The threshold for water shutoff: more than $150 and sixty days past due. According to the journalist Bill Mitchell, between March and August 2014 "nearly 19,500 Detroiters have had their water service interrupted."[6] The news of the shutoffs was widely covered in the media and prompted protests from residents and local, national, and international human rights activists. A panel of experts from the United Nations released a statement on June 25, 2014, saying, "Disconnecting water from people who cannot pay their bills is an affront to their human rights."[7] Many emphasized the cruel irony that a city within a state that is bordered by one of the largest freshwater reserves in the world is shutting off water to its residents.

The water shutoffs were part of the larger process of Detroit's bankruptcy plan, which was formally set into motion one year earlier. On Thursday, March 14, 2013, Michigan Governor Rick Snyder declared a state of emergency in Detroit and appointed Kevyn Orr as an emergency financial manager who would ultimately lead Detroit through a chapter 9 bankruptcy filing. Three days prior to this announcement, on Monday, March 11, former Detroit mayor Kwame Kilpatrick was convicted on federal charges of racketeering, fraud, and extortion, capping the end of a highly visible trial that outlined a salacious sexting scandal, a structure of financial kick-backs, and abuses of power.[8] One week before Kilpatrick's conviction thrust him and Detroit's derailment at the hands of corrupt city officials once again into national and international headlines, the *New York Times* ran the story "A Private Boom amid Detroit's Public Blight."[9]

As the city weaved its way through the bankruptcy filing and plan of adjustment to appease creditors, investors, and local elites alike, the resounding narrative of Detroit's troubles replayed again and again. Oftentimes blame was leveled at decades of mismanagement by city government.

And unsurprisingly, the blame of corruption and inept governance began with Mayor Coleman A. Young, the city's first black mayor, elected in 1973, and cycled all the way through to Kwame Kilpatrick. Mayor Kilpatrick began his term amid hope from supporters and fear from critics that his administration would bring a new energy to City Hall. He was nationally considered "one to watch" in the Democratic Party and his political future seemed so bright. However, even prior to the implosion of his career, Mayor Kilpatrick, dubbed by the media as "America's hip-hop mayor," was a frequent subject of racialized caricature, not for his work in City Hall but for the fascination of what reporters called his "bling" lifestyle.[10] Most media accounts of the state takeover of the city are preceded by a comment that links Kwame Kilpatrick's "irresponsibility" as contributing to the need for state takeover. While I am not suggesting that Kilpatrick was an excellent city executive, he stands in for the mainstream narrative as a prime example of the doggedly persistent narrative of black mismanagement in Detroit. And it is that narrative of mismanagement that undergirds the narrative need of the state to literally "take over" and discipline Detroit. The state and national media declared that Detroit's primarily black population and leadership cannot manage itself. In the midst of Detroit's slog through bankruptcy the city elected Mike Duggan as its seventy-fifth mayor. The most oft-cited headlines announcing Duggan's win did not include his plans for leading the city postbankruptcy or his plan for the first one hundred days; rather, the overwhelming news story of this election was "Detroit elects first white mayor in more than four decades."[11]

In September 2014 Detroit mayor Mike Duggan and the county executives of Wayne, Oakland, and Macomb Counties announced the formation of the Great Lakes Water Authority (GLWA)—a body that will lease the infrastructure currently owned by the Detroit Water and Sewerage Department. Critics and backers see this as the first step in the privatization of the public utility, arguably Detroit's most important resource. The memorandum of understanding approved on September 19, 2014, by Detroit City Council members in a 7-2 vote enabled metropolitan counties to lease the Detroit water system for the next forty years at $50 million a year. Although Detroit retains ownership of the system, each of the counties will have the authority to determine how the water is used and the rates of usage. The *control* of the system will now be placed with a six-member board representing the regional stakeholders: two members appointed by the mayor of Detroit, one member appointed by the governor, and one member appointed by each of the three counties involved in the agreement. The dilution of control from Detroit and the shared governance with the suburban counties that have long sought to distance themselves from the city represent a marked shift in the decades-long culture of divide between metropolitan Detroit and the city of Detroit.

The rationale for the GLWA regional agreement is seen as a compromise in the face of Detroit's bankruptcy. The politics are complex but the rationale for the city to enter into compromise often boils down to these facts: Detroit's system is old and in need of repair, as evidenced by the rash of water main breaks in the freezing temperatures of winter, and the bankrupt city has not performed the needed repairs and maintenance throughout the decades. Opponents see this as an assault under the cover of bankruptcy, the spiriting away of the control of one of the city's most valuable resources. Proponents insist that this move makes sense based on the idea that water delivery is not a city but a regional issue. I concur with both standpoints.

My concern here, however, is with the selectivity of metropolitan regional cooperation—compromise can be reached for a regional water system, but a compromise on a regional mass transit plan has never been possible. As discussed previously, the historic suburbanization of both home ownership and manufacturing was part of a willful division between metropolitan Detroit and the city, the legacies of which still reverberate today. More recently the conversation about the woefully inadequate regional transportation system was renewed when the *Detroit Free Press* ran a feature story about James Robertson, a man whose forty-six-mile round-trip commute from Detroit to his workplace in the suburbs includes a daily walk of twenty-one miles.[12] Part of the reason that Robertson's commute is so onerous is that for one seven-mile stretch there is no public transportation service at all. In Motor City, and especially if you are trying to get to and from its metropolitan suburbs, life without a car means a marathon commute each and every day. The point here is that cooperation for a regional transportation system to connect Detroit and metropolitan Detroit has failed again and again, yet this plan of regional cooperation for water was approved in such a rapid fashion with little time or space for public comment. The message is clear: metropolitan Detroit cooperation is hastened and easy to accommodate when it most benefits metropolitan Detroit.

As Detroit's present is in a moment of full-scale shift, the issue of water fuels both the promise of the city's past and the promise of the city's future. The beauty and fertility of the land that Antoine Laumet de la Mothe Cadillac noted over three hundred years ago was a direct result of both cultivation by the people who had long lived in the region and the sustainability of life provided by the river. The city will not be rebuilt because of the transport of finished goods and raw materials moving up and down the Detroit River, but if the last ten years are any indication it will rise again through the combination of innovation, entrepreneurial capital, and real estate development. This land is especially valuable since the December 2008 signing and ratification into state and federal law of the Great Lakes State Compact, which protects and keeps the water resources of the Great Lakes for the eight states and two Canadian provinces that border the lakes.[13]

The past haunts the future and the present in the devastatingly beautiful twentieth-century architecture and in the etymology of French and Native American place names pronounced with a distinctively Detroit twang. Most significantly, the vestiges of the past are apparent in the larger perception that Detroit is empty, potentially fertile land, barely populated and laid dormant, just waiting to be discovered and used to its full potential. Old Detroit is bankrupt, corrupt, unable to provide basic city services; new Detroit is gaining wealth, investment, and the invaluable cachet to draw a new population. The sticking point—the place through which this narrative of beautiful wasteland, Detroit as a renewed utopia, gets jammed up—is the legacy of Detroit for *all* Detroiters. As twenty-first-century Detroit is pointedly represented as "not about race" in the face of a twentieth century that was clearly about race, this past refuses to be silenced and made invisible. Even as we want to believe in the elemental power of the American Dream—the burning fire of determination, sustained by the life force of water—the centuries-old myths of the frontier are a place not only to foist dreams about possibility and growth but also to contain nightmares about discrimination and failure.

Acknowledgments

In a book about the narratives we tell, the backstory to this particular book is the kindness, generosity of spirit, and support that I have in my life.

This story begins first and foremost with the many Detroiters who have been in conversation with me. Although this list is too long to name, I want to thank a few people specifically: Darlene Hall, Deanna Neely, Jan and Jesse Adler, Jerry Glowzinski, Jessi Quizar, Scott Kurashige, and Michelle Cowin-Mensah. Thank you especially to my grandparents, the late Richard and Dorothy Hall. Growing up with their stories made postwar Detroit come to life as they regaled us with tales of their moves to Detroit, work in the auto plants, and the fun they had exploring the booming city. Thank you to Beverly Manick, the late Rowland Watkins, and the many students and staff I worked with at Young Detroit Builders in the late 1990s and early 2000s through an internship facilitated by the University of Michigan's residential college. The summers I worked there were a turning point for me in thinking about the power of place. Thank you not only for your frankness and acceptance all those years ago when "some Asian girl from Royal Oak" walked in the doors to learn with you but also for sharing your stories and listening to me as I shared my own.

I have benefited enormously from the generosity and mentorship of three wonderful scholars and people who have guided me through this career, as well as this book, with just the right amount of candor, critique, and kindness. I hope to one day be the kind of mentor that these three people have each been to me. George Lipsitz provided generous feedback on early drafts and encouragement in my growth as a scholar. His words of advice, and long view of both scholarship and career, have proven instrumental. Lisa Sun-Hee Park has traveled this decade-long road with me, navigating the way forward with sharp wit and candor. Her unfailing belief in me and reality checks dispensed with wry humor have proved crucial to my continued entanglement in academia. Natalia Molina's unwavering support and steadfast belief in my work has been essential to my development as a scholar. The hard questions and good advice dispensed over glasses of wine and in the hallways of conference hotels have helped me immeasurably throughout the years.

It is true that the relationships we build in graduate school are the ones to which we return again and again. My years at UC San Diego enabled the exploration of ideas and conversations that knew no boundaries. I thank the graduate students and faculty that I had the privilege to be in conversation with in the Department of Ethnic Studies. This book would not be possible without the learning that took place during the initial research and writing, deftly guided by a group of scholars that serves as an extraordinary example of the best kinds of scholarship and mentorship. That all-star group—Natalia Molina, Lisa Sun-Hee Park, Luis Alvarez, Yen Le Espiritu, and Adria Imada—was enormously generous in their critical engagement in getting me to think about that "first draft." Thank you to Martha Luna, Angela Kong, Myrna García, and Kate Levitt for friendship and support at that time and as it continues today. I thank my writing group—Mariola Alvarez, Tania Jabour, and José Fuste—who kicked my butt every other Tuesday night as we parsed our way through research, the job market, and life. I also thank Long Bui, who was a great writing partner and continues to be the best conference buddy ever. Adria Imada and Meg Wesling offered wise advice about how to go about publishing a book. Martha Escobar and Traci Brynne Voyles have been one step ahead of me in our postgraduate school careers and have shared generously their experiences of the process of book publication and navigating the tenure track.

At Bowling Green State University I have enjoyed working with the students, faculty, and staff in the School of Cultural and Critical Studies and the Department of Popular Culture. I would like to thank Marilyn Motz for her open door policy, one that I miss greatly since her retirement.

Thank you to Susana Peña and Andy Schocket for helpful guidance. Jolie Sheffer has been an invaluable mentor and friend. Thank you to the BGSU Women of Color Alliance for creating community and so much more. Thank you to Lisa Hanasono, Anne Mitchell, Clayton Rosati, Angela Nelson, Luis Moreno, Vibha Bhalla, Esther Clinton, Jeremy Wallach, DeeDee Wentland, Stephanie Rader, Sarah Smith Rainey, Thomas Edge, Bill Albertini, and Matt Donahue.

I have presented portions of the project at the University of Michigan's American Culture Colloquium, the University of California at Santa Barbara's School of Unlimited Learning, and Bowling Green State University's Popular Culture Colloquium, as well as at the American Studies Association, the Association of American Geographers, the Urban History Association, and Wayne State University's Humanities Conferences. I thank commentators, co-panelists, and audience members for the questions and comments I have received over the years. These forums have proven to be productive and constructive venues to take these ideas off the page and into the world. For financial support of the research I would like to thank the University of California's Fletcher Jones Fellowship, the Bentley Historical Library Bordin-Gillette Researcher Travel Fellowship, Bowling Green State University's Office of the Vice President for Research and Economic Development, Building Strength Grant, and the Stoddard and O'Neill Endowment for the Study of Popular Culture.

At the University of Minnesota Press, I would like to thank Richard Morrison for taking my book through the early channels, finding two excellent reviewers and ensuring that my book was well cared for during transition. Jason Weidemann picked up my project and shepherded it through the editorial process with kindness, candor, and skill. Erin Warholm-Wohlenhaus's attention to detail, organization, and timeliness of response to all my many questions was essential to the ins and outs of actually getting all the pieces to press, and I greatly appreciate her thoroughness. The two anonymous reviewers who read the manuscript gave generously of time and engagement to make this book all the better, and I appreciate their constructive critiques and support for the project. I would like to thank Alicia Gomez for overseeing the production side of publication and the many members of the production, design, and marketing teams that did the work of transmuting words into an actual book.

Thank you to Sheila McMahon for her sharp eye and careful copyediting of the manuscript.

I am thankful for many colleagues who have been in conversation with my work. I know that the finished book is much better for their engagement and I take full responsibility for any oversights and errors that may remain. Bill Albertini, Clayton Rosati, Jolie Sheffer, Martha Escobar, Traci Voyles, Kate Levitt, Anne Mitchell, Allie Tyler-Fristch, and Stephanie Langin-Hooper each read early drafts of chapters, and I thank them for helping to sharpen ideas. David Lobenstine's critical eye and keen sensibilities greatly improved the book. Thank you seems insufficient for the love, labor, and critical engagement that Mariola Alvarez and Tania Jabour provided over the years. I truly think that between the two of them, they may have read every single sentence (fragment and run-on alike!) that I have written since 2009. In addition to reading drafts of each chapter, they both also read and commented on the entire manuscript.

The long haul of writing the book was sustained by the good cheer and unyielding support of lifetime friends. I am so thankful for the ways in which my life is enriched by friendship and the enormous amounts of laughter and good food that come along with it. Thank you to Alanna Aiko Moore and Jan Estrellado, Jan and Jess Adler, Angela Ball, Jerry Glowzinski, Killy Scheer, Niketa Kulkarni, Shreya Shah Sasaki, Jenna Couzens, Rupa Patel, Amy and Marc Abrams, Erin and Chris Henson, and the extended Guanco-Atkinson-Mayo crew. Khine Aung, Colleen Hilton, and Rupal Shah are the best friends I could ever imagine. Their love, support, and sound advice are indispensable as we make our way through the decades.

At the heart of this tale is my own curiosity of how my family from the South and my sister and I, both adopted from Korea, all wound up in the inner-ring suburbs of Detroit. Although I don't actually address this question, the stories told throughout in so many ways begin there. And at the culmination of the biggest story I've told thus far, my biggest thanks of all go to my family. Good times spent sharing stories and our mutual love of history with Marsha, Marshall, Kathy, Ella, and Chloe Williams support and sustain me in so many ways. Joanne Kinney remains an inspiration as she lives her eighties like she did each every decade prior. I have learned so much from her grit, commonsense, unmatched fortitude, and tried and true method to making pie crusts. Robert Kinney has supported my educational aspirations from the earliest age, and I am thankful for his unwavering belief in me. Amanda, André, Archer, and Cresslin Guanco bring laughter, spontaneity, and dessert into my life. Their love, support, and reminders to have a little fun now and again are immeasurable. Thank you to my mom, Darlene Hall, for her unfailing support as I push my boundaries and in all the many steps I take. Her generosity in sharing her car, house, and time with me on my many research trips home were key to completing initial research, but it is her belief and encouragement to always pursue my biggest dreams that enabled me to embark on this work at all. My biggest thank you of all is to John Williams, the person who has lived not only with this book but with this author, each and every day. His unfailing support and boundless creativity motivate and inspire me. This book has his imprint all over it; indeed, it is a compilation of short stories and big ideas. Thank you for the laughter, love, and possibility that you bring into my world. Thank you for being you.

Notes

Introduction

1. John Huey, "To Our Readers: Assignment Detroit," *Time,* October 5, 2009, 4.

2. Ibid.

3. Jeff T. Watrick, "Time Puts Bow atop Their Assignment Detroit Project with Econ Club Panel," MLive, November 11, 2010.

4. Huey, "To Our Readers," 4.

5. Woodward Avenue, also known as M-1, starts at the Detroit River and runs twenty-seven miles to the city of Pontiac. Woodward is the geographic border between the east and west sides of Detroit. It also has the designation of being the location of the first paved concrete highway in the world and the site of the first three-color stoplight in the nation. MDOT, "Woodward Avenue: A Road to the Heart and Soul of America," *MDOT Today* (Winter 2003), https://www.michigan.gov/documents/MDOT_Woodward_Heart_and_Soul_170072_7.pdf.

6. The idea of "metro Detroiter" links to the idea of the metropolitan region more broadly, a designation that the U.S. Office of Management and Budget uses to refer to a central city "plus adjacent territory that has high degree of social and economic integration." OMB Bulletin no. 13-01 (February 28, 2013), http://www.whitehouse.gov/sites/default/files/omb/bulletins/2013/b13-01.pdf, 2. This murky designation of what the metropolitan region is has different "official" meanings but in my experience is primarily used to refer to the three counties—Wayne, Oakland, and Macomb—that include suburban communities within about a thirty-five-mile radius of the city of Detroit. Detroit is part of Wayne County. However, the Office of Management and Budget includes the three counties named above as well as the counties of Genesee, Lapeer, St. Clair, Livingston, Washtenaw, and Monroe, which are all within a seventy-five-mile radius of Detroit.

7. Yves Marchand and Romain Meffre, "Detroit's Beautiful, Horrible Decline," *Time,* March 2009; Nicole Hardesty, "Haunting Images of Detroit's Decline," *Huffington Post,* March 23, 2011; Olympia Snowe, "Detroit's Bankruptcy," *Colbert Report,* July 25, 2013.

8. David Harvey, *A Brief History of Neoliberalism* (Oxford: Oxford University Press, 2005), 2.

9. See Lisa Duggan, *The Twilight of Equality? Neoliberalism, Cultural Politics, and the Attack on Democracy* (Boston: Beacon Press, 2003), and Jodi Melamed, *Represent and Destroy: Rationalizing Violence in the New Racial Capitalism* (Minneapolis: University of Minnesota Press, 2011).

10. Ze'ev Chafets, *Devil's Night: And Other True Tales of Detroit* (New York: Random House, 1990). Though *Devil's Night* was quickly recognized by scholars and most everyday Detroiters as a highly sensationalistic account of the city by someone who hadn't lived within its vicinity for nearly two decades, it is still widely referenced and in print. In some ways, Chafets laid the groundwork for the contemporary genre of Detroit "returnee" books by former Detroiters moving back to write popular accounts of the city. See, for example, Mark Binelli, *Detroit City Is the Place to Be: The Afterlife of an American Metropolis* (New York: Metropolitan Books, 2012), and Charlie LeDuff, *Detroit: An American Autopsy* (New York: Penguin, 2013). Although these more contemporary accounts speak to larger institutional forces of race and class that contributed to Detroit's decline and are notable for the emphasis on possibility for Detroit's future, these books, like Chafets's account, often gain traction because of the author's credibility as a "Detroiter." And, as should be obvious from this introduction, I recognize my own position as a metropolitan Detroiter in writing this book. Yet I offer it not as an example of expert "truth" of the region based on my local experience but as a way to understand my relationship to the region as fundamental in influencing my worldview. In many ways I am most interested in how Detroit and its narrative is portrayed outside the region, asking how Detroit's narrative-at-large shifted, since this shift happened rather rapidly during the decade and a half I lived outside the region. In full disclosure, this book was written and researched in San Diego, Detroit, Ann Arbor, Royal Oak (Michigan), Bowling Green (Ohio), and various points in between.

11. See, for example, the August 27, 1965, *Life* magazine cover featuring the Watts Riot.

12. Reynolds Farley, Sheldon Danziger, and Harry J. Holzer, *Detroit Divided* (New York Russell Sage Foundation, 2000), 2.

13. See, for example, Catherine Cangany, *Frontier Seaport: Detroit's Transformation into an Atlantic Entrepôt* (Chicago: University of Chicago Press, 2014); Brian Leigh Dunnigan, *Frontier Metropolis: Picturing Early Detroit, 1701–1838*

(Detroit: Wayne State University Press, 2001); Denver Brunsman, Joel Stone, and Douglas Fisher, eds., *Border Crossings: The Detroit River Region in the War of 1812* (Detroit: Wayne State University Press, 2012); R. Alan Douglas, *Uppermost Canada: The Western District and the Detroit Frontier, 1800–1850* (Detroit: Wayne State University Press, 2001); Kenneth E. Lewis, *West to Far Michigan: Settling the Lower Peninsula, 1815–1860* (East Lansing: Michigan State University Press, 2002).

14. Kent Walker, "The Detroit River International Crossing Bridge: A Stakeholder Analysis of How One Wealthy Individual Could Exercise His Will against Many," *Administrative Sciences of Canada Conference* (June 8, 2013): 1–34 (quote on 4).

15. CBC News, "The Canada-U.S. Border: By the numbers," December 7, 2011, http://www.cbc.ca/news/canada/the-canada-u-s-border-by-the-numbers-1.999207.

16. See, for example, Olivier Zunz, *The Changing Face of Inequality: Urbanization, Industrial Development, and Immigrants in Detroit, 1880–1920* (Chicago: University of Chicago Press, 1982) for a social history of migration and growing population in the city of Detroit during the time of rapid industrialization.

17. Frank B. Woodford and Arthur M. Woodford, *All Our Yesterdays: A Brief History of Detroit* (Detroit: Wayne State University Press, 1969), 200–212.

18. See, for example, Donald Finlay Davis, *Conspicuous Production: Automobiles and Elites in Detroit, 1899–1933* (Philadelphia: Temple University Press, 1988).

19. Population statistics are from June Manning Thomas, *Redevelopment and Race: Planning a Finer City in Postwar Detroit* (Baltimore, Md.: Johns Hopkins University Press, 1997), 14. In 1900 Detroit's population was 285,704 people. The 1910 population was 465,766 and more than doubled by 1920 to 993,678. The population grew by over 50 percent by 1930 to 1,568,662, still grew slightly during the Depression to 1,623,452, and after World War II to an all-time high of 1,849,568 by 1950.

20. The Five Dollar Day, announced on January 5, 1914, was not the actual wage but included profit-sharing instituted by the company in hopes of investing workers with a sense of ownership in the product, and perhaps more importantly, Stephen Meyer argues that "the Five Dollar Day attempted to solve attitudinal and behavioral problems with an effort to change the worker's domestic environment" (6). Ford believed that every man was entitled to their base wage, which at that time was $2.50, but the balance of the amount that made up the other half of the Five Dollar Day was only available after proved and continued investigation to ensure that the workers demonstrated "thrift, good habits, and good home conditions" and were saving toward a home or

supporting a family adequately, as well as proving themselves to be punctual and effective workers. To that end, the average worker was not only observed on the job but also subjected to visits and investigations by the Ford Motor Company's sociology department. The investigations were carried out only for those who made $200 per month or less; anyone outside of that wage bracket was exempted and not subject to the company investigating their personal life. See, for example, Steve Babson, *Working Detroit: The Making of a Union Town* (1984; repr., Detroit: Wayne State University Press, 1986); Stephen Meyer III, *The Five Dollar Day: Labor Management and Social Control in the Ford Motor Company* (Albany: State University of New York Press, 1981); and Clarence Hooker, *Life in the Shadows of the Crystal Palace, 1910–1927: Ford Workers in the Model T Era* (Bowling Green, Ohio: Bowling Green State University Popular Press, 1997) for more information on Ford during the 1900s–1920s.

21. Jobs were readily available for American men, and increasingly so for white ethnic men. Nonwhite men were typically able to access work but found themselves frequently in the "hardest and dirtiest jobs." Women had varying opportunities for work and nonwhite women almost always worked as domestics or laundresses. See, for example, Forrester B. Washington, *The Negro in Detroit: A Survey of Conditions of a Negro Group in a Northern Industrial Center during the War Prosperity Period* (Detroit: Research Bureau, Associated Charities of Detroit, 1920); Babson, *Working Detroit*; John C. Dancy, *Sand against the Wind: The Memoirs of John C. Dancy* (Detroit: Wayne State University Press, 1966); Zunz, *The Changing Face of Inequality.*

22. In order to realize this idea of home ownership and through it access to the American Dream, steady work at a regular rate was required to allow the working class to enter into homeownership. Throughout the nineteenth century and into the early twentieth century, homes were typically purchased by the wealthy outright or by the working person through land contract. It was not until after World War I that mortgages were popularized, due to the fact that consumer credit was more readily available and the diminishing stigma attached to consumer debt and financing, as well as rising costs. See, for example, Kenneth T. Jackson, *Crabgrass Frontier: The Suburbanization of the United States* (New York: Oxford University Press, 1985), and Lendol Calder, *Financing the American Dream: A Cultural History of Consumer Credit* (Princeton, N.J.: Princeton University Press, 1999). In fact, the system set in place by the automotive industry provided a path to two important factors in the increase and availability of consumer credit: first, the mode through which some workers could earn a regular wage; and second, the increasing popularity and destigmatizing of buying on credit, resulting in the wide-scale financing of new cars. Car manufacturers were smart in that through financing they were able

to sell more cars to people who could not afford to buy them outright; as Lendol Calder's work reveals, "By 1924, almost three out of four new cars were bought 'on time.' . . . No other consumer durable good accounted for nearly as much consumer debt. . . . Without credit financing, the automobile would not so quickly have reached, and perhaps never have reached, a true mass market. . . . Installment credit and the automobile were both cause and consequence of each other's success" (*Financing the American Dream,* 184). As people began to buy cars, they were able to move farther out of the city center, farther away from jobs that before were accessible only by streetcar. As the less populated outer areas and neighborhoods with single-family homes became available, more and more people were interested in buying homes outside of the city center.

23. "Arsenal of democracy" refers to its role in producing munitions for World War I and World War II as the factories of the automobile producers were retooled to produce airplanes and ground vehicles.

24. Steve Macek, *Urban Nightmares: The Media, the Right, and the Moral Panic over the City* (Minneapolis: University of Minnesota Press, 2006), xii–xvi.

25. Neil Smith, *The New Urban Frontier: Gentrification and the Revanchist City* (London: Routledge, 1996).

26. Ibid., xvi.

27. George Lipsitz, "The Racialization of Space and the Spatialization of Race: Theorizing the Hidden Architecture of Landscape," *Landscape Journal* 26, no. 1 (1997): 10–23 (quote on 12).

28. George Lipsitz, *How Racism Takes Place* (Philadelphia: Temple University Press, 2011).

29. See Michael Omi and Howard Winant, *Racial Formation in the United States: From the 1960s to the 1990s* (New York: Routledge, 1994). Omi and Winant argue that racial formation is a "sociohistorical process by which racial categories are created, inhabited, transformed, and destroyed" through "a process of historically situated projects . . . and the evolution of hegemony" (55–56). They emphasize the idea that "race is a matter of both social structure and cultural representation" (56).

30. I am not trying to prove that cultural forces are more determinative than material forces, but cultural forces operate both within and outside material forces. I take a cue from Lisa Lowe and David Lloyd, who state: "Rather than adopting the understanding of culture as one sphere in a set of differentiated spheres and practices, we discuss 'culture' as a terrain in which politics, culture, and the economic form an inseparable dynamic." Lisa Lowe and David Lloyd, "Introduction," in *The Politics of Culture in the Shadow of Capital,* ed. Lisa Lowe and David Lloyd (Durham, N.C.: Duke University Press, 1997), 1–32 (quote on 1).

31. Lisa Lowe, *Immigrant Acts: On Asian American Cultural Politics* (Durham, N.C.: Duke University Press, 1996), 2.

32. Helen Heran Jun, *Race for Citizenship: Black Orientalism and Asian Uplift from Pre-Emancipation to Neoliberal America* (New York: New York University Press, 2011), 5.

33. The 2000 census for Royal Oak, Michigan, enumerated a population that was 94.8 percent white. See "Data Set: Census 2010 and Census 2000 Summary File 1," http://www.ci.royal-oak.mi.us/general-information/census-data.

34. Karen Dybis, "Five Years Ago, 'Time' Bought a House Here . . . and So Much Has Changed since Then," *Detroit Unspun* (blog), June 6, 2014, http://blog.thedetroithub.com/2014/06/06/five-years-ago-time-bought-a-house-here-and-so-much-has-changed-since-then/.

1. It's Turned into a Race Thing

1. See http://www.city-data.com/forum/detroit/925207-i-found-my-old-house-detroit.html. I am silently making minor spelling and typographical corrections to the quoted user posts from the City-Data.com forum. I have identified each post in the thread by numerical sequencing beginning with post 1 and extending as new posts are added. All times listed are local time, Eastern Daylight Time (EDT), which began on Sunday, March 14, 2010, and ended on Sunday, November 7, 2010, when Eastern Standard Time (EST) resumed. The verification of times and dates occurred during April 2016 when local time used was also EDT. When a user is logged on the posts are numbered. However, when viewing a thread without a member login the posts are not numbered. I have included both time and post number for ease of viewing. All posts can be accessed from this same URL.

2. Post 1, March 18, 2010, 6:30 p.m. I have attempted to write this chapter not using any gender pronouns unless the poster or other forum users identify a user with a gender pronoun. In the case of this user, Remisc, a gender pronoun is never self-identified, but SCBaker, another forum user, identifies Remisc as "she" in post 83, March 27, 2010 1:07 p.m.

3. Post 106, March 31, 2010, 5:50 p.m.

4. See Thomas J. Sugrue, *The Origins of the Urban Crisis: Race and Inequality in Postwar Detroit* (Princeton, N.J.: Princeton University Press, 1996), and David M. Freund, *Colored Property: State Policy and White Racial Politics in Suburban America* (Chicago: University of Chicago Press, 2007).

5. Svetlana Boym, "Nostalgia and Its Discontents," *Hedgehog Review* 9, no. 2 (Summer 2007): 7–18 (quote on 12).

6. Instagram went live in October 2010.

7. However, 2010 was a unique time for web design; as consumers increasingly began accessing the Internet on first-generation mobile devices, many websites had to be retooled as many early mobile devices could not run plug-in software.

8. As of March 25, 2016 the thread is still available and open to new posts.

9. During that time there were posts made by twenty-five different posters; however, the discussion was dominated by a handful of posters. Seven posters each made 6 or more posts during that time and collectively they posted 81 of these first 109 posts: MaryleelI, 20 posts; SCBaker, 14 posts; scolls, 13 posts; reconmark, 12 posts; Remisc, 10 posts; Heatherj43, 6 posts; usroute10, 6 posts. The other eighteen posters made the remaining twenty-eight posts.

10. The longest period of nonactivity is twenty-one months, between post 192, January 12, 2013, 5:37 p.m., and post 193, October 14, 2014, 10:18 a.m. The drop in activity on this thread, like most any Internet thread, is likely a result of the bump that the newest comments and most active threads receive.

11. On the thread the term *former Detroiter* refers to a former occupant of a house in the city proper, as opposed to someone that may still be living in metropolitan Detroit at large.

12. Post 84, March 27, 2010, 3:45 p.m.

13. One of the earliest community-wide experiments in Internet adoption is the Blacksburg Electronic Village. Formed in the early 1990s, the Blacksburg Electronic Village was a partnership between Virginia Tech, Bell Atlantic Company of Virginia, and the town of Blacksburg to wire the city and create a community network for government information, civic information, and business information specific to the city and community. See David Silver, "Margins in the Wires: Looking for Race, Gender, and Sexuality in the Blacksburg Electronic Village," in *Race in Cyberspace,* ed. Beth E. Kolko, Lisa Nakurma, and Gilbert B. Rodman (New York: Routledge, 2000), 133–50. Silver shows that even as the project had the goal to be a pioneer in the field of Internet and digital connectivity on a community-wide basis, the same structures of stratification and marginalization that appeared in real life were replicated in the formation of the Blacksburg digital structure.

14. Boym, "Nostalgia and Its Discontents," 7.

15. Renato Rosaldo, *Culture & Truth: The Remaking of Social Analysis* (Boston: Beacon Press, 1993), 69–70.

16. Ibid., 70.

17. Post 1, March 18, 2010, 6:30 p.m.

18. Joe T. Darden and Richard Thomas, *Detroit: Race Riots, Racial Conflicts, and Efforts to Bridge the Racial Divide* (East Lansing: Michigan State University Press, 2013), 314–17.

19. Population statistics are from Thomas, *Redevelopment and Race,* 14. See note 19 in the introduction for a breakdown of population by decades.

20. For example, the black population in 1910 was 5,741 people, accounting for 1.2 percent of the total population, and by 1940 the black population numbered 149,119 people and represented 9.2 percent of the total population. See U.S. Census Bureau, Table 23, "Michigan—Race and Hispanic Origin for Selected Large Cities and Other Places: Earliest Census to 1990," http://www.census.gov/population/www/documentation/twps0076/MItab.pdf. On racial segregation and clusters, see, for example, Zunz, *The Changing Face of Inequality.*

21. David Allen Levine, *Internal Combustion: The Races in Detroit, 1915–1926* (Westport, Conn.: Greenwood Press, 1976), 50.

22. Ossian and Gladys Sweet purchased a home in 1925 in an area that was widely assumed to be "all white." When the Sweets moved into the home a mob of whites surrounded the home and began stoning the house. After two days of physical and emotional attack, one of the ten people inside the Sweets' home shot into the mob, which resulted in the death of one man and the injury of another, and the arrest and trial of the Sweets and their friends. The first trial resulted in a hung jury and in the next trial the defendants were acquitted. This case set precedence, and is one of the first cases where blacks were not accused in the defense of their own property. While this defense of property had long been justifiable for white men, Dr. Sweet's case was shrouded by a city in which many felt that blacks did not have the right to buy property in a white neighborhood. Despite the eventual acquittal of the Sweets and their friends in 1926, the battle over housing access and right to property raged on for decades to come. See, for example, Kevin Boyle, *Arc of Justice: A Saga of Race, Civil Rights, and Murder in the Jazz Age* (New York: Henry Holt, 2004), and Phyllis Vine, *One Man's Castle: Clarence Darrow in Defense of the American Dream* (New York: Amistad, 2004), for in-depth examinations of the events and trial surrounding the Sweet case.

23. The 1933 National Industrial Recovery Act created the Housing Division of the Public Works Administration (PWA). The act "instructed the PWA to engage in construction, reconstruction, alteration, or repair under public regulation or control of low-cost housing and slum-clearance projects along with traditional government building projects such as highways and public buildings." Gail Radford, "The Federal Government and Housing during the Great Depression," in *From Tenements to the Taylor Homes: In Search of an Urban Housing Policy in Twentieth-Century America,* ed. John F. Bauman, Roger Biles, and Kristin M. Szylvian (University Park: Pennsylvania State University Press, 2000), 102–20 (quote on 104). On the heels of the passage of the National Recovery Act, the Detroit Housing Commission was established on November

24, 1933. Following the announcement, the Federal Emergency Housing Commission allocated the City of Detroit $3,200,000 for slum clearance and the construction of low-rent housing. The Detroit Housing Commission was officially charged with the development and administration of federally aided low-cost housing upon approval of the Detroit Common Council on January 15, 1934. "The History, Organization, and Function of the Detroit Housing Commission," July 1963, Carl Almblad Collection, Box 13, Folder 7, Detroit Housing Commission History, Walter P. Reuther Library, Wayne State University. The 1933 act ultimately laid the groundwork for the Wagner Steagall Act of 1937, which established the National Housing Authority.

24. For an in-depth discussion of race relations and the Sojourner Truth Homes situation, see Dominic Capeci, *Race Relations in Wartime Detroit: The Sojourner Truth Housing Controversy of 1942* (Philadelphia: Temple University Press, 1984).

25. Quoted in Bette Smith Jenkins, "The Racial Policies of the Detroit Housing Commission and Their Administration" (MA thesis, Wayne State University, Detroit, 1950), 146.

26. Freund, *Colored Property,* 15.

27. The Home Owners' Loan Corporation (HOLC) worked in conjunction with banks and real estate agencies across the country to draw up area maps that graded neighborhoods from A to D. The neighborhoods deemed in "decline" and a poor investment were given a D rating and colored in red on the map, hence the practice of "redlining." A key factor in determining the rating was race of the population. For example, as David Freund shows, "in the HOLC's 1939 survey of Detroit, neighborhoods described as having a 'Negro concentration' or viewed by appraisers as an 'area developing as a negro colony' automatically received a D rating" (114). More than a red code on a map, the D rating resulted in the widespread belief that these were "risky neighborhoods," meaning that it was difficult for individuals, builders, and developers to access mortgages or financing for properties located in the redlined area.

28. Freund, *Colored Property,* 177.

29. During the first 109 posts, MaryleeII contributes twenty separate posts and ultimately posts forty-two times during the entirety of the thread. Given the user name of "MaryleeII" and the multiple references of other posters to MaryleeII using the gendered pronouns of "her" and "she," for ease of the discussion I will also apply these gender pronouns to this user.

30. Post 14, March 20, 2010, 12:52 p.m.

31. Post 22, March 20, 2010, 10:37 p.m.

32. Post 20, March 20, 2010, 8:38 p.m.

33. Post 22, March 20, 2010, 10:37 p.m.

34. Freund, *Colored Property,* 23.

35. Sugrue, *The Origins of the Urban Crisis,* 43.

36. Melvin L. Oliver and Thomas M. Shapiro, *Black Wealth/White Wealth: A New Perspective on Racial Inequality* (New York: Routledge, 2006).

37. See, for example, George Lipsitz, *The Possessive Investment in Whiteness: How White People Profit from Identity Politics* (Philadelphia: Temple University Press, 1998), and Oliver and Shapiro, *Black Wealth/White Wealth.*

38. Lipsitz, *The Possessive Investment in Whiteness,* 6.

39. Post 64, March 25, 2010, 8:21 p.m.

40. See Sugrue, *The Origins of the Urban Crisis,* 194–97.

41. For example, June Manning Thomas shows that in 1940, "two-thirds of Detroit's central business district buildings were over fifty years old." Thomas, *Redevelopment and Race,* 14.

42. Ibid., 84.

43. Freund, *Colored Property,* 23.

44. Ibid.

45. Post 17, March 20, 2010, 7:02 p.m.

46. Becky M. Nicolaides and Andrew Wiese, "Postwar America: Suburban Apotheosis," in *The Suburb Reader,* ed. Becky M. Nicolaides and Andrew Wiese (New York: Routledge, 2006), 257–59 (quote on 257).

47. Ibid., 257–58.

48. Becky M. Nicolaides and Andrew Wiese, "Introduction," in Nicolaides and Wiese, *The Suburb Reader,* 1–10 (quote on 2).

49. Freund, *Colored Property,* 24. The house I grew up in, a ranch-style brick home built in 1956, is 1,240 square feet and representative of the architectural style and scale of the neighborhood.

50. East Detroit/Eastpointe is a small city, census 2000 population of 34,077, that borders Detroit. In 1992 the city officially changed its name to "Eastpointe" to clarify that it was not part of Detroit but an independent city.

51. Post 9, March 19, 2010, 4:15 p.m.

52. Although SCBaker does not directly say in this post or in later posts that he is white, the history of Eastpointe as a primarily white community is borne out in its census 2000 demographics, which counted a population that was 92.1 percent white, evidence of the long-standing majority white population of this city.

53. Post 9, March 19, 2010, 4:15 p.m.

54. Post 1, March 18, 2010, 6:30 p.m.

55. All population statistics in this paragraph are from Darden and Thomas, *Detroit,* 242 (suburbs), or U.S. Census Bureau, "Table 23" (city).

56. The *Shelley v. Kraemer* decision is widely considered a landmark ruling in equal housing and often touted as the end of racial restrictions to home ownership through the court's ruling that it is illegal to *enforce* racial covenants. However, in practice, the ruling made the enforcement of covenants inviolable by law but did not outlaw covenants themselves, only their enforcement.

57. Darden and Thomas, *Detroit*, 243, 242.

58. U.S. Census Bureau, State & County QuickFacts: Detroit (city), Michigan, http://quickfacts.census.gov/qfd/states/26/2622000.html.

59. Freund, *Colored Property*, 38.

60. Post 30, March 22, 2010, 9:40 p.m.

61. I do wonder if this is a slip of the brain/keyboard, as the Detroit area has a much larger population of immigrants from Iraq than Iran. According to Kim Schompeyer, "Using the 2005 American Community Survey (ACS) (U.S. Census bureau 2006) . . . the Detroit area Arab community was estimated to be 179,056" (35), and as detailed in the Detroit Arab American Survey of 2003, fully 32 percent of the Detroit Arab population is of Iraqi origin (36). Kim Schompeyer, "Arab Detroit after 9/11," in *Arab Detroit 9/11: Life in the Terror Decade*, ed. Nabeel Abraham, Sally Howell, and Andrew Shryock (Detroit: Wayne State University Press, 2011), 29–63.

62. Office of the United Nations High Commissioner for Refugees, "Refugees," http://www.unhcr.org/pages/49c3646c125.html.

63. Posts 17, 22, 26, March 20, 2010.

64. Posts 31–106, March 23–31, 2010.

65. Posts 31–74, March 23–25, 2010.

66. Post 31, March 23, 2010, 3:29 p.m.

67. Post 32, March 23, 2010, 4:41 p.m.

68. Post 33, March 23, 2010, 5:38 p.m.

69. This post in particular is filled with many typographical errors and is reproduced as originally typed.

70. Post 34, March 23, 2010, 11:28 p.m.

71. Post 36, March 24, 2010, 12:42 a.m.

72. In Detroit history, the role of the word *negro* lives large in the transcript and recall of the 1952 questioning and testimony of Coleman A. Young by the House Un-American Activities Committee (HUAC). As the Detroit mayor from 1974 to 1994, Young recalls the following exchange in his autobiography, *Hard Stuff: The Autobiography of Mayor Coleman Young* (New York: Viking Books, 1994). The HUAC's chief counsel, Frank Tavenner questioned Young as follows:

"'Have you been a member of the Communist Party?'

'For the same reason, I refuse to answer that question.'

'You told us,' said Tavenner in his plantation dialect, 'you were the executive secretary of the National Niggra Congress—'

'That word is "Negro," not "Niggra."'

'I said 'Negro.' I think you are mistaken.'

'I hope I am. Speak more clearly.'"

73. Post 36, March 24, 2010, 12:42 a.m.

74. Ibid.

75. Ibid.

76. Post 39, March 24, 2010, 9:08 a.m.

77. Posts 44, 47–58, 63, March 24–26, 2010.

78. Posts 62, 70–71, March 25, 2010 (reconmark); Posts 39–40, 42, 59, March 24, 2010 (SCBaker); Posts 41, 45–46, 61, 64–65, 67, March 24–25, 2010 (MaryleeII); Post 43, March 24, 2010, 4:07 p.m. (usroute10); Posts 69, 73, March 25, 2010 (ilovemycomputer90); Posts 37–38, March 24, 2010 (RememberMee); Post 68, March 25, 2010, 9:02 p.m. (meemy); Post 72, March 25, 2010, 9:34 p.m. (omckenzie710); Post 74, March 25, 2010, 11:06 p.m. (malamute).

79. Post 41, March 24, 2010, 12:59 p.m.

80. Post 43, March 24, 2010, 4:07 p.m.

81. Post 62, March 25, 2010, 8:01 p.m.

82. Post 73, March 25, 2010, 10:35 p.m.

83. Post 75, March 26, 2010, 2:58 a.m. While the City-Data forums are based on the individual contributions of users, there are moderators who exist within the community forums as both participants and people who monitor the discussions. Moderators have the ability to "close down" discussions, which in effect disables anyone from further posting on a thread. According to the forum FAQ section, each of the geographical states has approximately two moderators who monitor the threads and each moderator typically works 1–4 states. The Michigan forums, of which the Detroit forum is part, has two moderators, "Yac" and "magellan." In reply to a general website question as to how moderators are chosen, one of the moderators said, "Moderators are chosen by the current team when and where they are needed. There are no written criteria so I guess you're right—they're no different than the rest of us. We tend to choose calmer people who rarely engage in heated debates, are somewhat diplomatic and are able to spend a lot of time here." Moderator response in the "About the Forum FAQ," http://www.city-data.com/forum/faq/, May 18, 2007, 7:31a.m.

84. Post 76, March 26, 2010, 5:56 a.m.

85. Post 62, March 25, 2010, 8:01 p.m.

86. Posts 77–78, March 26, 2010.

87. Post 79, March 26, 2010, 12:50 p.m.

88. Ibid.
89. Ibid.
90. Ibid.
91. Post 80, March 26, 2010, 2:21 p.m.
92. Post 81, March 27, 2010, 9:53 a.m.
93. Post 82, March 27, 2010, 10:29 a.m.
94. Post 83, March 27, 2010, 2:07 p.m.
95. Post 100, March 28, 2010, 7:13 p.m.
96. Post 103, March 28, 2010, 10:11 p.m.
97. Post 104, March 28, 2010, 11:10 p.m.
98. Post 105, March 29, 2010, 2:50 a.m.
99. Post 106, March 31, 2010, 5:50 p.m.
100. The thread is still available as of March 25, 2016, and may at a later date be revived since at this point in time all of the threads remain active unless they are shut down by a moderator.

2. Picturing Ruin and Possibility

1. For example, then president Bill Clinton signed into law the Personal Responsibility and Work Opportunity Reconciliation Act (PRWORA) in 1996, which dramatically restructured the welfare system and embodied the triumph of neoliberalism.

2. On structural failure, see, for example, William Julius Wilson, *The Truly Disadvantaged: The Inner City, the Underclass, and Public Policy* (Chicago: University of Chicago Press, 1987), and Douglas S. Massey and Nancy A. Denton, *American Apartheid: Segregation and the Making of the Underclass* (Cambridge, Mass.: Harvard University Press, 1993). On the origins of the "culture of poverty" discourse, see, for example, Daniel P. Moynihan, *The Negro Family: The Case for National Action* (Washington, D.C.: Office of Policy Planning and Research, U.S. Department of Labor, 1965), and Oscar Lewis, *La Vida: A Puerto Rican Family in the Culture of Poverty* (New York: Random House, 1966). See Robin D. G. Kelley, *Yo' Mama's Disfunktional! Fighting the Culture Wars in Urban America* (Boston: Beacon Press, 1997), 15–42, for a discussion of how social scientists have constructed the underclass and the ghetto "as a reservoir of pathologies and bad cultural values" (16).

3. Wilson, *The Truly Disadvantaged.*

4. Massey and Denton, *American Apartheid;* William Julius Wilson, *When Work Disappears: The World of the New Urban Poor* (New York: Knopf, 1996).

5. Macek, *Urban Nightmares,* xii, 38, 152–53, 183.

6. Jason Hackworth, *The Neoliberal City: Governance, Ideology, and Development in American Urbanism* (Ithaca, N.Y.: Cornell University Press, 2007).

7. Camilo José Vergara, *The New American Ghetto* (New Brunswick, N.J.: Rutgers University Press, 1995), 220.

8. As the writer Mark Binelli states, "Everyone seemed to agree that Camilo Vergara's work was not ruin pornography, though he'd arguably been the Hefner of the genre." Binelli, *Detroit City Is the Place to Be,* 272. "Ruin porn" appears to have no agreed upon etymological genealogy but is bandied about quite frequently. It is sometimes used interchangeably with "ruin photography" and at other times to reference a particular type of ruin photography that is intentionally exploitive in its aesthetic posturing of ruin-gazing as a mode of pleasure. John Patrick Leary deems the Detroit imagery frequently considered "pornographic" as sensationalist. Leary and others critique that makers of "ruin porn" do not interact with the built environment but rather produce an image overly concerned with visual representation to the omission of the larger context. John Patrick Leary, "Detroitism," *Guernica Magazine*, January 15, 2011.

9. See, for example, Yves Marchand and Romain Meffre, *The Ruins of Detroit* (Göttingen: Steidl, 2010), and Andrew Moore, *Detroit Disassembled* (Akron, Ohio: Akron Art Museum, 2010). Of note, *Time* magazine used one of Marchand and Meffre's images for the cover photo for the 2009 story "The Tragedy of Detroit" (see Figure 2).

10. However, the role of the documentary photographer is one that is not without challenge. Martha Rosler has taken up this critique throughout the last four decades. In her 1981 essay "In, Around, and Afterthoughts (On Documentary Photography)," Rosler raises the questions of meaning, credibility, and aim in documentary photography both historically and contemporarily. She also brings up questions about the personal motivations and goals of documentary—as a means for career as well as an attempt to present (and represent) "authentic images." Martha Rosler, "In, Around, and Afterthoughts (On Documentary Photography)" (1981), in *Decoys and Disruptions: Selected Writings, 1975–2001* (Cambridge, Mass.: MIT Press, 2004), 151–206. She continues to make this critique, as we see in the epigraph that opens this chapter. See Martha Rosler, "Post-Documentary, Post-Photography" (1999), in *Decoys and Disruptions: Selected Writings, 1975–2001* (Cambridge, Mass.: MIT Press, 2004), 207–44 (quote on 209–10).

11. Timothy J. Gilfoyle, foreword to *Harlem: The Unmaking of a Ghetto*, by Camilo José Vergara (Chicago: University of Chicago Press, 2013), vii–ix. Gilfoyle likens Vergara's work to Riis's work in "exposing the differences between segregated and marginalized urban communities and those of 'normal America'" as well as Vergara's use of "shock-and-awe" as reminiscent of Riis (vii–viii).

However, Gilfoyle is quick to point out that in contrast to Riis, Vergara is very clear about his recording of people and poses; he also emphasizes Vergara's record of intense photography over decades rather than years (viii).

12. Alan Trachtenberg, *Reading American Photographs: Images as History, Mathew Brady to Walker Evans* (New York: Hill and Wang, 1989).

13. Dianne Harris, *Little White Houses: How the Postwar Home Constructed Race in America* (Minneapolis: University of Minnesota Press, 2013); George Lipsitz, *How Racism Takes Place* (Philadelphia: Temple University Press, 2011); Mike Davis, *Magical Urbanism: Latinos Reinvent the U.S. Big City* (New York: Verso, 2001).

14. National Endowment for the Humanities, "Awards and Honors: National Humanities Medals," 2012 Award Year, http://www.neh.gov/about/awards/national-humanities-medals.

15. Emily Deruy, "Camilo Jose Vergara Receives National Humanities Medal," ABC News, July 10, 2013.

16. See, for example, Massey and Denton, *American Apartheid,* and Sugrue, *The Origins of the Urban Crisis.*

17. Vergara, *The New American Ghetto,* xxii–xxiii. When *The New American Ghetto* was published, Vergara enumerated this archive as including more than 3,000 slides of the South Bronx, New York; 1,200 slides of Chicago, Illinois; 1,100 slides each of Harlem, New York, North Central Brooklyn, New York, and Newark, New Jersey; 300 slides each of Gary, Indiana, and Camden, New Jersey; 260 slides of Detroit, Michigan; 200 slides of Los Angeles, California; and about 600 slides of "other urban areas" including nine other geographically marked locations. *The New American Ghetto,* 227–29.

18. Ibid., 229.

19. Ibid., xiii–xiv.

20. However, in the conclusion to *The New American Ghetto,* Vergara writes, "For a month I lived in the city's desolate northwest section, immediately west of Grand Circus Park" (210). This statement conflicts with his prior statement indicating that he made only a few trips at five days per trip.

21. Ibid., xiii.

22. Ibid., xv.

23. Ibid., 2.

24. Ibid., 2.

25. See, for example, Chad Heap, *Slumming: Sexual and Racial Encounters in American Nightlife, 1885–1940* (Chicago: University of Chicago Press, 2009), and Catherine Cocks, *Doing the Town: The Rise of Urban Tourism in the United States, 1850–1915* (Berkeley: University of California Press, 2001).

26. J. Paul Getty Museum, "Artists: Camilo José Vergara," http://www.getty.edu/art/gettyguide/artMakerDetails?maker=31302.

27. Camilo José Vergara, *Silent Cities: The Evolution of the American Cemetery,* in collaboration with Kenneth T. Jackson (Princeton, N.J.: Princeton Architectural Press, 1989); *The New American Ghetto* (New Brunswick, N.J.: Rutgers University Press, 1995); *American Ruins* (New York: Monacelli Press, 1999); *Twin Towers Remembered* (Princeton, N.J.: Princeton Architectural Press, 2001); *Unexpected Chicagoland* (New York: New Press, 2001); *Subway Memories* (New York: Monacelli Press, 2004); *How the Other Half Worships* (New Brunswick, N.J.: Rutgers University Press, 2005); *Harlem: The Unmaking of a Ghetto* (Chicago: University of Chicago Press, 2013).

28. U.S. Census Bureau, "Population of the 100 Largest Cities and Other Urban Places in the United States: 1790 to 1990," June 1998, Table A, https://www.census.gov/population/www/documentation/twps0027/twps0027.html#tabA.

29. Vergara, *The New American Ghetto,* 17.

30. It is difficult to tell where precisely Vergara was photographing; however, the suggestion that this was the epicenter of the Detroit rebellion is likely elided in terms of geography. A more precise location (i.e., the crossroads) might reveal an area slightly outside the infamous Twelfth Street location depicted in national media images of the 1967 Detroit rebellion.

31. See Macek, *Urban Nightmares,* 139–98, for an analysis of news coverage of the U.S. postindustrial cities in the 1980s and 1990s.

32. Detroit was the sixth largest city in 1980 and the seventh largest in 1990. U.S. Census Bureau, Table 23, http://www.census.gov/population/www/documentation/twps0076/MItab.pdf.

33. Vergara, *American Ruins,* 11.

34. Although the images I show here do not demonstrate this, he is famous for what he calls the "rephotographic method," also referred to as time-lapse. In this he returns to the same vantage point and photographs it over time to provide a temporal narrative of change of a location. The relationship that Vergara suggests between space and time is an important device to construct a narrative of change over time. While Vergara is well known for this method, his Detroit collection in *The New American Ghetto* only has one such example featuring two images. *American Ruins* has ten separate locations showing the rephotographic method. Each of the locations features anywhere from two to four images showing change to a location over time.

35. Nick Yablon. *Untimely Ruins: An Archaeology of American Urban Modernity, 1819–1919* (Chicago: University of Chicago Press, 2010), 5.

36. Caitlin DeSilvey and Tim Edensor, "Reckoning with Ruins," *Progress in Human Geography* 37, no. 4 (2012): 465–85 (quote on 467).

37. Ibid., 467.

38. Vergara, *American Ruins,* 14.

39. Ibid., 61.

40. Eric Hill and John Gallagher, *AIA Detroit: The American Institute of Architects Guide to Detroit Architecture* (Detroit: Wayne State University Press, 2003), 116.

41. Vergara, *American Ruins,* 13.

42. Ibid., 12–13.

43. Ruth Wilson Gilmore, *Golden Gulag: Prisons, Surplus, Crisis, and Opposition in Globalizing California* (Berkeley: University of California Press, 2007), 55–56.

44. Reynolds Farley, Sheldon Danziger, and Harry J. Holzer, *Detroit Divided* (New York: Russell Sage Foundation, 2000), 161.

45. Ibid., 1, 2.

46. Farley, Danziger, and Holzer, in their landmark study of Detroit, write, "When one takes into account the overwhelmingly white suburban ring, one finds that the Detroit metropolitan area is among the nation's most prosperous. In terms of the earnings of employed men and women, Detroit ranked 7th out of 281 metropolises in 1990; in terms of per capita income, it was 24th of 281. In 1997, the average income of families in metropolitan Detroit was 13 percent above the national average . . . the stark inequality between poor blacks living in the central city and the more affluent whites in the suburbs makes metropolitan Detroit unusual. A few numbers convey this polarization. In 1990, the city's population was 76 percent African American; the suburban ring was only 5 percent African American. The poverty rate for the city was 32 percent; for the ring, 6 percent." Farley, Danziger, and Holzer, *Detroit Divided,* 2.

47. Andrew R. Highsmith, "Beyond Corporate Abandonment: General Motors and the Politics of Metropolitan Capitalism in Flint, Michigan," *Journal of Urban History* 40, no. 1 (2014): 31–47.

48. Vergara, *American Ruins,* 68–69.

49. Ibid., 64.

50. N. Smith, *The New Urban Frontier.*

51. See Leary, "Detroitism."

52. Vergara, *American Ruins,* 205.

53. Vergara, *The New American Ghetto,* 216; Vergara, *American Ruins,* 48.

54. Michel de Certeau, "Walking in the City," in *The Certeau Reader,* ed. Graham Ward (Oxford: Blackwell, 2000), 101–18 (quote on 105); Vergara, *American Ruins,* 48.

55. Vergara, *The New American Ghetto,* xiii. Vergara comments in the introduction to *The New American Ghetto,* "Until 1986 I usually shot pictures from the street level, but with crack dealers selling on every other corner, this became very dangerous" (xiii).

56. James Scott, *Seeing Like a State: How Certain Schemes to Improve the Human Condition Have Failed* (New Haven, Conn.: Yale University Press, 1998), 2–3.

57. Ibid., 6.

58. The 2010 census data on Detroit was released at the end of March 2011. For a few days after, the news was abuzz with the historic population loss for Detroit and Michigan. These numbers were released on the heels of the early March 2011 theatrical release of *Vanishing on 7th Street,* an apocalyptic thriller in which the entire city of Detroit, except for a handful of survivors, disappears—vanishing overnight. In the end, the only two people who survive the shadows of darkness are two children—one preteen African American boy and a six-year-old white girl who, when the film closes, are seen riding a horse down the middle of a deserted freeway littered with abandoned cars—heading out of Detroit toward Chicago, in hopes of finding other people. According to news media, the census bureau, and the film, Detroit is disappearing and its people are not simply *leaving,* in the words of the *New York Times,* but are *vanished.* Katherine Q. Seelye, "Detroit Census Confirms a Desertion Like No Other," *New York Times,* March 22, 2011.

59. Vergara, *The New American Ghetto,* xii.

60. Ibid., 2.

61. Vergara, *American Ruins,* 208.

62. I have intentionally decided not to reproduce the photo of this particular building. My point here is not to ask the reader to decide whether the building is a ruin/non-ruin, which I feel like the inclusion of the image might do. In my opinion, Vergara includes the image to prove to his reader his estimation of the building as a ruin, despite the person on the phone.

63. Vergara, *American Ruins,* 52–55. *The Top of the David Broderick Tower, Detroit, 1998* appears on page 55.

64. Ibid., 55.

65. Ibid., 54.

66. Ibid.

67. Vergara, *The New American Ghetto,* 220.

68. Ibid., 215.

69. James Bennet, "A Tribute to Ruin Irks Detroit," *New York Times,* December 10, 1995.

70. Although Curtis died in 1952 without fame or fortune, and separated from his wife, in the 1970s his work received renewed attention and he is now considered one of the most important photographers of the American West. See, for example, Edward S. Curtis, *The North American Indian: The Complete Portfolios* (Cologne: Taschen, 2015); Edward S. Curtis, *The Master Prints* (Santa Fe, N.M.: Arena Editions, 2001); Edward S. Curtis, *Portraits from North American Indian Life* (New York: Dutton, 1972). His image titled *Vanishing Race* is arguably one of his most oft-cited photographs. According to the Curtis biographer Timothy Egan, "On this trip [to Navajo land in the Southwest] alone Curtis shot over 600 images including *Vanishing Race* and *Cañon de Chelly*." Timothy Egan, *Short Nights of the Shadow Catcher: The Epic Life and Immortal Photographs of Edward Curtis* (New York: Houghton Mifflin Harcourt, 2012), 94.

71. Derick Hutchinson, "Ilitch Organization Releases Plans for New Red Wings Arena District," ClickOnDetroit, July 21, 2014.

72. David Muller, "Ilitch Holdings' Chris Ilitch Details New Detroit Red Wings Arena & District, 15 Years in the Making," MLive, September 18, 2014.

73. Adjacent to these vacant lots owned by Olympia Development are the Park Avenue Hotel and the Hotel Eddystone, both frequently photographed, making appearances in Vergara's work as well as serving as the location of iconic tagging by the Hygenic Dress League (as discussed in chapter 4) and the area from which a portion of Anthony Bourdain's *Detroit: Parts Unknown* is also filmed (as discussed in chapter 5).

74. Jan Thibodeau, "See Bird's-Eye View of New Red Wings Arena Construction Progress," MLive, March 15, 2016.

75. "Detroit's David Broderick Tower Completes Financing Plan, Renovation Begins," *DBusiness,* December 26, 2010.

76. David Muller, "Five Days after Opening to Residents, Detroit's Broderick Tower Fully Leased," MLive, November 8, 2012.

77. See www.brodericktower.com for current availability and rates.

3. Fanning the Embers

1. The ad was two minutes long and took up four thirty-second spots. Chrysler had to get special permission from the NFL as the typical commercial break consists of three thirty-second spots for a total running time of one minute and thirty seconds. The following year, Chrysler ran another two-minute commercial as part of the "Imported from Detroit" campaign, this one starring Clint Eastwood.

2. Tim Nudd, "Chrysler's 'Born of Fire' Wins Emmy for Best Commercial: Third Straight W+K Spot to Win," *Adweek,* September 13, 2011.

3. Tim Nudd, "The 10 Best Commercials of 2011," *Adweek,* November 28, 2011.

4. Effie Worldwide, "Wieden+Kennedy and Chrysler's Imported from Detroit Wins the Grand Effie at the North American Effie Awards Gala in New York," *Effie Press Release,* May 23, 2012, www.effie.org/pressroom/5_23_12.

5. Nielsen, "Super Bowl XLV Most Viewed Telecast in U.S. Broadcast History," February 7, 2011.

6. Although there are more up-to-date statistics on the viewership of the commercial, it is important to note the popularity of its reception in the days directly following its debut. In the twenty-six days following its initial appearance during the Super Bowl, as of 7:50 a.m. PST on March 4, 2011, the YouTube version of the full-length commercial had 9,018,848 views. This does not include the commercial's posting in other forms and formats on the Web in addition to the shorter, thirty-second version that Chrysler also ran.

7. "Lose Yourself" won the 2003 Academy Award for Best Original Song and the 2003 Grammy for Best Rap Song.

8. The Chrysler 200 is a remodeled and reengineered version of the Chrysler Sebring. The Chrysler 200 was chosen as the featured vehicle since it is manufactured in metropolitan Detroit.

9. Ashley C. Woods, "'Born of Fire' Chrysler 200 Ad Featuring Eminem Was Simply the Best of 2011," MLive, December 23, 2011.

10. Jane Jacobs, *The Death and Life of Great American Cities* (New York: Random House, 1961).

11. Bedrock Corporations, also referred to as Bedrock Manufacturing, is the privately held company founded by Tom Kartsotis. Kartsotis is also the founder of Fossil, Inc., a Texas-based company primarily known for its namesake line of fashion watches. Shinola's parent company, Bedrock, is not to be confused with the Dan Gilbert subsidiary Bedrock Real Estate, discussed in chapter 5.

12. Anne VanderMay, "Think You Know Shinola? Think Again," *Fortune,* July 9, 2013.

13. Shinola, "Why Open a Watch Factory in Detroit?," http://www.shinola.com/our-story/about-shinola.

14. Brent Snavely and B. J. Hammerstein, "Chrysler Super Bowl Ad: How It All Came Together," *Detroit Free Press,* February 8, 2011.

15. I thank Stephanie Salerno for engaging in conversations with me about the sonic palette of this commercial.

16. The 1950s population figure is from Joe T. Darden, Richard Child Hill, June Thomas, and Richard Thomas, *Detroit: Race and Uneven Development,* (Philadelphia: Temple University Press, 1987). The 2011 population figure is

from U.S. Census Bureau, State & County QuickFacts: Detroit (city), Michigan, http://quickfacts.census.gov/qfd/states/26/2622000.html.

17. The *Forbes* annual list of Fortune 500 companies had Chrysler LLC in the number 59 spot in 2011. See http://fortune.com/fortune500/2011/chrysler-group-llc-59/.

18. Charles K. Hyde, *Riding the Roller Coaster: A History of the Chrysler Corporation* (Detroit: Wayne State University Press, 2003), 242–46. "Big Three" is an automobile industry and Detroit regional shorthand reference for the three American car companies all headquartered in metropolitan Detroit.

19. Numerous commentators, politicians, and business people leveled this critique; see, for example, Bryce Hoffman, *American Icon: Alan Mulally and the Fight to Save Ford Motor Company* (New York: Crown Business, 2012); Bill Vlasic, *Once Upon a Car: The Fall and Resurrection of America's Big Three Automakers—GM, Ford, and Chrysler* (New York: William Morrow/HarpersCollins, 2011); Hyde, *Riding the Roller Coaster.* The Detroit-born Mitt Romney, an eventual Republican nominee for president, notably weighed in with an editorial in the *New York Times.* Mitt Romney, "Let Detroit Go Bankrupt," *New York Times,* November 18, 2008. Romney is the youngest son of a prominent Michigan politician, the late George Romney. George Romney served as the past chairman and the president of the American Motors Corporation. He was the former governor of Michigan as well as the secretary of the U.S. Department of Housing and Urban Development.

20. Raymond Williams, "Advertising the Magic System," in *Problems in Materialism and Culture* (London: NLB, 1980), 170–95 (quote on 183).

21. Snavely and Hammerstein, "Chrysler Super Bowl Ad."

22. Harry C. Katz, "Recent Developments in US Auto Labor Relations: The Decline of the Big Three and the United Automotive Workers," in *Globalization and Employment Relations in the Auto Assembly Industry: A Study of Seven Countries,* ed. Roger Blanpain (Alphen aan den Rijn: Kluwer Law International, 2008), 131–42 (quote on 134).

23. Ibid.

24. Paul Ingrassia, *Crash Course: The American Automobile Industry's Road from Glory to Disaster* (New York: Random House, 2010), 63.

25. Dana Frank, *Buy American: The Untold Story of Economic Nationalism* (Boston: Beacon Press, 1999), 161.

26. And tellingly, the U.S. market share abroad continues to be robust as "General Motors sells more vehicles in China than in the United States." Gregory W. Noble, "The Chinese Auto Industry as Challenge, Opportunity, and Partner," in *The Third Globalization: Can Wealthy Nations Stay Rich in the*

Twenty-First Century, ed. Dan Breznitz and John Zysman (New York: Oxford University Press, 2013), 57–81 (quote on 58).

27. See Christine Choy, dir., *Who Killed Vincent Chin* (New York: Filmakers Library, 1988); Helen Zia, *Asian American Dreams: The Emergence of an American People* (New York: Farrar, Straus and Giroux, 2000); "The Politics of Remembering," special issue, *Amerasia Journal* 28, no. 3 (2002).

28. The final sentence for the assailants remained probation and a fine, which were the stipulations of the initial plea bargain.

29. Brian Henderson, "Toward a Non-Bourgeois Camera Style," in *Film Theory and Criticism,* ed. Leo Braudy and Marshall Cohen (New York: Oxford University Press, 2009), 57–67 (time and space discussed on 59).

30. For a look at life on the line in the late twentieth century, see Lolita Hernandez, *Autopsy of an Engine: And Other Stories from the Cadillac Plant* (Minneapolis: Coffee House Press, 2004).

31. See Zunz, *The Changing Face of Inequality,* 311–13; Hooker, *Life in the Shadows of the Crystal Palace,* 107–23; Heather Ann Thompson, *Whose Detroit: Politics, Labor, and Race in a Modern American City* (Ithaca, N.Y.: Cornell University Press, 2001); Dan Georgakas and Marvin Surkin, *Detroit: I Do Mind Dying* (Cambridge, Mass.: South End Press, 1998); Richard Thomas, *Life for Us Is What We Make It: Building Black Community in Detroit, 1915–1945* (Bloomington: Indiana University Press, 1992).

32. Washington, *The Negro in Detroit.*

33. Washington's report outlines a coded reference to the rape of a theater employee by a supervisor; incessant harassment at an auto-parts factory by a supervisor who insisted that one of the respondents, a worker on the line, become his mistress; and a hotel that had to change its policy of "hiring only good-looking mulatto girls" due to the fact that these women faced such harassment on the job and subsequently quit that the hotel could not keep in its employ a stable workforce.

34. See David Boje, "The Sexual Politics of Sneakers: 'Common Ground' and Absent-Referent Stories in the Nike Debate," *Organization & Environment* 14, no. 3 (September 2001): 356–63.

35. Terry Smith, *Making the Modern: Industry, Art, and Design in America* (Chicago: University of Chicago Press, 1993), 206.

36. Linda Bank Downs, *Diego Rivera: The Detroit Industry Murals* (New York: Detroit Institute of Arts in association with W. W. Norton, 1999), 29.

37. Ibid., 35.

38. David Craven, *Diego Rivera: As Epic Modernist* (New York: G. K. Hall, 1997), 138.

39. Amy Pastan, *Diego Rivera: The Detroit Industry Murals* (London: Scala, 2006).

40. Craven, *Diego Rivera,* 138.

41. Downs, *Diego Rivera,* 96.

42. See, for example, Jennifer Baichwal's *Manufactured Landscapes* (New York: Zeitgeist Films, 2006), featuring the work of the photographer Edward Burtynsky. The opening scene, which features a Chinese factory that produces irons, is notable for its quiet, precise, and starkly antiseptic interior.

43. Downs, *Diego Rivera,* 175.

44. Ibid., 29.

45. Ibid., 23.

46. Steve Babson, *Working Detroit: The Making of a Union Town* (Detroit: Wayne State University Press, 1986), 53.

47. Joann Muller, "Eminem's Super Bowl Ad for Chrysler Had CEO Worried," *Forbes,* February 7, 2011, www.forbes.com/sites/joannmuller/2011/02/07/eminems-super-bowl-ad-for-chrysler-had-ceo-worried.

48. Loren Kajikawa, "Eminem's 'My Name Is': Signifying Whiteness, Rearticulating Race," *Journal of the Society for American Music* 3, no. 3 (2009): 341–63.

49. Ibid., 352.

50. Eric King Watts, "Border Patrolling and 'Passing' in Eminem's 8 Mile," *Critical Studies in Media Communication* 22, no. 3 (2005): 187–206; Liam Grealy, "Negotiating Cultural Authenticity in Hip-Hop: Mimicry, Whiteness and Eminem," *Continuum* 22, no. 6 (2008): 851–65.

51. Watts, "Border Patrolling and 'Passing' in Eminem's 8 Mile."

52. U.S. Census Bureau, State & County QuickFacts: Detroit (city), Michigan, http://quickfacts.census.gov/qfd/states/26/2622000.html.

53. See Shana Redmond, "Detroit's Idle: The Domestic Sounds of Labour's Foreign Landscape," *Race & Class* 55, no. 1 (2013): 60–77, for an important analysis of the sonic representation within the commercial that, she argues, "dislocates the manual and cultural labours of Black Detroit."

54. "Lose Yourself," 2002. Musical credits: Jeff Bass, Marshall Mathers, and Luis Resto; lyrics by Marshall Mathers. Eminem is the stage name used by Marshall Mathers. In the film the actor Mekhi Phifer plays a character by the name of David "Future" Porter, B-Rabbit's best friend.

55. "The 50 Greatest Hip-Hop Songs of All Time," *Rolling Stone,* December 5, 2012.

56. "Lose Yourself," 2002.

57. Elisha Anderson, "Michigan Man Performs Voice-Over for Eminem Chrysler Ad," *Detroit Free Press,* February 7, 2011.

58. See, for example, Ted Johnson, "'Saturday Night Live' Parodies Clint Eastwood's Chrysler Ad," *Variety,* February 12, 2012; Sarah Anne Hughes, "'30 Rock' Spoofs Clint Eastwood 'Halftime in America' Ad," *Washington Post,*

April 20, 2012; Verne Gay, "Clint Eastwood's 'Halftime in America': Parodies Begin!," *Newsday,* February 8, 2012.

59. Brian Monroe, "Were Politics Buried inside Eastwood's 'Halftime' Commercial?," CNN, February 7, 2012.

60. See, for example, the multipronged advertising and media campaign of Shinola Detroit, a U.S.-based watch and bicycle manufacturer, as well as the August 2014 debut of the Apple iPad commercial featuring Detroit community activist Jason Hall. David Muller, "Detroit Slow Roll Cofounder Jason Hall Featured in New Apple iPad Spot," MLive, August 11, 2014.

4. Flickers of the American Dream

1. See, for example, the list of films that screened at the event "Imaging Detroit" in September 2012: http://www.imagingdetroit.org/screen.html. Mireille Roddier, one of the event organizers, discussed the event during a paper presentation at the Association of American Geographers Annual Meeting in April 2013. A rundown of some of the most well-known films, including the two I discuss here, is included in Julie Hinds, "Motor City Movies Take Film World by Storm," *Detroit Free Press,* April 22, 2012.

2. Dustin Dwyer, "Our How-To Guide for Making a Hardscrabble, Gritty, Post-Industrial Documentary about Detroit," Michigan Radio, February 2, 2012.

3. See, for example, Patricia Nelson Limerick, *The Legacy of Conquest: The Unbroken Past of the American West* (New York: W. W. Norton, 1988), 26, for a discussion of Frederick Jackson Turner's frontier thesis as a process, not a place, and Richard Slotkin, *Gunfighter Nation: The Myth of the Frontier in Twentieth-Century America* (Norman: University of Oklahoma Press, 1992), for a discussion of the role of the frontier in popular culture.

4. The same time that both of these films were released there was also a growing genre of Detroit books by former Detroiters. See, for example, Mark Binelli, *Detroit City Is the Place to Be: The Afterlife of an American Metropolis* (New York: Metropolitan Books, 2012), and Charlie LeDuff, *Detroit: An American Autopsy* (New York: Penguin Press, 2013). Although these more contemporary accounts speak to institutional forces of race and class that contributed to Detroit's decline and are notable for the emphasis on the possibility for Detroit's future, they also often gain traction because of the authors' credibility as a Detroiter.

5. Hinds, "Motor City Movies."

6. Mike Rubin, "A Battered City, through Local Lenses," *New York Times,* April 27, 2012.

7. *Deforce* release schedule, 2010, http://www.deforcemovie.com/release-schedule. As of May 1, 2014, *Deforce* was available for instant streaming via

iTunes and for DVD purchase on Amazon. In contrast, on this same date *Detropia* was available for instant streaming via Netflix, Amazon Instant Video, Google Play, and iTunes. It was also available for DVD purchase on Amazon.

8. See, for example, Jeannette Catsoulis, "Moody Shots of Detroit's Urban Decay," *New York Times,* September 6, 2012; Andrew O'Hehir, "'Detropia': Can Detroit Be Saved?," *Salon,* September 7, 2012; Whitney Matheson, "'Detropia': PBS Airs Powerful Detroit Doc," *USA Today,* May 24, 2013; David Denby, "Good Fights: 'Detropia' and 'The Eye of the Storm,'" *New Yorker,* September 10, 2012; Kristin McCracken, "What Can Detroit Teach the Nation? Heidi Ewing on Detropia," *Huffington Post,* September 5, 2012.

9. David Wilson, *Cities and Race: America's New Black Ghetto* (New York: Routledge, 2007). Wilson situates the contemporary moment as the "third wave" of the U.S. black urban ghetto, which is directly linked to globalization (5–6).

10. Robin D. G. Kelley, *Yo' Mama's Disfunktional! Fighting the Culture Wars in Urban America* (Boston: Beacon Press, 1997), 16.

11. The title screens are not as extensive as the DVD chapter breakdown, which includes: (1) Opening; (2) Why?; (3) Foundation; (4) Centrally Planned Segregation; (5) Black Progress & The Rebellion; (6) Riot: Causes and Effects; (7) Coleman Young; (8) Corruption & Mismanagement; (9) Living Standards; (10) Kwame Kilpatrick; (11) Blight; (12) Broken City Services; (13) Black Ownership; (14) War on Drugs; (15) Jail & Justice; (16) Looking Forward; (17) Credits.

12. Louise Spence and Vinicius Navarro, *Crafting Truth: Documentary Form and Meaning* (New Brunswick, N.J.: Rutgers University Press, 2001), 24.

13. Ibid.

14. In an interview, Falconer reveals that he was introduced to this group of interviewees by one of his other subjects, Dr. Luke Bergmann, who had lived in this community and wrote a book about his experiences. Hillary Eschenburg, "'Deforce' Director Daniel Falconer on Documenting the Rise and Fall of Detroit," *BoxOffice,* March 28, 2012.

15. Eschenburg, "'Deforce' Director Daniel Falconer."

16. ActNow Foundation, "Q&A with DEFORCE director Daniel Falconer," February 11, 2012.

17. Eschenburg, "'Deforce' Director Daniel Falconer."

18. ActNow Foundation, "Q&A with DEFORCE director Daniel Falconer."

19. "In the life" is a slang reference to working within the drug trade.

20. Luke Bergman, *Getting Ghost: Two Young Lives and the Struggle for the Soul of an American City* (Ann Arbor: University of Michigan Press, 2010).

21. Fairlane is a local mall.

22. Wilson, *Cities and Race,* 86.

23. In this chapter I use the term *text-over* to refer to on-screen text that appears as a narrative tool rather than simply an on-screen caption. In *Deforce* this device is used rather sparingly. In *Detropia* this is the primary narration tool, as this film does not rely on a voice-over narration; therefore, the "text-over" serves as the primary narrative device of the film, standing in as the narrative voice.

24. His exact role in the drug trade is not revealed in the film.

25. See the film's website at http://www.detropiathefilm.com/news.html.

26. Babson, *Working Detroit,* 31. See also Meyer, *The Five Dollar Day,* and Hooker, *Life in the Shadows of the Crystal Palace.*

27. Beth Tompkins Bates, *The Making of Black Detroit in the Age of Henry Ford* (Chapel Hill: University of North Carolina Press, 2012), 41.

28. This is a colloquial name for towns and cities that barred nonwhites from living within their limits but relied on people of color as part of their workforce. The name itself comes from signs that some of these towns posted in warning, such as the sign in Anna-Jonesboro, Illinois, that read: "Nigger, Don't Let the Sun Go Down on You in Anna-Jonesboro." See James W. Loewen, *Sundown Towns* (New York: Simon & Schuster, 2005), 1–2.

29. See Sugrue, *The Origins of the Urban Crisis,* 76–77, and Freund, *Colored Property,* 284–327, for a more complete discussion of Dearborn's housing policies.

30. Melamed, *Represent and Destroy.*

31. Starr works at the coffee shop across from Orchestra Hall, attends the town hall meeting with Bing, guides the filmmakers through the "ruins," and questions the European tourists who have come to see the decay.

32. This representation of the present recurs so frequently that a 2012 film addresses the life, work, and actual presence of Detroiters. Mark Dworkin and Melissa Young, dirs., *We Are Not Ghosts!* (Oley, Penn.: Bullfrog Films, 2012), 52 minutes.

33. See Isabel Wilkerson's *The Warmth of Other Suns* (New York: Vintage Books, 2010), which provides a counternarrative to the idea of the South as a primary location of racism through her accounts of racism faced in the cities of the North, Midwest, and West for those seeking life outside the brutal realities of the Jim Crow South. For a Detroit-specific case study of the post–World War II battle for racially equal access to labor, see Heather Ann Thompson, *Whose Detroit?: Politics, Labor, and Race in a Modern American City* (Ithaca, N.Y.: Cornell University Press, 2001).

34. James N. Gregory, *Southern Diaspora: How the Great Migrations of Black and White Southerners Transformed America* (Chapel Hill: University of North Carolina Press, 2005).

35. The Detroit plant closed in February 2012. However, despite the suggestion that all jobs were moved overseas, according to news reports most of the Detroit plant's jobs were moved to a plant in Three Rivers, Michigan, a town about 165 miles west of Detroit. See Ziati Meyer, "American Axle to Close Detroit Plant in February," *Detroit Free Press,* July 1, 2011, and Dustin Walsh, "American Axle Hopes Demolition of Detroit Complex Will Spark Interest in Property," *Automotive News,* June 18, 2013.

36. The Hygienic Dress League Corporation has a Tumblr page (http://hygienicdressleague.tumblr.com/) with many photos and very little information, but it has been the subject of numerous news articles. See John Zemke, "Hygienic Dress League Art Project Goes Public with IPO," *modelD*, October 14, 2014; Travis R. Wright, "Going Corporate: The Hygienic Dress League Reinvents Street Art by Mocking Advertising," *Detroit Metro Times,* September 14, 2011; Jaime Rojo and Steven Harrington, "HDL 'American Gothic' and 'Walden' on Michigan Barns," *Huffington Post,* July 10, 2013.

37. O'Hehir, "'Detropia': Can Detroit Be Saved?"

5. Feeding Detroit's Rise

1. Anthony Bourdain, "Kick Out the Jams," November 8, 2013, http://anthonybourdain.tumblr.com/post/66383936226/kick-out-the-jams.

2. The hour-long episodes have the standard forty-three-minute running time with seventeen minutes of commercials.

3. In his itinerary of eating and drinking, he constructs a nostalgic narrative of Detroit's past—first visiting a Coney Island–style restaurant, which features a more-than-century-old Detroit take on a chili dog. This particular food and type of diner established by early twentieth-century Greek immigrants is a unique staple of Detroit food culture. Then he has a drink and a burger with the political strategist Adolph Mongo, at a bar and grill adjacent to Eastern Market where neither man even mentions the food and drink; instead, conversation focuses on the corruption of city government, highlighting the infamous actions of former Detroit mayor Kwame Kilpatrick. Bourdain then rejoins Charlie LeDuff and they drive around the city looking at more blight and abandonment before stopping at "Greedy Greg's," a soul food barbeque set up in the yard of a private home, with ribs on a grill outside and greens and mac and cheese on the stovetop in the kitchen. His next stop is a Detroit firehouse where he takes a tour of the station and pitches in to prep the family meal for the guys on shift that evening. Lighthearted vegetable chopping and joking around with the firefighters in the kitchen peppers an otherwise bleak portrayal of Detroit: the city's blighted homes, fire-crazy arsonists, and the poorly protected and paid firefighters. The next scene serves as an

interlude wherein Bourdain addresses the audience as discussed in the main text of this section. As he talks we see artists painting murals on old brick, and a bunch of shots of young people on bikes and walking down streets, before transitioning to the pop-up restaurant discussed in this section. From here Bourdain travels to the *pupusería*. After this stop he climbs atop a riding lawn mower, beer in hand, and joins the members of the Detroit mower gang in mowing a park overgrown with tall summer grass, since funding for park maintenance was slashed by the city. Finally the show closes with an interview with Malik Yakini, executive director of the Detroit Black Community Food Security Network at the D-Town Farm, for a discussion of urban agriculture and farming.

4. Dustin Walsh, "Warren Buffett Tells *Crain's:* I'm Ready to Buy in Detroit," *Crain's,* September 18, 2014.

5. Miriam Greenberg, *Branding New York: How a City in Crisis Was Sold to the World* (New York: Routledge, 2008), 12.

6. Ibid., 13–14.

7. Bourdain, "Kick Out the Jams."

8. Ben Austen, "The Post Post-Apocalyptic Detroit," *New York Times Magazine*, July 13, 2014, 22–29, 37–38.

9. Joann Muller, "Quicken Billionaire Dan Gilbert on Giving Back to Detroit," *Forbes,* September 18, 2012.

10. For a listing of Dan Gilbert's affiliate companies, see http://www.bedrockmgt.com/family.php. Bedrock Real Estate Services serves as Dan Gilbert's public-facing real estate arm. As described on Bedrock's website, Bedrock Real Estate is part of the larger network of Gilbert-affiliated business ventures: "Bedrock Real Estate Services is affiliated with a great family of companies, including Quicken Loans, the Cleveland Cavaliers, Fathead.com, Title Source, Veritix and dozens more. We are constantly looking for opportunities to collaborate among our companies. We call these opportunities 'threads.' We look forward to talking to you about the threads that might weave with your business and our businesses." The list that follows shows the extensive reach, in terms of geography and industry, of Gilbert's investments.

11. This includes a September 2014 announcement that Gilbert will finance the expansion of a freeway off-ramp, which will serve the entire city. In an effort to solve a bottleneck of cars exiting to downtown Detroit, Gilbert's subsidiary will finance the $1.25 million dollar project, which will widen the ramp from one to three lanes. Incidentally, the expansion will result in the exit dropping cars right along the service drive that runs adjacent to the Gilbert-owned Greektown Casino. See Sherri Welch, "Gilbert Funds Plan to Widen I-375 Ramp to Lafayette," *Crain's,* September 21, 2014.

12. Rock Ventures LLC/Bedrock Real Estate, "Detroit Fast Facts," July 9, 2014, http://www.quickenloans.com/press-room/wp-content/uploads/2013/10/2014-07-09-DetroitFastFacts-July2014-blue-and-orange.pdf. An updated version of the "Fast Facts" can be downloaded from http://www.quickenloans.com/press-room/detroit-timeline/.

13. Quicken Loans, "Detroit Engagement Timeline," http://www.quickenloans.com/press-room/detroit-timeline/.

14. Sharon Zukin, *The Culture of Cities* (Malden, Mass.: Blackwell, 1995), 7, 3.

15. Suzanne Smith, *Dancing in the Street: Motown and the Cultural Politics of Detroit* (Cambridge, Mass.: Harvard University Press, 1999), 6, 14.

16. Austen, "The Post Post-Apocalyptic Detroit," 26.

17. Rock Ventures LLC/Bedrock Real Estate, "Detroit Fast Facts" (2014).

18. Quicken Loans, "Detroit Engagement Timeline."

19. Muller, "Quicken Billionaire Dan Gilbert on Giving Back to Detroit."

20. Greenberg, *Branding New York,* 13–14.

21. In February 2013 a report focused on this area called "7.2 SQ MI: A Report on Greater Downtown Detroit" was released by a consortium of private groups: the Hudson-Webber Foundation, the Detroit Economic Growth Corporation, the Downtown Detroit Partnership, Midtown Detroit Inc., D:hive, and Data Driven Detroit. For a copy of the report, see http://detroitsevenpointtwo.com/resources/2013-Full-Report.pdf.

22. "7.2 SQ MI," 31. For example, age group 35–54 is 26 percent of the population and 55+ is 27 percent of the population. Of the 2010 Greater Downtown population, age group 18–24 is 17 percent and age group 25–34 is 18 percent of the total.

23. Ibid., 34.

24. The first graphic reveals statistics for the following: "Age 25–34 and College-Educated, of the Total Population, 2006–2010." The accompanying percentages reveal 8 percent of the Greater Downtown, 1 percent of Detroit as a whole, 3 percent of Michigan, and 4 percent of the United States. Ultimately, the takeaway is that although this particular population of young and college educated is a small segment of the overall population, they are overrepresented in Greater Detroit in comparison to the city, state, and country as a whole. Yet it is the graphic just below this information that for me causes the confusion in interpretation. The second graphic's title reads: "College-Educated, of the 25–34 Population, 2006–2010." This data shows a markedly different intersection of age and education, with 42 percent of the Greater Downtown, 11 percent of Detroit as a whole, 29 percent of Michigan, and 31 percent of the United States. It takes a moment to digest what these statistics are symbolizing,

which is that of all the twenty-five- to thirty-four-year-olds in a particular subset, this is the total percentage of that group that has a college education. This language also raises the question of whether this means some college or a college degree.

25. "7.2 SQ MI," 32, bold in the original.

26. Although the report doesn't state it specifically, the conception of "foreign-born" is likely a nod to Richard Florida's "melting pot index." See Richard Florida, *The Rise of the Creative Class* (New York: Basic Books, 2002), 261, 334.

27. "7.2 SQ MI," 32, 34.

28. Governor John Engler in 2000 announced a plan to "recruit young skilled workers," and Governor Jennifer Granholm in 2003 announced, "We want to create cool cities, hip places to live and work." Curtis M. Hoffman and Jeremy Pyne, "The Brain Drain Wars: Characteristics of Recent Movers into and out of Michigan," in *Sustaining Michigan: Metropolitan Policies and Strategies,* ed. Richard W. Jelier and Gary Sands (East Lansing: Michigan State University Press, 2009), 281–306. Although the work of Hoffman and Pyne shows that this is somewhat of an overstatement, they conclude unilaterally that "Michigan is not suffering from an unprecedented mass creative class exodus" (292).

29. See June Manning Thomas, "Michigan's Urban Policies in an Era of Land Use Reform and Creative-Class Cities," in *Sustaining Michigan: Metropolitan Policies and Strategies,* ed. Richard W. Jelier and Gary Sands (East Lansing: Michigan State University Press, 2009), 261–80, and Hoffman and Pyne, "The Brain Drain Wars."

30. Hoffman and Pyne ultimately conclude that even though Cool Cities is a high-profile program that might have potential to change perceptions, the money garnered by cities through the program "is dwarfed by losses in state revenue sharing" ("The Brain Drain Wars," 301). Yet they are prescient in their assertion that "only a revitalized Detroit–Ann Arbor metro area could conceivably compete with Chicago" (301). Most notably in Detroit, Eastern Market received a $100,000 development grant as part of the initiative, and there were other smaller grants awarded. Unfortunately, because of the discontinuation of the program the State of Michigan no longer features information about the program on its website.

31. "7.2 SQ MI," 9.

32. Ibid., 4.

33. Megan Krigbaum, "Soul Food for a Hungry City," *Food & Wine,* June 2012, 94–101.

34. Max Taves, "Detroit's Tiger Stadium Redevelopment Project Turns to 'Crowdfunding,'" *Wall Street Journal,* February 10, 2015. See the site plans at http://www.revivethecorner.com/.

35. According to Michael Hodges, "In 1945 thirty-two trains arrived and departed daily. By 1966 that number had dropped to eighteen." Michael H. Hodges, *Michigan's Historic Railroad Stations* (Detroit: Wayne State University Press, 2012), 57.

36. John C. Dancy, *Sand against the Wind: The Memoirs of John C. Dancy* (Detroit: Wayne State University Press, 1966), 55.

37. Phyllis Vine, *One Man's Castle: Clarence Darrow in Defense of the American Dream* (New York: Amistad, 2004), 62.

38. Vergara, *The New American Ghetto,* 214; Vergara, *American Ruin,* 56–59.

39. The companies behind both magazines have invested money in Detroit in recent years. As discussed in the introduction, Time Inc.'s flagship publication, *Time* magazine, purchased a house in Detroit with the assignment for reporters to live in and report from Detroit for one year in 2009. More recently, Condé Nast served as the title sponsor for a photography exhibit of Bruce Weber's Detroit images that ran from June 20 to September 7, 2014, at the Detroit Institute of Arts, titled "Detroit—Bruce Weber."

40. The restaurant was so successful that by early 2013 it expanded, which resulted in more seating and lessened wait times. Even so, on a night when any of the Detroit sports teams are in town, wait times are regularly in the one-hour range. For those who want just to eat the food, Slow's opened a second, "to go" location in Midtown in 2010 that served an abbreviated menu to meet demand for catering and take-out orders, which it could much better accommodate with a bigger kitchen and counter-only service.

41. *Man vs. Food,* November 4, 2009; *Best Sandwich in America,* July 25, 2012.

42. Frederick Douglas Opie links the origin of the term *soul food* to the black power movement of the 1960s and 1970s. See Frederick Douglas Opie, *Hog and Hominy: Soul Food from Africa to America* (New York: Columbia University Press, 2008), xi. Krishenendu Ray suggests that "soul food" was first mentioned in the *New York Times* on September 18, 1966. Krishenendu Ray, "Ethnic Succession and the New American Restaurant Cuisine," in *The Restaurant Book,* ed. David Beriss and David Sutton (Oxford: Berg, 2007), 110.

43. Although the etymology of "soul food" originates in the late twentieth century, the practice and way of cooking that it calls to mind has origins in West Africa, moving alongside transatlantic slavery to the American South. In addition to Opie, *Hog and Hominy,* see Adrian Miller, *Soul Food: The Surprising Story of an American Cuisine, One Plate at a Time* (Chapel Hill: University of North Carolina Press, 2013), and Anne L. Bower, ed., *African American Foodways: Explorations of History and Culture* (Urbana: University of Illinois Press, 2007).

44. See, for example, Karen Hess, *The Carolina Rice Kitchen: The African Connection* (Columbia: University of South Carolina Press, 1992).

45. Food Research and Action Center, "SNAP Access in Urban America," January 2011, http://frac.org/wp-content/uploads/2011/01/urbansnapreport_jan2011.pdf. This document has differing groups of comparison; for SNAP (food stamp) benefits it includes county-level statistics and for poverty the statistics are at the city level.

46. Nathan Skid, "Whole Foods Moving into Midtown," *Crain's,* July 27, 2011.

47. Dale Buss, "Whole Foods Opens in Detroit, but Don't Get Maudlin over It," *Forbes,* June 5, 2013; Kai Ryssdal, "Whole Foods CEO: Detroit Is a Long-Term Investment," Marketplace, June 5, 2013; Sonari Glinton, "Re-invigorating a Detroit Neighborhood, Block by Block," NPR, July 28, 2013; Sarah Hulett, "What Whole Foods' Opening Means—and Doesn't Mean—about Midtown Detroit," Michigan Radio, June 5, 2013.

48. Troy, West Bloomfield, Rochester Hills, and two Ann Arbor locations.

49. The news of Whole Foods was highlighted nationally and internationally, whereas the opening of a Meijer, a regional supermarket chain, on July 25, 2013, received much less attention. This is likely due to several factors, including the reputation of the Whole Foods brand as an upscale market. Meijer broke ground on a second Detroit store in June 2014.

50. As of September 28, 2014. See Bloomberg Business, "Whole Foods Market Inc.," http://investing.businessweek.com/research/stocks/snapshot/snapshot_article.asp?ticker=WFM.

51. Michael Serazio, "Ethos Groceries and Countercultural Appetites: Consuming Memory in Whole Foods' Brand Utopia," *Journal of Popular Culture* 44, no. 1 (2011): 158–77 (quote on 166).

52. See, for example, regarding food consumption in particular, Josee Johnston, Michelle Szabo, and Alexandra Rodney, "Good Food, Good People: Understanding the Cultural Repertoire of Ethical Eating," *Journal of Consumer Culture* 11, no. 3 (2011): 293–318.

53. Ashley Woods, "Walter Robb, Whole Foods CEO, on Opening Detroit Store: 'We're Going after Elitism, Racism,'" *Huffington Post,* April 30, 2013.

54. U.S. Census Bureau, State & County QuickFacts: Detroit (city), Michigan, http://quickfacts.census.gov/qfd/states/26/2622000.html.

55. At the time of this writing I live in Ann Arbor, a city that has two Whole Foods Markets, one of which I count, along with a Trader Joe's, as one of my two regular grocery stores. I situate myself as such in order to be clear that at the same time that I analyze the process of the Midtown store, I am a longtime regular customer of the corporation in both Ann Arbor and San Diego (my

prior home). In fact, by my count I have patronized at least twenty different Whole Foods Markets, across the United States.

56. Courtney Subramanian, "Whole Foods Stretches Low-Income Strategy," *Time,* September 19, 2013.

57. Emily Badger, "Why Whole Foods Is Moving into One of the Poorest Neighborhoods in Chicago," *Washington Post,* November 14, 2014.

58. Tom Ryan, "Whole Foods Grows Smaller," *Forbes,* February 14, 2012.

59. Scott Davis, "Whole Foods' Holistic Growth Plan," *Forbes,* April 30, 2014.

60. See, for example, Bill Ruthhart, "Englewood Whole Foods Store Represents Bet by Emanuel, Company," *Chicago Tribune,* July 1, 2014, and Mark Guarino, "Whole Foods Repackages Itself for Poor Neighborhoods," *Al Jazeera,* July 31, 2014.

61. John Gallagher, "In Detroit, Whole Foods Working to Serve Whole Community," *Detroit Free Press,* November 10, 2013.

62. David Muller, "Whole Foods CEO Says Second Detroit Location Is in the Works," MLive, September 18, 2014.

63. Danny Devries and Robbie Linn, "Food for Thought: Addressing Detroit's Food Desert Myth," Data Driven Detroit, September 8, 2011; James Griffioen, "Yes There Are Grocery Stores in Detroit," Urbanophile, January 25, 2011; "Detroit Grocery Stores, 'Food Desert' Myth Examined in Noah Stephens' Photography Survey," *Huffington Post,* October 22, 2012.

64. Woods, "Walter Robb, Whole Foods CEO."

65. Renee E. Walker, Christopher R. Keane, Jessica G. Burke, "Disparities and Access to Healthy Food in the United States: A Review of Food Deserts Literature," *Health & Place* 16, no. 5 (September 2010): 876–84. This article reviewing the literature on food deserts concurs that there is no definitive usage and the phrase is used differently by different researchers. According to Walker, Keane, and Burke, the phrase is used to refer to "urban areas with 10 or fewer stores and no stores with more than 20 employees" as well as "poor urban areas, where residents cannot buy affordable, healthy food." In so doing the authors point to differing conceptions of access to food as both quantity of stores as well as type and quality of foods available. They go on to state that in general, "there is a lack of consensus on the definition of food deserts and what measures are required for identifying food deserts, thereby contributing to the debate about their actual existence" (876).

66. Paula Dutko, Michele Ver Ploeg, and Tracey Farrigan, *Characteristics and Influential Factors of Food Deserts,* Economic Research Report 140 (Washington, D.C.: U.S. Department of Agriculture, Economic Research Service, 2012), 1.

67. The report explains that "low-income tracts are characterized by either a poverty rate equal to or greater than 20 percent, or a median family income that is 80 percent or less of the metropolitan area's median family income (for tracts in metropolitan areas) or the statewide median family income (for tracts in nonmetropolitan areas). . . . Low access is characterized by at least 500 people and/or 33 percent of the tract population residing more than 1 mile from a supermarket or large grocery store in urban areas, and more than 10 miles in rural areas." Ibid., 5.

68. USDA, "Food Access Research Atlas," http://www.ers.usda.gov/data-products/food-access-research-atlas/go-to-the-atlas.aspx; "Detroit Zip Codes and 2010 Census Tracts," Data Driven Detroit, July 2012. The tracts include in zip code 48223: 5439, 5437, 5438, 5436, 5441, 5440, 5441, 5443; in zip code 48228: 5458, 5457, 5464; in zip code 48209: 5249, 5250; in zip code 48238: 5301; in zip code 48203: 5383, 5079, 5080; in zip code 48211: 9851; in zip code 48226: 5208, 5207.

69. Devries and Linn, "Food for Thought."

70. Brightmoor and Warrendale are in the zip codes 48223 and 48228, respectively.

71. USDA, "SNAP Retailer Locator," http://www.fns.usda.gov/snap/retailerlocator.

72. Tracie McMillan, "Can Whole Foods Change the Way Poor People Eat?," *Slate,* November 19, 2014.

73. Ibid.

74. Ibid.

75. Woods, "Walter Robb, Whole Foods CEO."

76. Maura Webber Sadovi, "Whole Foods Bets Detroit," *Wall Street Journal,* June 4, 2013. The Whole Foods Market is part of a mixed-use project initially developed by Ram Realty Services of Florida that included the Ellington, "a fifty-five-unit condominium complex, a parking garage structure that was built in partnership between Ram and Wayne State University and Detroit Public Schools, as well as 12,623 square feet of ground level retail space." Ram Realty Services, "The Ellington, Detroit, Michigan," http://www.ramrealestate.com/listings/The_Ellington/Ellington_Flyer.pdf. As of a July 30, 2014, visit, the retail spaces were leased by a Starbucks, FedEx/Kinko's, Bank of America, Great Expressions Dental, and a T-Mobile. While the lot where the Whole Foods was located was not developed alongside the Ellington and the parking garage, the other pieces of the development were complete in 2006 and heralded as one of the earlier mixed-use developments of the Midtown redevelopment. Daniel Duggan, "Location, Prices a Draw in Midtown," *Crain's,* August 13, 2007. In addition to the Ellington, Ram owned the adjacent lot.

77. Jason Hackworth, *The Neoliberal City: Governance, Ideology, and Development in American Urbanism* (Ithaca, N.Y.: Cornell University Press, 2007), 128.

78. Ibid.

79. Annie Gasparro, "Detroit May Be Bankrupt, But at Least It Has Whole Foods," *Wall Street Journal,* August 1, 2013.

80. Alison Gregor, "A Detroit District Thrives by Building on the Past," *New York Times,* August 31, 2010.

81. "Ilitches Reveal Plans for Detroit's New 'Sports and Entertainment' District," *Detroit News,* July 21, 2014.

82. And, in the case of Detroit's development, the most blighted and ill-cared-for areas historically were the areas in which the city's poor, immigrant, and black communities lived in the nineteenth and twentieth centuries. As the city's "Master Plan" for development was revealed in 1946, it was no surprise that the areas slated to be razed and redeveloped were the same areas where the city's overcrowded black population was ghettoized.

Conclusion

1. A French–English dictionary gives the French pronunciation as "detRWA," for those familiar with French-language rules.

2. Detroit Historical Society, "Section 1: Before 1701—The People of the Three Fires," http://detroithistorical.org/buildingdetroit/curriculum_3fires.php.

3. Cangany, *Frontier Seaport,* 9–10.

4. Kenneth E. Lewis, *West to Far Michigan: Settling the Lower Peninsula, 1815–1860* (East Lansing: Michigan State University Press, 2002), 24–27.

5. United States Environmental Protection Agency, "The Great Lakes," http://epa.gov/greatlakes/basicinfo.html.

6. Bill Mitchell, "In Detroit, Water Crisis Symbolizes Decline, and Hope," *National Geographic,* August 22, 2014.

7. UN News Centre, "Widespread Water Shut-Offs in US City of Detroit Prompt Outcry from UN Rights Experts," June 25, 2014, http://www.un.org/apps/news/story.asp?NewsID=48129#.VCAcSi5dUhw.

8. Mary M. Chapman, "Former Mayor of Detroit Guilty in Corruption Case," *New York Times,* March 11, 2013.

9. Monica Davey, "A Private Boom amid Detroit's Public Blight," *New York Times,* March 4, 2013.

10. See, for example, Gus Burns, "Downsized: Kwame Kilpatrick Swaps 5,000-Square-Foot Texas Home for Milan Jail Cell," MLive, March 12, 2013. To this day, media stories frequently reference the "flashy suits" and diamond-studded earring he wore through his first term, "club crawls" that followed his

first inauguration, and rumors that he frequently hosted strippers in the mayoral mansion.

11. Eliott C. McLaughlin, "Detroit Elects First White Mayor in More Than 4 Decades," CNN, November 6, 2013.

12. Bill Laitner, "Detroiter Makes Supersize Commute with Heart and Sole," *Detroit Free Press,* February 1, 2015. Robertson has been making this commute five days a week, in the blistering heat of summer and the frigid temperatures of winter, for over a decade. His one-way trip from his home in Detroit to his job in suburban metropolitan Detroit is twenty-three miles. His journey to work takes four and a half hours as he walks nine of the miles and is able to take bus service for some of the remaining miles. His 10 p.m. end time means that the limited bus service is even more limited, so his return home takes six hours as he must walk twelve of the twenty-three miles. News media outlets and everyday people have overwhelmingly responded to this story, raising hundreds of thousands of dollars in donations to this determined and persistent hardworking Detroiter.

13. Great Lakes—St. Lawrence River Basin Water Resources Council, "The Great Lakes—St. Lawrence River Basin Water Resources Compact: Resource Kit," 2015, http://www.glslcompactcouncil.org/Docs/Download/GLCompact ResourceKit-1-5-15.pdf.

Index

REBECCA J. KINNEY is assistant professor in the School of Cultural and Critical Studies and Popular Culture at Bowling Green State University. Dr. Kinney's work has appeared in the journals *Race & Class, Transformations,* and *Media Fields.* She grew up in metropolitan Detroit and earned her doctorate in ethnic studies from the University of California, San Diego.